PRINCIPLES OF COMPUTER ORGANIZATION

A first course using the 68000

Principles of Computer Organization
A first course using the 68000

Colin Charlton and Paul Leng

Lecturers in the Department of Computer Science
University of Liverpool

McGRAW-HILL BOOK COMPANY

London · New York · St Louis · San Francisco · Auckland · Bogotá
Caracas · Colorado Springs · Hamburg · Lisbon · Madrid · Mexico
Milan · Montreal · New Delhi · Oklahoma City · Panama · Paris
San Juan · São Paulo · Singapore · Sydney · Tokyo · Toronto

Published by
McGRAW-HILL Book Company (UK) Limited
SHOPPENHANGERS ROAD · MAIDENHEAD · BERKSHIRE
ENGLAND SL6 2QL
TEL: 0628-23432; FAX: 0628-35895

British Library Cataloguing in Publication Data
Charlton, Colin
  Principles of computer organization: a first course using the 68000.
  1. Computer systems
  I. Title II. Leng, Paul
  004

  ISBN 0-07-707217-0

Library of Congress Cataloging-in-Publication Data
Charlton, Colin.
  Principles of computer organization: a first course using the 68000 /
Colin Charlton and Paul Leng.
      p.   cm.   •
  ISBN 0-07-707217-0
  1. Computer organization. I. Leng, Paul. II. Title.
QA76.9.C643L46   1990
004.2'2--dc20   89-78243

12345 RC 93210

Typeset by Charlton and Leng and printed and bound in Great Britain by
Richard Clay Ltd, Bungay, Suffolk

For
Margaret, Zoe, Daniel and Caroline,
Gwynne, William, Mary and Thomas,

and in memory of
Ivor J. Leng
(1917–1989)

Contents

Preface

The study of the discipline of computing begins with an understanding of the idea of a *program*, and of how programs are performed by computers. This in turn requires us to understand something of the nature of the machines that are used for this purpose. For most people who are involved in the programming and application of computers, this understanding is essentially at a *functional* level: we are interested in the computer as a machine for executing programs.

The principal purpose of this book is to help develop an understanding of how computers fulfil this primary function. It is presumed that the reader will have already begun to learn how to write programs for computers, probably using a high-level language such as Pascal. No specific level of prior knowledge is assumed, however, and the book is intended to serve as a text for a course that might immediately follow, or proceed concurrently with, an introduction to high-level language programming.

Our aim is to underpin this introduction with an explanation of the relationship between high-level languages and systems, and the machines on which they are implemented. This requires an examination of the organization of the physical components of the computer, the way in which programs are represented within the machine, and the steps involved in their execution. The most satisfactory way to do this is to study the programming of computers at this primitive level through the medium of a simple assembly language. However, although assembly-language programming is central to the theme of this book, the purpose of this is not so much as an end in itself but rather as a means to describe machine behaviour. We try in particular to show how a study of their machine-level equivalents enables us to understand the control and data structures of high-level languages and their implementation.

Because we are interested in establishing the *principles* of how a computer functions, and how programs are performed, we have tried to avoid basing our explanations on a description of any particular computer. The characteristics of 'real' computers inevitably derive from a compromise between their idealized objectives and a variety of practical considerations. Too close a concentration on the specific details that result from this can obscure the important general principles that apply. In the most significant aspects of their behaviour, however, almost all present-day digital computers are essentially similar, all being derived from a common model of computation. We have therefore tried, as far as possible, to present our description of the organization and programming of computers in a machine-independent way, emphasizing concepts and principles that will apply to most or all current computers. Where necessary, we have used the device of an imaginary 'paper' computer to illustrate the ideas we introduce through simple examples.

This approach has its limitations. Computing is an essentially practical discipline, and to attain a satisfactory understanding of the ideas we wish to explore it is important to write programs and to study them in execution. For us to extend the design of our paper machine for this purpose would be self-defeating. Instead, we include in the book a description of the popular 68000 microprocessor and its assembly language. We use these both to provide a concrete illustration of the concepts discussed, and to enable them to be developed further in practical programming. Because, however, we wish to separate the description of concepts from the description of their realization in the 68000, we have, quite deliberately, isolated the latter in separate sections of each chapter. As each new topic is introduced, it is presented first in as general and machine-independent way as possible, before we go on to describe the corresponding features of the 68000 machine. We hope by this separation to emphasize the general principles of computer organization and machine-level programming, reinforced by a practical study of a 'real' computer.

This book derives, in part, from courses that have been taught by the authors to undergraduate students at Liverpool University over a number of years. We owe our thanks to them, and to our colleagues: Jim Watt, for all the advice and support he has given throughout this time, Janet Little, Ken Chan, and the other members of the Department of Computer Science.

Chapter 1

Elements of the computer

1.1 Introduction

This book is about computers, and how they perform the tasks for which
they are used.

Different people, of course, use computers for different purposes, and
these different uses lead to different views of the machines. At one ex-
treme, a businessman or woman may be using a computer to keep records
of customers. For this user, the computer may appear to be no more than
a rather sophisticated card-index system. Conversely, the electrical engineer's view of a computer is of a complex electrical circuit, the behaviour of
which can only be described properly in terms of its physical characteristics.
Somewhere in between we have the picture of the computer as it appears
to the person who is using it to perform **programs**, written in a language
such as BASIC or Pascal; for him or her, the computer is a machine that
will solve any of a very large class of problems that can be described using
this programming language.

One way of resolving these different views of the computer is to place
them in a hierarchy; from this we derive what is often called an **onion-
skin model** of a computer (Figure 1.1). There are many different forms of
this model, and the number and significance of the different 'skins' of the
onion are quite arbitrary. The common characteristic of onion-skin models
is their view of a computer system as a series of layers. At each level in this
hierarchy, we have a coherent picture of the computer described in terms
of what it does and how it is used at that level. So, for example, if we
are using the computer only to perform word-processing, it is possible to
provide a completely adequate functional specification of the machine by

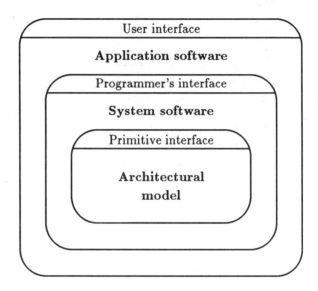

Figure 1.1   An 'onion-skin' model of a computer system

describing all the word-processing operations it can perform, and how we can induce it to perform them. We often call this sort of description an **interface**, since it separates an external, user's, view of the machine from whatever is required to make that machine function as it is required to do. If we peel away this interface, or skin of the onion, however, we will find revealed a layer of **software**, i.e. programs that have been written to provide this functionality and to support this user interface. This software is in turn written by users of the machine, programmers, who are themselves making use of a different view of the computer defined at a lower level in the hierarchy.

This book is written for people who are already, or perhaps have just begun, using computers to perform programs written in high-level languages. For a programmer, the functional specification of the computer—the programmer's interface—is very well-defined: it is, for most purposes, equivalent to a definition of the programming language being used. If we wish to use a computer only to perform Pascal programs, then it is sufficient to define the functionality of the computer by saying that it will perform any program that has been written according to the grammatical rules of the Pascal language, and that the result of this program being performed will be defined by the semantics of this language. All that we need further to this is some information on the practicalities of the computer, and we can quite adequately make use of it as a machine for running Pascal programs.

This view of the computer may be quite sufficient for most practical programming purposes. If we wish to go further, however, to begin to understand a little of *how* the computer works as well as *what* it will do, then we must strip away this layer of the onion. Beneath it, we find a level of 'system' software—compilers, operating systems, and more—which serves to create this convenient programming interface for the machine. We will from time to time throughout this book be making reference to aspects of this software, although any detailed study of it is well outside our scope. Our real purpose is to examine the machine level on which this layer of software is based: the level that in Figure 1.1 we have described as the **primitive interface**.

The primitive programming level

The computer, at this level of description, is still a programmer's machine, but, as we have suggested, the programming interface that it provides is a primitive one. Once again, we can define the functions of the computer at this level by describing the programming language that we use to make it perform these functions; but in this case the language we must use will not be BASIC or Pascal, but a much more primitive, 'low-level' language. Unlike BASIC and Pascal, this language will not be intended primarily as a notation for expressing solutions to problems, but will, rather, define at an elementary level the operations that the computer can perform, i.e. it will be what we call a **machine-oriented** language rather than one that is **problem-oriented**. Below this primitive programming interface is a machine that is, in essence, a **hardware** construction, i.e. (with some limited exceptions that need not concern us here) the primitive interface is the lowest level at which we can write software, or programs, for the machine. The picture we have of the machine at this level is sometimes called the **architectural model**, and is largely defined by this primitive programming language.

Why should we study the machine at this level? Some people, of course, must do so; those programmers who write the software that creates the next upward layer of the onion will need to understand and use the machine on which their programs will depend. Equally, the engineers charged with the task of creating the physical machine will use this architectural model as a design specification, just as a building engineer uses an architect's drawings for the same purpose. These, however, are specialists; for the great majority of users of the computer, including most professional programmers, there will be no need to make use of the machine at any level lower than that of a high-level programming language. To *understand* the machine, even at these higher levels, however, we must recognize that whatever tasks the computer performs—a Pascal program, perhaps, or a word-processing operation—will, at a lower level, be effected by actions that can only be described in terms of this primitive architectural model.

The justification of this book is that users of computers, and especially programmers in high-level languages, need, and want, to understand something of the underlying machine on which their use of the computer depends. If we wish to go further in a study of computer science, this understanding will become essential; but even if we do not, it will help us to become better high-level language programmers if we have a clear and well-founded understanding of how our programs make use of the machines on which they are performed. We will try, therefore, throughout this book, to use our discussion of the architectural model of the computer and the primitive programming interface to explain how higher-level programs are performed. We will assume that the reader has, or is in the process of acquiring, some understanding of programming in a language such as Pascal, although no specific high-level language will be assumed.

High-level and low-level programming

The best way to learn about the primitive interface is to learn how to write programs to execute at this level, and to understand what these programs do. Programming at this level is rather different from using a language such as Pascal: the language we will need to use is less easy to learn than Pascal, and the programs we write will be more difficult to understand and more likely to contain errors. For these, and other, reasons, most people prefer to write software in high-level languages, and it is generally better to do so whenever this is possible. However, low-level language programming still has a place, albeit a limited one, in programming practice. As we shall find, there are some things that it is possible to do at this level that would be difficult or impossible in most high-level languages. It is also, sometimes, possible to write programs in a low-level language that are much smaller in size, or execute much more quickly, than their high-level language equivalents, and in some applications these optimizations may be very important. Nevertheless, it is equally important not to exaggerate these advantages; people are more important than computers, and, in general, it is more important that we should use the computer in ways that are convenient for us than fit in with the requirements of the machine. So our real purpose in studying low-level programming is not, principally, as an end in itself but to give us a greater insight into the computational process on the machines we are using.

1.2   The von Neumann model

We have identified the machine level in which we are interested by describing it, rather loosely, as the lowest level at which we can write programs for the computer. To define this level fully, it will be necessary to describe in detail the primitive programming language in which these programs must be written. Here we encounter a problem, however, as there is no single, universal language that will apply; in reality, computers are manufactured articles that are marketed commercially, and each type and model of computer has its own individual characteristics. These differences mean that, in contrast to problem-oriented, high-level languages, which are generally **machine-independent**, low-level languages are generally specific to particular computers.

Nevertheless, although these differences of detail between different computers, and their languages, may be great indeed, there remains also a great deal in common between most computers. In fact, the design of almost all present-day digital computers is based on an architectural model the essential features of which are common to all. We call this common model the **von Neumann machine**, after the mathematician John von Neumann who was one of the major figures in the early development of the concepts that led to the first computers being built.

The principal features of the von Neumann model, illustrated in Figure 1.2, are derived from our view of the computer as a *machine for performing programs*. A computer program, in whatever language it is written, defines a series of steps by which the solution to a problem is reached. If we are to build a machine to perform programs, then it must include some active part that will perform these program steps. In the von Neumann machine, we call this active component the **processor**.

We know that the execution of a program may require the same sequence of steps to be repeated several times, and we know also that many programs will involve the manipulation of quantities of information, or **data**; think of our word-processing system, for example. For this to be possible, we will require some means of retaining both program steps and other data until the program's task is complete. In the von Neumann machine, both program steps and data are held in the computer's **memory**, also called its 'store'. The use of the word 'memory' reflects the analogy with human thought, and the way in which we ourselves solve problems. In order to perform a task such as, for example, baking a cake, it is necessary to remember both the recipe from which we are working (the program) and also other details such as the time when the cake went into the oven (the data). We may imagine, perhaps, that while the task is being performed, some active part of the brain (the processor) is busy using these remembered details to bring

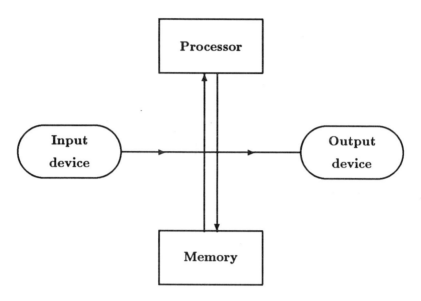

Figure 1.2   Elements of the von Neumann machine

the task to its conclusion.

We cannot bake a cake unless we have at some time learned how to do so, perhaps by reading the recipe from a book. Equally, there must be some means by which the computer obtains the information it needs to perform its tasks. An **input device** provides a means by which information can be transmitted from the user of the computer into the computer's memory, and an **output device** performs the reverse function, enabling us to see the results of the program being performed. For the desk-top microcomputers that most of us use, the usual input device is a keyboard, pressing a key on which transmits some information into the computer, and the usual output device is a television screen or visual display unit (VDU), which allows us to read text or examine other information produced by the operation of the computer.

Abstract machines and physical hardware

If we look inside the casing of our desk-top microcomputer, we will find an electronic component which is the processor, and one, or more usually several other components which together constitute the memory. These components take the form of **integrated circuit** packages, or '**chips**' as they are commonly called (Figure 1.3). Other chips are present to control

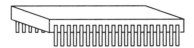

Figure 1.3 An integrated circuit package

and communicate with the input and output devices. Processor, memory, and input and output components are connected together via a **bus**, which is a channel along which information can pass between these units.

The fact that we can identify physical components corresponding to the elements of the von Neumann model illustrated in Figure 1.2 is a reflection of the close relationship between this model and the actual construction of computers. It is, nevertheless, an **abstract** model, the purpose of which is not so much to describe the physical construction of a computer but rather to provide a framework on which to base our understanding of the way in which the computer performs its functions. It is these functional characteristics of the computer as a program-performing machine on which we shall concentrate in this book, and we shall say as little as possible about the physical hardware.

In fact, the von Neumann model defines a general program-performing machine which we can apply equally well to explain the execution of programs in high-level languages. If we try to describe how a Pascal program is performed, we will need to introduce the idea of a 'memory' to explain how program variables are maintained and we will need to hypothesize a 'processor' to explain how, for example, a conditional statement can be performed, i.e. we will need to define something like a von Neumann model in order to provide an explanation of the **semantics**, or 'meaning' of the program. Putting it another way, the abstract 'Pascal-program-performing' machine to which we referred in Section 1.1 is itself, in its broad essentials, a kind of von Neumann machine. The von Neumann model thus provides a basis for understanding not only most digital computers but also most high-level programming languages (although not all; for some languages, such as LISP, it is a less satisfactory model). We shall here be using the von Neumann model as a starting point for our description of the primitive-level architecture of the computer, but the relationship between the low-level and high-level 'abstract machines' is one to which we will constantly return.

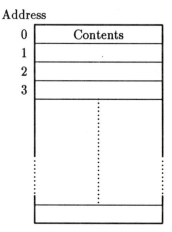

Figure 1.4   Representation of the memory

The memory

One of the central features of the von Neumann model—and hence of all the real computers we will be discussing—is the presence of a single main memory which is used to store both programs being performed and data needed by these programs. Here we arrive at a difference between this model and our picture of the execution of high-level language programs. In a Pascal program, for example, we can distinguish clearly between the program steps (statements) and data (variables and constants). In the simple von Neumann architectural model, however, the central memory is used to store both programs and data uniformly.

We visualize the memory (Figure 1.4) as taking the form of an ordered set of cells, or **words**, each of which is capable of storing, or 'remembering', an item of information, such as, perhaps, a number. Each word is itself numbered; this 'location number', or **address**, provides a way of identifying each word uniquely for reference. Location numbers for a particular computer conventionally start at address 0 and go on up to a value that defines the **memory size** of the machine. We often call the information stored in a word its **contents**; this terminology ('address' and 'contents') reflects our mental picture of the memory as a row of lockers or pigeonholes, each with its own identifying number.

Bits and bit-patterns

Within each word, we have a further subdivision into smaller units of memory which we call **bits**. A bit is in fact the smallest conceivable memory-unit, as it can store only one piece of information which can have only two possible values. We can think of various different ways of interpreting these two values: for example, as states of a switch ('on' or 'off'), or as answers to a question ('yes' or 'no'). One particularly useful interpretation is to think of these two values as being numeric digits, 0 or 1. It is this interpretation which gives rise to the term 'bit', which is a contraction of 'binary digit'.

With this interpretation, our picture of a bit is of an elementary memory cell the contents of which may only be either of the values 0 and 1. A **word** is a row of these cells (Figure 1.5), conventionally numbered from 0 again. The **word length**, or number of bits in a word, will be different in different

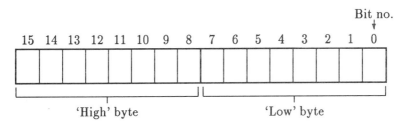

Figure 1.5   A 16-bit word

real machines; in Figure 1.5 we have shown a word of 16 bits, which is typical of many modern microcomputers. In fact, the term 'word' is sometimes used specifically to refer to a memory unit of size 16 bits, as well as, more generally, to describe the unit of memory that is addressed and operated upon by the processor. Because (with this latter meaning) a 'word' is not a uniform quantity defined for all machines, we often make use of another quantity, a **byte**, which is a unit of 8 bits. In some computers, those which operate on 8-bit words, the terms 'word' and 'byte' are effectively synonymous; conversely, Figure 1.5 illustrates a word containing 2 bytes. Because a byte is a well-defined quantity, it is often used as a standard unit of memory capacity; when a computer is described as having '32K' of memory, this will usually be taken to mean a store of size 32 768 bytes. Here, the symbol 'K' stands for the number 2^{10}, or 1024; for reasons that will become clear, the size of a computer store is almost invariably a power of 2.

For any particular word, the set of values of the bits which make up the word defines the value, or contents, of the word. This set of bit-values, or **bit-pattern**, can be described by writing it down as a sequence of 0 and 1 symbols. Thus the 8-bit word shown in Figure 1.6 may be said to contain the value 00000101. If we ignore the redundant zeros at the

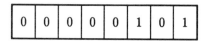

| 0 | 0 | 0 | 0 | 0 | 1 | 0 | 1 |

Figure 1.6 A byte containing the binary representation of the number 5

start of the bit-pattern, this is, of course, the way in which we write the number 5 in binary notation, so it is clear that we can, if we choose to do so, think of the word shown in Figure 1.6 as 'containing' the number 5. This correspondence between 'bit-patterns' and binary arithmetic notation is the reason for our numbering the bit positions in a word starting from 0 on the *right* (Figure 1.5). We often refer to bit 0, the rightmost bit, as the 'least significant bit', while the leftmost bit (bit 15 in Figure 1.5) is the 'most significant bit'.

We will return in later chapters to look in more detail at the way information is represented within computer 'words'. We will need to consider not only how numbers can be stored, but also other kinds of information handled by the computer, including the steps of the program itself which must also be stored in this medium. For the moment, however, it will be sufficient to note that when, in a Pascal program, we perform an assignment such as:

$$A := 5$$

this can be interpreted, at the architectural level, as causing a particular memory location to assume the bit pattern 101.

Abstract and physical memory

This interpretation of a bit pattern as representing a binary number is, of course, an **abstraction**, i.e. we can choose to interpret it in any other way we wish, and we will indeed find ourselves using different interpretations as we come to look at how other kinds of information are to be represented. We could go further and say that the picture we have of a 'word' as containing a row of 'bits' is itself an abstraction, or model of reality. Within the physical machine, a bit is an electronic component that can assume either of two states. However, in describing our architectural model of the computer, we need not concern ourselves with the details of this physical implementation;

it will be sufficient to use our abstraction of this in the form of a binary digit that can be written as 0 or 1.

One other characteristic of physical computer memory may be mentioned at this point. In many microcomputer systems, some parts of the memory are reserved for storing constant information, such as essential system software, which is part of the permanent configuration of the machine. To protect this information from being accidentally lost, it is often held in memory devices ('chips'), the physical construction of which is such as to prevent the information they hold being altered. This kind of memory device is called a Read Only Memory, or ROM, because we can inspect (read) the information it holds, but this cannot be changed by any action within the computer. Memory whose word-values can be changed as well as inspected is, rather misleadingly and inaccurately, usually called RAM. RAM stands for Random Access Memory, although a more useful and accurate term would be 'Read and Write Memory'. Although these two kinds of memory will have some significance within the organization of the actual computers we use, in describing the architectural model it will be easier to assume that all memory is uniform RAM.

1.3 Introduction to the paper machine

We have, so far, presented a description of the von Neumann machine model in broad outline only. The essential characteristic of the machine is its ability to perform programs, the details of which are stored as a series of steps within the computer's memory. If we are to go further, to examine this function more closely, we will need to define the nature of these program steps, and to describe other details of the machine that are necessary to show how it performs programs. To do so, we will need to depart from our completely general model, and begin to describe the details of a *particular* computer architecture.

One way of doing this would be to select a specific real computer system, and to use the details of this as a way of introducing and illustrating the topics we wish to discuss. The disadvantage of this is that all real computers are different, and these differences mean that no one machine provides a satisfactory illustration of the properties of computers in general. Furthermore, many of the specific details of real computers are quite arbitrary, or are present for reasons that are irrelevant to our understanding of the way in which programs are performed. These extraneous details tend to clutter up the picture of the machine, making it more difficult to learn how to use it, and obscuring the important principles that we want to expose.

For these reasons, we shall base our description of the computer's primitive programming interface not on any particular real computer, but on an artificial 'paper' computer, the design of which we will develop as we go along. The advantage of this is that, because we have no intention of building a real computer to this design, we will have no need to worry about practical considerations such as cost, speed, or even technical feasibility. This will leave us free to introduce into the computer's design whatever features are useful to exemplify the general principles of computer organization and low-level programming. Furthermore, since our purpose is illustrative rather than practical, we will not worry too much if some aspects of our design are incomplete, impracticable, or even inconsistent. It will be sufficient if our paper machine is defined to the point at which we can write programs for it, and that we understand what these programs will do.

The characteristics of this 'paper' machine will be introduced as we need them to illustrate the topics we will be dealing with in this book. For the moment, all we need say is that the architecture of this computer is based on the von Neumann model that we have outlined, with a simple memory consisting of a single array of memory cells, or words. Whenever we need to do so, we will assume that these words are 16 bits, or 2 bytes long, although many of the machine's properties can be described without requiring us to make this assumption. Computers are traditionally given names, or frequently, more or less meaningless numbers, so we shall call our computer 'Papyrus', a name that suggests a primitive form of paper.

Useful though Papyrus will be, we hope, as a vehicle for introducing each topic in turn, this approach has its limitations. Computer science is, essentially, a practical discipline, and to understand the principles of computer architecture and machine-level programming it is important to be able to study them in a practical context, by writing and running real programs. Although we shall be able to write programs for Papyrus, we have no real computer to perform them. To allow us to write programs that can be performed on real computers, we shall also describe in this book some of the details of a real processor, the Motorola MC68000. As each new topic is introduced, we shall try, as far as possible, to describe it with as little reference as possible to the specific characteristics of real machines; our 'paper' machine, Papyrus, will help us do this. Having dealt with general principles and concepts, however, and illustrated them using Papyrus, we shall go on to look at their practical application on a real computer, using the MC68000 as our example.

Because we want to try to separate general principles (which are largely machine-independent) from practical details, those sections of the book that describe the particular characteristics of the MC68000 will be kept separate. The intention behind this approach is to introduce concepts and principles in a context that does not depend on any particular real machine, and to avoid any association of these ideas with a specific architecture. For the same reason, we have avoided making Papyrus (which is not really a computer, but rather a pedagogic device) look particularly like the 68000; we wish to emphasize, throughout the book, the distinction between general *concepts* and their specific *realization*. The sections of the book that deal with the 68000 come at the end of each chapter, with title-headings prefaced by an asterisk *, and will describe, quite briefly, the way in which the topics introduced in that chapter are implemented within the 68000. Sections that are not 'starred' in this way (apart from this one!) will not refer to any specific machine other than Papyrus.

1.4   *Introduction to the Motorola MC68000

The 'real' computer described in this book is the MC68000 (often referred to simply as the '68000') designed by the Motorola company of the USA, and manufactured by Motorola and a number of other companies.

Strictly speaking, the MC68000 is not really a computer, but a **processor**, i.e. its function is to perform program steps. To enable it to perform this function usefully, it must be combined with memory and with input and output devices in some configuration based on the model outlined in Figure 1.2. Very many computer systems, marketed commercially by different companies all over the world, are constructed in this way using the MC68000. In the simplest case, the system might include a single 68000 processor, some memory, and a keyboard and VDU screen to provide input and output capability, with perhaps a disk unit to facilitate software storage. This kind of system is often called a 'packaged' microcomputer, or simply a microcomputer. The MC68000 itself is a **microprocessor** because it is a computer processor that has been miniaturized to the extent that it can be manufactured as a single 'chip'.

The 68000 is in fact the first in a 'family' of microprocessors from Motorola (the 68000, 68008, 68010, 68012, 68020, 68030, 68040). The 68000 is the 'base' machine of this family, and Motorola have designed the series of microprocessors so that upward code compatibility is maintained. This means that 68000 code will run on all of these microprocessors, and the 68000 instruction set forms the essential nucleus of each of these instruction sets. Within the text of this book, we shall use the 68000 'base machine' architecture for the purpose of description and in our examples, although all of this will also be applicable to other processors of the 68000 family.

In order to carry out practical programming exercises based on the topics covered in this book, you will need to have access to some 68000-based computer system. As all the different systems marketed by different companies will have their own individual features, there is no point in our trying to describe this system in detail: to use it, you will need some information, specific to the particular type and model of computer, which will probably be provided in the form of a 'user guide' by the manufacturer. Fortunately, however, most modern microcomputers are designed for ease of use, and most of the operations required to use the computer and to perform programs on it can be learned very quickly. If you have already learned how to use the computer to perform programs in a high-level language, then most of these operations will already be familiar to you; the 'mechanics' of preparing and executing a program in a low-level language will not be very different from those required for, say, Pascal programs.

Writing low-level language programs is, of course, very different from writing programs in Pascal. Fortunately, however, in this respect there are few differences between all the different computers based on the 68000. Because the 68000 is the 'processor' component, it is this that defines what program steps can be performed. Hence, at this 'primitive' programming level, the characteristics of all the 68000-based computers will be principally those of the MC68000 itself. We shall be describing the properties of the 68000 processor, and writing programs to execute using this processor; almost all of this should be applicable to any computer that has a 68000 processor. We shall have to assume that the actual computer in use has some memory and input and output devices, but otherwise we need not consider its particular characteristics.

Details of the MC68000 will be introduced in the course of the book, generally following our introduction of the relevant concepts in a more general way. So far, the major concept we have introduced is the idea of the von Neumann machine model, a representation of the computer as a machine for performing programs the steps of which are stored in its memory. All the 68000-based computers we are likely to meet fit into this pattern. The memory of the computer is, of course, not part of the 68000 itself; however, the **word length** of the computer is a property not just of the memory but also of the processor, since it defines the size of the unit of information which is processed at each step. In a von Neumann machine, the processor inspects or alters information in the memory using the **address** of the word in which the information is located. Physically, this involves placing the address of the word on the **bus**, which connects the processor to the memory; the **contents** of the word will then be returned on the bus to the processor. In 68000-based machines, the address of a word may be up to 23 bits in length, allowing for a memory of up to 2^{23} words to be attached and used (although the amount of memory actually

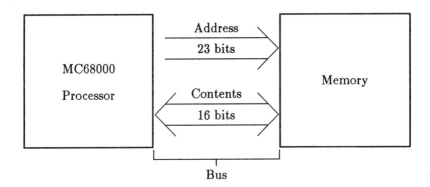

Figure 1.7   The 68000 processor–memory relationship

available may be much less than this). The value that is returned on the bus—the contents of the addressed location—is 16 bits in length, so we can describe the 68000, like Papyrus, as having a 16-bit word length. Figure 1.7 illustrates the 68000 processor–memory relationship.

In fact, although the 68000 is essentially a 16-bit machine, it is also capable of dealing with values that are both smaller and larger than this would imply. In particular, we shall find that it is often useful to deal in values that are 8 bits in length, i.e. in **bytes**. To facilitate this, a 68000 address is, in general, up to 24 bits in length, and identifies not a 16-bit word, but a byte. A **word** comprises 2 bytes, and the address of a word must be an even number. Thus, the picture we have of the 68000 store is illustrated in Figure 1.8.

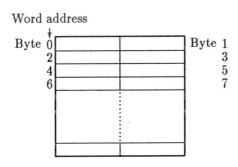

Figure 1.8   The 68000 memory

1.5   Exercises

1. How many different bit-patterns can be expressed in the form of a single byte?

2. If we require to represent 12 different cases by expressing each in the form of a unique bit-pattern, how many bits will be needed for each pattern? Write down the 12 bit-patterns.

3. Investigate the 68000-based computer you will be using. What is its **memory size**? Does this include any ROM? If so, which memory addresses represent ROM? What input and output devices are attached?

Chapter 2

Instructions and their execution

2.1 Registers and instructions

The central function of our von Neumann machine is to perform the series of steps that make up the execution of a program. In this respect, high-level and low-level programs are alike: both involve the representation of an **algorithm** in the form of a sequence of such steps. In Pascal, and many other high-level languages, we call these individual program steps 'statements'. A Pascal statement can be arbitrarily complex; for example, we can write:

$$a := b + c$$

or we can write:

$$a := (b + c) * d + (e - f)/g$$

or, indeed, much more complex statements than these. At the primitive architectural level, however, the individual program steps that are performed are necessarily much simpler than this. These elementary program steps are called **instructions**. Unlike a high-level language statement, an instruction usually involves only a single operation, such as an addition or subtraction.

The form an instruction takes will vary from machine to machine. On our Papyrus computer, which is typical of many, most instructions involve an operation, such as addition, taking place between two **operands**. One of these operands is usually a value obtained from a location in the memory, and the other is held in a **register**.

For our purpose, a register can be thought of as simply a special kind of storage cell. A register is part of the processor, rather than the memory, but it has the same general characteristics as a single word of memory, i.e. it can 'contain' a bit-pattern, or value, which can be altered as a result of program actions. Unlike a memory cell, however, a register does not have a location number, or address, but is usually referred to by a 'name'. Papyrus has a number of registers, but for the moment we need only mention one, which we will call the 'A register', or simply 'A'. Like a word of memory, the Papyrus A register is 16 bits long.

The Papyrus addition instruction adds a value obtained from a memory location to the value contained in the A register, leaving the result in A, i.e. it is the equivalent of a Pascal statement performing:

$$A := A + operand$$

where 'A' is the A register, and 'operand' refers to a memory location. How this addition is performed by the Papyrus processor need not concern us. We know that we can represent an integer number in binary notation by a bit-pattern, which can be stored in a memory word or register. So if the A register initially contains the bit-pattern 101, representing the number 5, and the value of the operand is the bit-pattern 10, i.e. the binary representation of the decimal number 2, then we will expect the result of the instruction to leave the A register containing the bit-pattern 111, representing the decimal number 7 (Figure 2.1). Because the addition

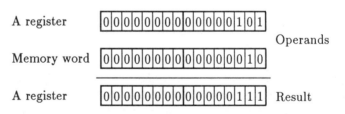

Figure 2.1   An addition into the A register

takes place into the register, this sort of register is sometimes given the rather old-fashioned name of 'accumulator'.

Representation of instructions

We know that the memory of the computer is used to store not just data values, such as integers represented in binary notation, but also the program steps, or instructions, themselves. How is our Papyrus addition instruction to be represented in the store? Let us consider an instruction that will add into the A register the value obtained from memory location number 65. The representation of this instruction divides naturally into two parts: one to signify that the operation required is an addition into the A register, and the other to specify the address, 65, of the operand. We can obviously represent the address as a number in binary notation and hence store it as a bit-pattern. Equally we can represent the operation required, or **function**, of the instruction, by encoding it as a bit-pattern. In this case, there is no generally recognized representation of functions by bit-patterns, as there is for integers in binary notation, so the **function code** used will be quite arbitrary and different for different computers. On Papyrus, the function meaning 'add into the A register a value obtained from a memory location' will be represented as an 8-bit pattern by the function code 00001001. The operand address, 65, is represented in binary notation by the 8-bit pattern 01000001. So we can represent the complete instruction in one 16-bit word containing the bit-pattern 0000100101000001 (Figure 2.2). We

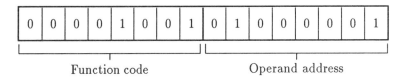

Figure 2.2 A 16-bit instruction word

have divided this instruction word into two 8-bit **fields**, one to contain the function code, and the other to contain the address of the operand. If we regard the latter as an unsigned integer, then 8 bits is sufficient to allow us to represent addresses in the range 0–255. This is unlikely to be sufficient for our purpose, but we will return to consider this problem later. The 8-bit function code field can also contain binary values in the range 0–255, allowing 256 different functions to be represented. If we were designing a real computer, we would have to give considerable thought to the size of this field and to the allocation of codes for the functions to be implemented. For Papyrus, however, we will not worry about such details; we will assume that 8 bits is sufficient to allow us to represent all the functions we wish to implement, and we will not try to design any coherent system for encoding them. In fact, many real computers, particularly microcomputers, find it convenient to use an 8-bit function code. This is not universal, however, and some larger computers have a more complex division of the instruction word into several fields.

The instruction **format**, and also the coding of functions within it, are design decisions of practical concern to the engineers who create the physical hardware of the computer. For our purposes, however, they are arbitrary details with little useful significance. We will, especially, not wish to have to remember that the Papyrus addition instruction is represented by the bit-pattern 00001001. Instead, we will use a more meaningful **mnemonic** code to describe an instruction. If we see an instruction written in the form:

$$ADD \quad A, 65$$

it will be easy to understand this as meaning 'add into the A register the value obtained from location number 65', and this representation of the instruction will be much easier to remember than the binary coding given in Figure 2.2. So, in this book, we will usually represent an instruction by writing it in a mnemonic form like this. We will, as far as possible, avoid mentioning the binary codings of instructions, although we will, of course, have to keep in mind that it is a binary representation that is used in the computer's memory and interpreted by the processor when instructions are executed.

2.2   The execution of instructions

Consider, again, a simple Pascal statement of the form:

$$result := first + second - third$$

where, for simplicity, we will assume that the identifiers 'result', 'first', 'second', and 'third' all refer to integer variables. To achieve a similar effect to this at the primitive architectural level requires the execution of several instructions to perform the elementary addition, subtraction, and other steps implied in the high-level language statement.

Since the **operands** involved in the statement are all simple integers, it will be possible to represent each in the form of a bit-pattern within a single word of memory (assuming, of course, that none of the values involved is too large to be represented in a word of the size we are using). Let us suppose that word number 65 is being used for the variable that we have called 'first'. Locations 66 and 67 will be used for 'second' and 'third', and the 'result' will be stored at address 69 (Figure 2.3). Notice the correspondence between the variable **names** used in the high-level language, and the **addresses** of locations in the memory; both are used to identify locations in the abstract machine store. The **contents** of a word is the equivalent,

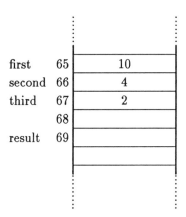

first	65	10
second	66	4
third	67	2
	68	
result	69	

Figure 2.3   Part of the memory used to store program variables

in the architectural model, of the **value** of the variable stored at that location. In this illustration we have given the three operands values of 10,
4, and 2, which for convenience are shown in Figure 2.3 as decimal numbers, although we know that these will actually be stored in the locations
as bit-patterns. No value is shown in location 69, representing the result
variable. In fact, some unknown bit-pattern will be stored there, but we
wish this to be replaced by the binary equivalent of the number 12, as the
result of performing $10 + 4 - 2$.

We can achieve this with the following sequence of Papyrus instructions:

$$
\begin{array}{lll}
LOAD & A,\ 65 & ;\ A := first \\
ADD & A,\ 66 & ;\ A := A + second \\
SUB & A,\ 67 & ;\ A := A - third \\
STORE & A,\ 69 & ;\ result := A
\end{array}
$$

Here we have written the Papyrus machine instructions in the mnemonic
form introduced in Section 2.1. Following the semicolon after each instruction is a Pascal-like statement describing the effect of the instruction. The
first instruction copies, or **loads**, the value obtained from address 65 into
the A register. The next is an addition instruction of the type explained in
Section 2.1; its effect is to add to the value already in the A register, the
value obtained from address 66. Remembering the relationship between
variable names and addresses illustrated in Figure 2.3, this will leave A
containing the equivalent of first+second, i.e. the value 14. The next in-

struction is a subtraction from the A register, leaving A with the value 12. Finally, this value is copied into the memory with a **store** instruction which places the result in the required location, 69.

The Papyrus LOAD and STORE instructions perform the equivalent of **assignment** operations in Pascal and other high-level languages. Because most of the **arithmetic** (and other) operations in Papyrus will take place using at least one operand contained in a register, the important assignments are those *to* a register (LOAD) and *from* a register (STORE). These kinds of instruction are typical of the many computers which, like Papyrus, cannot perform arithmetic operations directly on two values in memory without first fetching one into a register. Generally the STORE instruction is the only one which changes the value of a memory location.

The cycle of instruction execution

The sequence of four instructions described above could form part of a **program** being performed by the Papyrus processor. We know that, in this case, the instructions will be stored within words of the memory as bit-patterns. Let us suppose that these four instructions are stored in the locations whose addresses are 120, 121, 122, and 123. In the illustration of this in Figure 2.4, the 'high' byte of each instruction word is shown as containing the function code, and the 'low' byte the operand address of the instruction. For clarity, we have written the function code in its mnemonic

120	LOAD	A	65
121	ADD	A	66
122	SUB	A	67
123	STORE	A	69

Figure 2.4   Instructions in the store

form and the operand address as a decimal number; we will not need to keep repeating that the actual representation of both fields within the store is in the form of a bit pattern.

When these instructions are performed, the processor will need to know where they are located in the memory. For this purpose, it needs another register: the **program counter** register, PC. The bit-pattern contained within PC is interpreted as a positive integer which represents the **address** of an instruction. The purpose of the PC register is to contain the address of the instruction that is about to be performed (executed) by the processor. All von Neumann machines have a register of this kind, usually called PC.

We can now describe the steps performed by the processor in the execution of a sequence of instructions. For the sequence shown in Figure 2.4, the PC register must first contain the value 120, indicating the address of the first instruction to be performed. Execution of this instruction will proceed in a series of well-defined stages, characteristic of the von Neumann family of machines.

1. **Fetch instruction** The instruction whose address is contained in PC is fetched from the memory into the processor, where it will be stored in the **instruction register** (IR). In the example of Figure 2.4, this will result in IR containing the representation of the instruction LOAD A,65.

2. **Increment PC** Once the instruction to be executed has been fetched, there is no need to 'remember' the address from which it came. Because a program is executed as a sequence of instructions taken (usually) from consecutive memory locations, the processor now **increments** the value contained in the PC register, i.e. 1 is added to it, to indicate the expected address of the next instruction to be performed. In our example, this will leave PC containing the value 121.

3. **Decode instruction** The instruction contained in IR is analysed by the processor to determine what action is required next. In this case, the function code of the instruction specifies a LOAD A operation, so the operand address (65) is extracted from IR, to be used to fetch the operand.

4. **Fetch operand** The value of the operand of the instruction is fetched from memory into the processor. In Papyrus, this value will be stored in a register called the **memory data register** (MDR). In our example, the operand address is 65, and location 65 (Figure 2.3) contains the value 10, so MDR will be assigned this value.

5. **Execute instruction** Now that all the values of operands are contained in processor registers, Papyrus can proceed to execute the instruction whose function code is held in the high byte of IR. In this

case, the instruction is a simple LOAD A, so the 'execute' stage simply involves transferring the operand value (10) from MDR into the A register.

6. **End** The steps required to perform the instruction are now complete, so the processor returns to stage 1 of the cycle to begin the next instruction in the sequence. Notice again that, as a result of stage 2 above, PC now contains the value 121, so the next pass through the cycle will perform the instruction at address 121.

Figure 2.5 illustrates the interaction between processor and memory during the execution of this cycle. In this illustration broken arrows are used

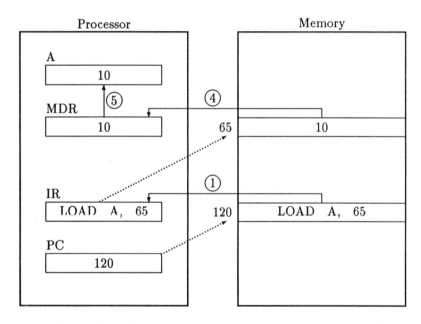

Figure 2.5 Some stages in the instruction-execution cycle

to show when a value held in a register **points** to an address of a memory location. The solid arrows, numbered to refer to stages in the cycle, show actual transfers of data values. The details of this cycle will vary, to some extent, depending on the instruction being performed; for example, a STORE instruction will require a stage to be included for a value to be placed in a memory location. In its broad outline, however, this characteristic instruction–execution cycle is the same for all instructions and for all von Neumann-type machines.

Two of the new registers we have introduced, IR and MDR, need to be described only in order to explain how this instruction cycle works. The instruction register, IR, contains the current instruction once it has been fetched from memory by the processor's **instruction fetch unit**, and the memory data register, MDR, contains the relevant current operand value. The 'execute' stage of the instruction is carried out by the processor's **execution unit**, also called the **arithmetic logic unit**, or ALU. In most cases, execution will involve application of the operation defined by the instruction in IR to operands whose values are contained in MDR and A. Figure 2.6 illustrates these functional units and the relationships between registers.

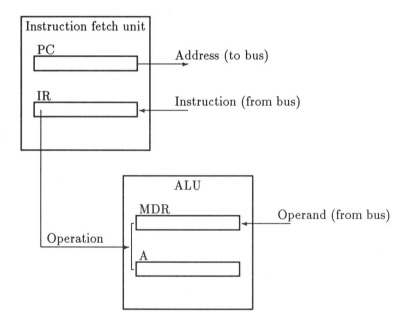

Figure 2.6 Relationship between processor registers and functional parts

The IR and MDR registers cannot be referred to explicitly by program instructions, and their operation is 'behind the scenes', i.e. *below* the 'primitive interface' at which we write programs. For this reason, these are sometimes called 'invisible' registers, and we will not often need to refer to them again. The program counter register, however, is not 'invisible', as we shall see later on.

2.3   Writing a simple program

We now know almost enough about how Papyrus works to be able to write a very simple program that (if it were a real machine) it could perform. The basic elements of the program will be the instruction steps that we require to be executed in sequence. These instructions will be written using the mnemonic notation introduced in Section 2.1.

Because Papyrus, like other computers, represents instructions internally using binary codes, it will be necessary for the mnemonic instructions of our program to be translated into this form and stored in locations in the computer's memory before they can be executed. In the case of a high-level language such as Pascal, this translation is performed by a program called a **compiler**. The task of a compiler (Figure 2.7) is to translate a **source program** written in, for example, Pascal, into an equivalent **object program** which is in a form which the computer can execute — i.e. in the form of binary-coded instructions and values.

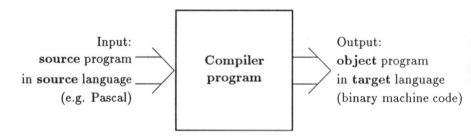

Figure 2.7   The function of a compiler

Because the form of the Pascal Language is very different from the primitive instructions that the computer can execute, a Pascal compiler is quite a complicated program. The programs we shall be writing, however, are in a notation that is much closer to the primitive machine level. In general, each instruction written in the mnemonic form we are using corresponds to an equivalent simple instruction which can be represented in binary form and stored in a word in the store. Hence, the translation from mnemonic form into binary form is relatively simple. The program that performs this translation is called an **assembler**, and the simple language that it translates is called an **assembly language**. We will call the Papyrus assembly language 'PASS', and we will assume the existence of a PASS assembler that can translate a source program written in the PASS language into an object program in the form of binary machine-code instructions for the Papyrus machine.

Declarations and directives

In the PASS language, we can write an instruction in the mnemonic form
we have been using, i.e.

$$ADD \quad A, 65$$

could be an instruction in a program, which would be translated by the
assembler into the binary-coded form 0000100101000001. Although this
mnemonic form is much more convenient than using the binary notation,
it will still require us to decide exactly which location in the memory is to
be used for each program variable. In a large and complicated program, we
might find ourselves having to remember hundreds of location addresses,
with a correspondingly high risk of making mistakes which would cause the
program to execute incorrectly.

In a high-level language program, of course, this problem is resolved
by making use of meaningful **identifiers** to refer to program variables.
Mistakes are much less likely to arise if we can use names like COUNT,
MAXIMUM, and TOTAL rather than having to remember the location
numbers that are being used to store these quantities. We know, however,
that there is a direct relationship between variable **names** and location
addresses, so there is no reason why, even in a simple assembly language,
we should not use identifiers in place of numeric addresses.

When we use variable names in high-level languages, we usually have to
declare them in the program, so that the compiler can interpret their use
correctly when the program is being translated. This will also generally be
the case in assembly languages. In the PASS language, there are a number
of different forms of **declaration**; the simplest, which we will use here,
takes the form of a **labelled** location. We can write this as, for example:

$$RESULT: \quad WORDS \quad 1$$

This declaration tells the assembler that we wish the next available location
(a WORD) to be set aside for use as a program variable. This location will
be referred to using the **label**, or identifier, 'RESULT'.

When the PASS assembler translates our program, it will deal with this
declaration by reserving a word in the memory accordingly. If this word is
location number 51, for example, then an instruction in the program which
is written as:

$$ADD \quad A, RESULT$$

will be translated by PASS into binary form exactly as if we had written:

$$ADD \quad A, 51$$

that is, the **label** 'RESULT' and the **address** 51 are exactly **equivalent**.

In making this declaration, we wrote 'WORDS 1' to instruct the assembler to set aside one word for the variable which we called 'RESULT'. This kind of 'instruction' to the assembler is rather different from an instruction such as ADD A, 51. The latter is translated into a binary instruction which will be executed by the Papyrus processor, whereas 'WORDS 1' does not represent any **executable** instruction, but simply tells the PASS assembler to take some particular action. To distinguish the two, we call this kind of 'instruction' an **assembler directive**, reserving the term **instruction** to refer to executable instructions that will be obeyed as steps in the object program.

Input and output operations

Before we can go on to write a complete program for Papyrus, we will need to find some means by which the results of the program can be displayed for our examination on our imaginary **output device**, i.e. the program will have to include instructions that will send information from the processor and memory to this device. For almost any program, moreover, we will want to make use of data which we present via an **input device**, i.e. we will usually expect to type in data on a keyboard for use within the program. Again, there will have to be instructions in the program to **read** this data from the input device.

Unfortunately, the instructions we need to control and communicate with these **peripheral devices** are rather more complicated in their operation than the simple READ and PRINT statements that we find in high-level languages. Their details will also need to allow for differences between different kinds of physical peripheral devices, i.e. the instructions will be not only machine-dependent but also device-dependent.

For these reasons, we will defer a close examination of input and output operations until much later in the book. Meanwhile, to allow us to write some sensible programs, we will make use of some **system functions** to perform simple input and output of data. These system functions have the same status as READ and PRINT statements in high-level languages, i.e. they are not themselves primitive instructions, but perform the actions required by making use of standard pieces of program (software) which are stored somewhere in the memory. The precise nature of these system functions will be easier to understand when, in Chapter 5, we introduce the topic of **subroutines**. In our programs, however, we can make use of a system function just as if it were a primitive instruction.

For the moment, we will introduce just two Papyrus system functions:

> *read_integer*   ; *reads an integer into the A register*
> *print_integer*   ; *prints the value of A on the screen*

When the *read_integer* function is performed in the program execution sequence, Papyrus will wait for some numeric keys to be struck on its (imaginary) keyboard. As soon as the first non-numeric key is struck, marking the end of the number being input, the program will continue with the binary value of this number stored in the 'A' register. Similarly, the effect of the *print_integer* function is to cause the binary value contained in the A register to be printed in the form of a decimal number, i.e. the bit-pattern 101 will be printed as the number 5. Notice that we have written these **function names** in lower case; this is a convention we will use in PASS to distinguish between the use of system functions, and primitive instructions, which will normally be written in upper-case characters.

An example program

We can now describe the form of a simple program written in the PASS assembly language. Before we do this, however, let us first look at how the program might be written in a high-level language. Figure 2.8 represents a very simple program written in Pascal; many other high-level languages use a very similar notation, and even if you are familiar only with, for example, BASIC, you will probably have little difficulty recognizing what this program is intended to do. Notice in particular the section headed 'VAR' which introduces a number of **declarations** of variables that will be used in the program. All these variables are of **type** 'integer', so we know that they can be represented within the memory of the computer as binary words.

The part of the program between the words 'BEGIN' and 'END' is the **statement part**. These statements will be translated by the Pascal compiler into instructions to be executed on the **target machine**—in this case, Papyrus. The statements of this program will cause three values to be read from whatever input device is being used for Pascal, and the result of a simple calculation using these values will be written to the output device.

Figure 2.9 shows the equivalent of this program written in PASS. The first line of this is similar to that of the Pascal program; it introduces a title 'FIRST_ONE' for the program. This, in the assembly-language version, is an instance of an assembler **directive**. The 'PROGRAM' line does not translate into any executable Papyrus instruction, but is present only to indicate the start of the program text to the assembler.

The next line, STARTADDRESS 50, is another directive. In this case,

---

```
PROGRAM   FIRST_ONE;

    VAR
        FIRST, SECOND, THIRD: INTEGER;
        RESULT: INTEGER;

    BEGIN
        READ(FIRST,SECOND,THIRD);
        RESULT := FIRST + SECOND - THIRD;
        WRITE(RESULT)
    END.
```

Figure 2.8   A simple high-level language program

the assembler is being directed to translate succeeding instructions into binary words which will be stored in successive memory locations, starting at address 50. Usually, it will not matter to us where instructions, and data words, are located in the memory, so we need only use the START-ADDRESS directive if, for example, we want to avoid overwriting some area of memory that is being used for some special purpose. In this program, however, we have chosen to direct the assembler to place instructions at addresses starting from word number 50, and to use locations starting at 100 for the program variables, so another directive STARTADDRESS 100 is present for the latter.

Most of the other lines of the program contain instructions (including in this category the special 'instructions' which make use of system functions and are written in lower case). As is usually the case in assembly languages, only one instruction is written on each line; this makes the program rather long, but helps us, perhaps, to remember the one-to-one relationship between assembly-language instructions and the binary-coded instructions that will be executed by Papyrus when the program has been translated and stored in the memory. Some of the lines contain comments that we have used to annotate the program and explain its actions. Comments in PASS are preceded by semicolons, so anything written after a semicolon on a line is used for documentary purposes only, and has no effect on the way the program is translated or the form of the object program. Comments are

```
PROGRAM   FIRST_ONE
STARTADDRESS   50          ;This is a DIRECTIVE

;Begin by reading in three values
        read_integer       ;using the system function to read into A
        STORE   A, FIRST   ;and storing the result in memory
        read_integer
        STORE   A, SECOND
        read_integer
        STORE   A, THIRD

;Now perform the calculation
        LOAD    A, FIRST
        ADD     A, SECOND
        SUB     A, THIRD
        STORE   A, RESULT

;Print the result and finish
        LOAD    A,RESULT   ;Not really necessary, as RESULT still in A
        print_integer

        stop

;Declarations

STARTADDRESS   100
FIRST:      WORDS   1
SECOND:     WORDS   1
THIRD:      WORDS   1
RESULT:     WORDS   1

END
```

Figure 2.9 The program of Figure 2.8 written in PASS

used in high-level languages also, but are even more important in low-level programming, where sequences of instructions can rapidly become quite incomprehensible without them.

The last 'instruction' of our example program in fact uses another system function, the 'stop' function. This is needed because, when the program has completed its task, we will expect its execution to terminate, and (probably) the machine's operating system to take over. Remember, however, the cycle of instruction execution described in Section 2.2: whenever Papyrus completes the execution of an instruction, the **program counter** will have been incremented, and the processor will go on to execute the instruction that it finds in the next memory location. It may be that no instruction has been placed in this location; however, *some* bit-pattern will be present, and this bit-pattern will be fetched, decoded, and executed just as if it were part of the program, with (probably) unfortunate results! If we are to avoid this happening, we must make sure that the program's execution terminates properly—in this case, using the system function 'stop' which returns **control** to the Papyrus operating system.

The 'stop' function is the last 'instruction' to be executed in our program. It is followed, in the program text, by a number of declarations of the variables we have used. The presence of the STARTADDRESS 100 directive ensures that the variable we have called FIRST will occupy location 100, SECOND location 101, and so on, i.e. the **label** FIRST is equivalent to the address 100. In our Pascal program it was necessary to declare the variables *before* we used them in the program, but this is not usually the case in assembly languages, which allow declarations to be included anywhere in the program. It is usually sensible, however, to keep them separate from instructions of the program, for the reason introduced in the previous paragraph: if we allow it to happen, the processor can 'execute' a data word just as if it were an instruction, with unpredictable results. This is an important, but dangerous, characteristic of von Neumann machines: there is no *intrinsic* difference between a bit-pattern that represents an instruction and one that represents, for example, an integer, so our programs must take care to distinguish one from another.

The final line of the program is another directive, END. Notice the difference between this and the 'stop' function. The latter is translated by PASS into an instruction which, when executed by the Papyrus processor, will bring the program's execution to an end by returning control into the operating system. The END directive, conversely, marks the **textual** end of the source program, i.e. it tells the assembler that its task is now complete.

The two programs in Figures 2.8 and 2.9 look rather different, but will perform similar tasks. Since we know that assembly-language programs have a very close relationship to the binary machine-code that is executed by the computer, we can use the program of Figure 2.9 as a representation not just of a **source** program in the PASS language, but as a way of describing the object program to which it is equivalent. Because we know that Pascal programs, too, must be translated into machine-code instructions before they can be performed, we can use our assembly-language program as an illustration of the form into which a Pascal program will be compiled for execution. In fact, the actual instructions that the Pascal compiler will produce when translating the program of Figure 2.8 may be very different from this. Even so, our examination of the low-level forms of program through the medium of the PASS assembly language should help us to understand the forms into which programs in high-level languages must be translated.

Long and short instructions

So far, we have assumed that all Papyrus machine instructions are exactly one word long. However, as we noted in Section 2.1, this instruction **format** allows us only 8 bits of the instruction word in which to specify the address of the instruction's operand. With this restriction, it would be possible to refer to operands with addresses in the range 0–255 only.

In order to allow Papyrus programs to make use of the whole of the available memory, we will need to extend the instruction word so that larger operand addresses can be specified. The simplest way to achieve this is for instructions that need this extended addressing capability to be two words long, occupying two consecutive locations in the memory. In this case, the first 8 bits of the first word defines the function code, as before, and the remaining 24 bits (8 bits from the first word, plus the whole of the succeeding word) specifies the operand address (Figure 2.10). Twenty-

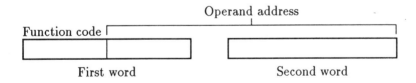

Figure 2.10   A 'long' instruction

four bits is sufficient to allow us to refer to 2^{24} different memory addresses, allowing Papyrus to make effective use of a memory of up to this size.

In Papyrus, in general, all instructions have both a 'short' and a 'long' form. For example, the 'ADD A,operand' instruction which we have been

using for illustration is present in two versions, for 8-bit and 24-bit operand
addresses respectively. The two versions have different **function codes**;
this is necessary because the Papyrus processor, when **decoding** the instruction in the course of its execution cycle, will need to know whether
to use the lower byte of the instruction word as its operand address, or
whether to go on to fetch the next word from memory in order to construct
a 24-bit address. In the latter case, the execution cycle of Section 2.2 will
be extended accordingly, with the program counter being incremented *twice*
to make sure the *next* instruction is fetched from the correct location.

When writing programs for Papyrus, we rarely need to worry about
whether an instruction is one or two words long. For this reason, the same
mnemonic function code will be used for both long and short forms of an
instruction, and we will rely on the PASS assembler to work out which
binary instruction code is needed. For example, the instruction:

$$ADD \quad A, ITEM$$

will be assembled into a one-word (short) instruction only if the assembler
finds that the identifier ITEM refers to an address in the range 0–255. If
ITEM labels a word with a larger-numbered address, the long form of the
instruction will be generated.

Not all computers have as clear-cut an instruction set as Papyrus: some
make use of instructions that may be one, two, three, or more bytes long,
and, often, not all instruction lengths are used for every different function.
The Papyrus instruction set, however, is **orthogonal**: that is to say, every
different form of an instruction, in general, applies equally to each different
instruction type. In particular, each instruction has both a short and a
long form. Non-orthogonal instruction sets are more difficult to remember,
but in a real machine, which has to make efficient use of a limited number
of function codes, it may not be possible to allow every instruction to
be present in every form required. The alternative would be to eliminate
'short' instructions altogether, and use a 32-bit format for every instruction;
however, this would mean that programs would take up more memory than
necessary, and the execution of instructions would be slowed by the need
to fetch two words for every instruction.

2.4   *68000 programs

Registers and instructions

Like all von Neumann machines, the 68000 has a **program counter** register
to indicate the address of the next instruction to be executed. On the

68000, this register, PC, is 32 bits long. In fact, only the lower 24 bits of PC are used, because of the limitation on the 'width' of the address bus along which addresses are sent from the 68000 processor to the memory (Figure 1.7). The 32-bit size of PC is maintained for consistency with the size of other processor registers, and to allow for future expansion in the size of the address bus. Recall, also, that a 68000 address identifies a **byte** of memory. Instructions, however, are always one or more whole **words** in length, and the address of a 68000 word is always an even number. Thus, the least significant bit (bit 0) of PC is ignored when an instruction is fetched, and is assumed to have the value 0, indicating an even-byte address. In the 68000 equivalent of the instruction-execution cycle outlined in Section 2.2, the program counter is always incremented in steps of 2.

In the description of Papyrus, we introduced a single 'accumulator', the 'A' register. The 68000 has eight registers of this type, the **data registers**, D0–D7. Whereas a single accumulator makes for a simpler machine design, we will often find it useful to have several such registers to hold values being worked on in a program. Each of the 68000 data registers is 32 bits long, since, as we mentioned in Chapter 1, the 68000 processor has the capability to deal in quantities which are both *smaller* than one word (i.e. a byte) and *larger* than one word (a **longword**, of 32 bits). When performing operations on single-word values, however, only the lower 16 bits of the register are used, and in this case the registers D0–D7 all appear like the Papyrus 16-bit A register. The characteristics of the program counter and data registers are illustrated in Figure 2.11. For the moment, we will concentrate on single-word operations on the 68000; **longword** and **byte**

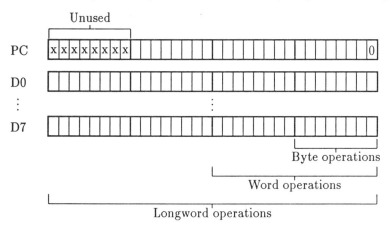

Figure 2.11   68000 PC and data registers

discussed in later chapters.

000 instruction, like Papyrus, performs an operation using from a register and one from memory. For example, an adds the value obtained from an address 'ITEM' into a r the 68000, be written as:

$$ADD \quad ITEM, D1$$

Notice that, for the 68000, we write the 'destination' register into which the result will be stored after the operand identifier 'ITEM'. This is the other way round from Papyrus, which is probably more typical of most machine instruction forms. One of the reasons for the difference is that the 68000 is more powerful than many machines in that it can perform operations in both 'directions', i.e. we can both ADD into a register, and also ADD the value of a register into a memory location. These two forms are written, for example:

$$ADD \ COUNT, \ D3 \quad * \ D3 := D3 + COUNT$$
$$ADD \ D2, \ TOTAL \quad * \ TOTAL := TOTAL + D2$$

Note again that, in both cases, the 'destination' of the result is written *second*. Both the destination and the other operand may be either the address of a memory location or any of the registers D0–D7, and there are also other operand forms which will be introduced in later chapters. In fact, both operands may be registers, in which case we can write:

$$ADD \quad D1, \ D5 \quad * \ D5 := D5 + D1$$

We cannot, however, add together values in two memory locations without making use of a register.

We have introduced these 68000 instructions using a **mnemonic** notation to represent the function code, with symbolic **identifiers** for the registers and operand addresses used. In fact, the examples we have given use the notation and conventions of the standard Motorola MC68000 assembly language. We will continue to use this form both to introduce the instructions of the 68000 and to write example programs for illustration. The assembly language you will use in writing programs for a 68000-based computer is likely to be almost, if not completely, the same as this, although sometimes assemblers for particular systems may have minor differences from or additions to this 'standard' form.

68000 machine code

Whatever assembler language is used, the instructions of a program must be translated into an internal binary coded form before they can be executed by the 68000 processor. The number of words occupied by the binary-coded instruction will vary depending on the instruction and the operands used; for example, an ADD instruction using two registers as operands will occupy a single word, while the instruction:

$$ADD \quad LABEL, D4$$

will be assembled into two 16-bit words (Figure 2.12). Notice that in this

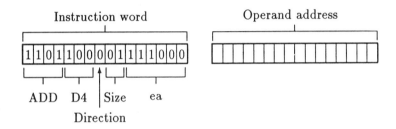

Figure 2.12   Machine code for the 68000 instruction ADD   LABEL, D4

case, the whole of the first word defines the instruction code (including as part of this the specification of the register, D4, which is being used). The operand address corresponding to the identifier LABEL occupies the whole of the following word. The instruction-word for the 68000 is divided into a number of **fields**; the first of these defines the function being performed, in this case ADD, which on the 68000 is coded as 1101.

Because the ADD instruction may make use of any of the eight data registers, a 3-bit field is required to define which one is being used; in this case this is D4, so the appropriate field is coded with the binary value of 4, i.e. 100. Another 1-bit field is required to specify that the 'direction' of the addition is into the register, rather than into the memory location specified for the other operand, and another field to specify that the operands used will be each of size one **word**.

The remaining bits of the instruction word (bits 0–5) are used to define the **effective address** (ea) of the operand. We will find, as we uncover the capabilities of the 68000 in later chapters, that there are many different ways in which the operand of an instruction such as ADD can be defined. For the time being, however, we will say only that the code 111000 included in this field in Figure 2.12 specifies that the operand of the instruction is to be obtained from memory using the address given in the following word. The whole of this instruction, therefore, is necessarily two words in length. If we wish to ADD together the values in two registers, however, it is possible to encode this instruction in one word (Figure 2.13). In this case,

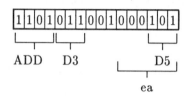

Figure 2.13   Machine code for the instruction   ADD   D5, D3

the fact that the second operand of the instruction is register D5 is included in the coding of the 'effective address' field, ea.

It is also possible that 16 bits may be insufficient to represent the address of the operand that we require; in this case, two words will be used for the operand address of the instruction, and the 'ea' field will be coded to signify this. Thus, the ADD instruction may, in different versions, be one, two, or three words in length. However, we will not usually have to worry about this, and certainly we will very rarely, when writing programs for the 68000, need to be concerned with the coding of the instructions we are using. So (as with Papyrus), having introduced the elements of the instruction-code representation in use, we will in future use, instead, the mnemonic representation of instructions to describe them and illustrate their application.

Other simple instructions

The 68000 subtraction instruction has exactly the same forms as ADD; for example:

$$SUB \quad D5, TOTAL \qquad * TOTAL := TOTAL - D5$$

Note that the instruction subtracts the value of the first operand (in this case, D5) from that of the second, storing the result in the location of the second operand (TOTAL).

The LOAD and STORE instructions which we introduced for Papyrus are, on the 68000, replaced by a single general MOVE instruction which enables values to be copied (assigned) between memory locations and registers. The general form of this instruction (for operands of length one word) is:

$$MOVE \quad (ea), (ea)$$

i.e. we can 'move' a value from any **effective address** to any other effective address. As we have seen from the example of ADD, an 'effective address' may be either a memory location or one of the data registers. Hence, examples of MOVE instructions include:

MOVE D1, STORE	** STORE := D1*
MOVE VAL, D3	** D3 := VAL*
MOVE D2, D3	** D3 := D2*
MOVE SOURCE, DESTINATION	** DESTINATION := SOURCE*

The last of these is an example of a 'store-to-store' operation, which transfers a value between two memory locations without making use of a register. We did not find this instruction on Papyrus, and indeed many less powerful processors than the 68000 do not have an instruction of this type. On the 68000, MOVE is the only instruction which has this completely general form; ADD, SUB, and most other instructions require at least one of the operands to be in a register.

An example program

Figure 2.14 shows a 68000 assembly-language version of the program that we have been using, in Figures 2.8 and 2.9, to contrast high-level and low-level language programming. It can be seen at once that the 68000 program is very similar in its general form to the PASS assembly-language program of Figure 2.9, although the details of the instructions and directives used are different. As we have mentioned before, there are differences, mainly quite minor, between various different assembly languages used for the 68000, and it is possible that the language in use on the machine you are using will have some differences from the notation we are using. We have also assumed, again, the existence of system **functions** to perform simple input and output operations, in this case using the register D0. The existence and form of these functions is not standard to the 68000, but will depend on the particular machine in use. For this reason, we have written these 'instructions' in a different typeface to signify that, in a real program, they will have to be replaced by whatever instructions are required to perform these operations on the particular machine you are using.

Like our PASS assembly-language program, this program in 68000 assembler includes **instructions**, **directives**, **declarations**, and **comments**.

```
TTL      FIRST_ONE
ORG   1100                          * The 'start address' directive

* Begin by reading in three values. We will assume that a
* System function 'read_integer' is available to help us

              read_integer          * read into D0
              MOVE   D0, FIRST       * store the number in memory
              read_integer
              MOVE   D0, SECOND
              read_integer
              MOVE   D0, THIRD

* Now perform the calculation
              MOVE   FIRST, D0       * D0 := FIRST
              ADD    SECOND, D0
              SUB    THIRD, D0
              MOVE   D0, RESULT

* Print the result and finish
              MOVE   RESULT, D0
              print_integer          * function to print the value in D0

              TRAP   #0              * The 'stop' instruction

* Declarations

ORG   1200
FIRST:        DS   1
SECOND:       DS   1
THIRD:        DS   1
RESULT:       DS   1

END
```

Figure 2.14   A simple 68000 assembler-language program

We have already discussed the form taken by the simple instructions ADD, SUB, and MOVE for the 68000. In this program, we have not attempted to take advantage of any of the more powerful features of the machine; for example, we have used only the one data register, D0. This enables us to compare more readily the programs of Figures 2.9 and 2.14, without, so far, exploiting the fuller capabilities of the 68000.

One other instruction is used in Figure 2.14; this is the TRAP instruction which brings the program's execution to a halt by returning control into the machine's operating system. In fact, the 68000 TRAP instruction has a wider role than this, determined by the value of its operand. In Figure 2.14, the operand is written '#0', the # symbol signifying that the number 0 which follows is an integer **value**, rather than the **address** of an operand. We are assuming that the TRAP instruction with operand value 0 will have the effect of terminating program execution, but this, too, is something that, because it depends on the operating system software, may be different on the machine you are using. We will return to explain the TRAP instruction fully in a later chapter.

The directives, declarations, and comments of our 68000 program all follow the pattern introduced earlier for PASS. The TTL (TITLE) directive introduces the program name, and ORG (ORIGIN) defines a starting address for a section of the program. Declarations make use of the directive DS (define storage) to set aside one or more **words** for a labelled variable. Comments, in this assembly language, are preceded by the * symbol; again, however, it is necessary to be aware that in different versions of the 68000 assembly-language for different 68000-based computers, these details may change.

2.5   Exercises

1. Section 2.2 described, in general terms, the sequence of steps involved
   in the execution of a single instruction. Write down a corresponding
   sequence which would be required for the execution of a 68000 instruction:

   ADD   D1, MEMLOC

   The sequence must allow for the length of the instruction (2 words) and
   for the fact that it involves storing a result in the memory.

2. What would be the nearest high-level language equivalents (in Pascal or whatever other language you are familiar with) to the following
   assembly-language elements?

   (a) The instruction MOVE   P, Q

   (b) The directive TTL

   (c) The declaration NUM: DS 1

3. Write the program of Figure 2.14 in a form that is suitable for execution
   on the computer you are using. You will need to investigate (a) how to
   express equivalents to the system functions read_integer and print_integer;
   (b) how to bring the program's execution to an end (possibly replacing
   the TRAP instruction used); and (c) any other differences in the assembly language you will be using. When the program has been converted
   into the appropriate form, assemble and run it on the computer.

4. Modify the program to perform the equivalent of the Pascal assignment

   *answer := 2 * alpha + beta*

   for some numbers *alpha, beta* read as data. Assemble and run your
   modified program, testing that it produces the correct answer for various
   cases. Investigate the consequence of executing the program for *alpha*
   = 30 000, *beta* = 10 000. Do you understand the reason for this result?

5. Find out how much memory is occupied by your program, in two ways:
   (a) by adding up the sizes of the instructions used, and (b) from information produced by the system when your program is assembled and/or
   executed.

Chapter 3

Arithmetic and control

3.1 Simple arithmetic on the computer

To illustrate the simple instructions that we have introduced so far, we have been assuming that operand values of **type** integer can be represented as bit-patterns within words of memory or registers, and that instructions like ADD and SUB will perform operations using these bit-patterns to produce the expected results. To understand how this is so, we must examine more closely the way in which integers are represented in binary notation.

Any **positive** integer can be expressed as a sum of powers of 2: for example, the number $25 = 16+8+1$, i.e. $2^4 + 2^3 + 2^0$. Another way of writing this would be $1 \times 2^4 + 1 \times 2^3 + 0 \times 2^2 + 0 \times 2^1 + 1 \times 2^0$, from which we derive the binary representation of the number: 11001.

Notice the way in which each **bit position** in this representation is associated with a particular power of 2; the rightmost, or **least significant bit** has the power 2^0, the next 2^1, and so on. This **positional notation** is essentially the same as we use for decimal numbers: in writing the decimal number 25 we are using a positional notation to represent a number whose value is $2 \times 10^1 + 5 \times 10^0$. The **binary** positional notation is the basis for representing integers within words in the computer's memory (Figure 3.1).

The computer **processor** performs arithmetic on these values in just the same way as we would do so (in binary or in decimal notation). To perform an addition of two binary numbers, we, or the computer, must start by adding the least significant bits. If the result of this is greater than 1, then a **carry** of 1 must be taken into the next addition stage, in which the bits of power 2^1 are added. This procedure is repeated for each

43

bit position in turn, from right (least significant) to left (most significant) until the end of the word is reached.

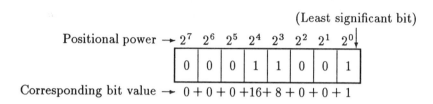

Figure 3.1   The number 25 represented in a byte of store

Negative numbers

How are we to represent a negative integer within a word of memory? In everyday usage, we identify a negative number by prefixing it with a minus sign; thus, for example, -84 is a negative decimal number. We sometimes also use the plus sign as a prefix to show that an integer is positive.

We *can* do something similar using bits within memory words. Recall that the interpretation of a 'bit' as being a numeric value, 0 or 1, is only one way of thinking about it; we can, equally validly, think of the two states of a particular bit as representing the signs, $+$ and $-$. This is, in fact, the basis of the way in which negative numbers are represented in most computers. When a word of memory is used to contain a signed integer, the leftmost (most significant) bit is interpreted as containing the sign of the number. Conventionally, the bit-value 0 is equivalent to a '$+$' sign, and 1 stands for '$-$'.

It might appear that, using this convention, the number -1 would be represented in 8 bits by the bit pattern 10000001. In fact, while this form of representation would be possible, it is not the one used by nearly all computers. The drawback of this so-called **sign and magnitude** representation is that in order to carry out, for example, an addition between a positive and a negative number, a quite different **procedure** is required from that used in adding two positive numbers. When *we* carry out arithmetic, we understand that the addition of a negative number to a positive one is equivalent to a subtraction. For the computer processor to make this observation and act on it accordingly, however, would lead to additional complexity and consequent slower operation of its arithmetic circuitry.

For this reason, almost all computers make use of an alternative **twos complement notation** to represent signed numbers. In this notation, the leftmost bit of the word is again used as the **sign bit**; but in this case, the

presence of a minus sign is not interpreted as negating the value of the rest
of the word. Instead, the sign bit alone is interpreted as carrying a negative
power of 2, while all other bits are positive, as before.

Figure 3.2 should help to make this clear. Notice that in this 8-bit

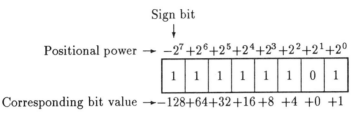

Figure 3.2   A negative number in a byte of store

representation, the leftmost, or sign bit, is associated with the **negative**
power 2^7, i.e. a 1 in this position has the bit-value -128. The other bits are
all positive, as before, so that had the sign bit in Figure 3.2 had the value 0,
the number encoded would have been evaluated as $64+32+16+8+4+0+1$
$= 125$. The presence of a negative sign does *not* mean that this number
becomes -125; instead, we evaluate it as $-128+64+32+16+8+4+0+1 =$
$-128+125 = -3$.

The advantage of this form of representation is that the operations of
addition and subtraction can be carried out, bit-by-bit, on these numbers
without the need to distinguish between different cases of positive and negative sign. It is easy to confirm this. Try, for example, adding the binary
number 4 (100) to the bit-pattern shown in Figure 3.2, using the bit-by-bit
addition procedure we used for positive integers. You should find that, if
you ignore a final **carry out** from the most significant bit, you are left with
the correct answer, $-3+4 = 1$ (Figure 3.3).

Carry and overflow

The form of number representation we are using is called **twos complement notation** because we negate a number by inverting (**complementing**) all its bits to form the **ones complement**, and then adding a further
1 to the result. Thus:

$$
\begin{aligned}
3 &= 00000011 \\
\text{(ones complement)} &= 11111100 \\
(+1) &= 11111101 \Rightarrow -3 \text{ in twos complement form}
\end{aligned}
$$

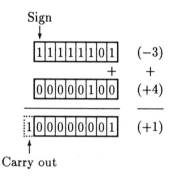

Figure 3.3   Addition of signed 8-bit numbers

In performing this conversion, we must ignore any **carry out** that results from the addition, just as we did when performing the addition in Figure 3.3. In general, when performing twos complement arithmetic, a carry out from the sign bit does not indicate an incorrect result of the operation. It is clear, however, that incorrect results *can* sometimes arise if we perform arithmetic within words of fixed size. Suppose, for example, we add the numbers +127 and +1 within 8-bit (signed) words:

$$
\begin{aligned}
+127 \;&=\; 01111111 \\
+\,1 \;&=\; \underline{00000001} \\
\text{result} \;&=\; \overline{10000000}
\end{aligned}
$$

The answer we get *should* be +128, and indeed, in unsigned binary notation, that is the interpretation of the bit-pattern we have obtained. However, if the leftmost bit is interpreted as a sign, the number we have must be (in twos complement notation) evaluated as −128!

The problem has arisen because, in a **signed** 8-bit word, the largest positive integer we can represent is +127. If we add 1 to this, the consequence is a carry into the sign bit leading to an incorrect result. We call this sort of carry an **overflow** condition. Overflow (in signed 8-bit arithmetic) will arise if we add two positive numbers whose sum is greater than 127, or two negative numbers whose sum is less than −128. More precisely, and in general, an overflow condition arises when there is a carry *in* to the sign bit but no carry *out* (as, for example, when we add two positive numbers which overflow into the sign bit), or if there is a carry out from the sign bit when there has been no carry into it (as happens when we add two negative numbers whose sum cannot be represented in the number of bits we have available).

Status bits

The conditions of **carry** and **overflow**, which arise in certain cases of twos complement arithmetic, may appear to be similar but have very different meanings. As we have seen, the fact that a carry out has occurred as a result of an arithmetic operation does not imply that the bit-pattern remaining within the word is an incorrect representation of the result required. An overflow condition, conversely, *does* imply that the result obtained is incorrect, because the correct result cannot be represented using the number of bit-positions available.

Clearly, it will be important for us to know when overflow has occurred during an arithmetic calculation. As we shall see later, it is also sometimes important to know when a carry condition has arisen. To allow us, in our programs, to detect these conditions, the processor must record their occurrence within a special register: the **status register**, SR.

In order to record whether or not a single condition has arisen, a single bit only is required; we can mark the occurrence of the condition by setting the bit to the value 1. Within the status register, particular bits are used to record each of the conditions, carry and overflow, which we have been discussing. When a carry or overflow condition arises from an arithmetic operation, the processor will automatically record this fact by setting the appropriate bit in SR.

Carry and overflow are not the only 'conditions' that may arise which we may wish to know about; in particular, we will often want to know whether the result of a calculation is positive, negative, or zero. To help us do this, Papyrus also records within its status register two further conditions, to mark when the result of the previous arithmetic operation is negative or zero. The **carry**, **overflow**, **sign**, and **zero** conditions are recorded as separate **status bits** within SR, which, as we shall see shortly, can be examined individually within our programs. In general, these arithmetic status bits will refer to the previous arithmetic operation, and will be reset when the next such operation is performed.

The Papyrus status register, illustrated in Figure 3.4, is 16 bits long. The particular bit-positions used to record each different condition are not at all significant; nor, for the moment, will we consider the use of the other bits in this word, except to observe that they will provide a means of recording the occurrence of other 'conditions' beyond those that we have been discussing.

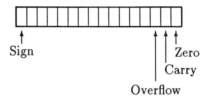

Sign   Zero
              Carry
          Overflow

Figure 3.4   The Papyrus status register, showing some status bits

Numbers in the store

One thing we very often want to do, in both high- and low-level programs, is perform calculations in which some of the terms are not program 'variables' but actual numeric values. A simple example of this occurs when we want to increment a variable. In Pascal, this could take the form of the statement:

count := count+1;

One way of doing this in assembly language would be to use a memory location that we know to contain the binary representation of the number 1. If this location has the identifier, or label 'ONE', (for example), then the PASS equivalent of the Pascal statement would be:

LOAD   A,   COUNT
ADD   A,   ONE
STORE   A,   COUNT

The PASS language allows us to define a location that contains a particular numeric value by simply writing that value on a separate line of the program: we can attach an identifier, or label, to that location if we wish, just as we did when we were declaring program variables using the WORDS directive. In fact, the only difference between a declaration of the form:

SOMENUM :   WORDS   1

and one of the form:

SOMENUM :   17

is that in the first case, no defined bit-pattern is placed in the memory location allocated, whereas in the latter, the location labelled 'SOMENUM' will contain the representation of the number 17.

We can, in this way, define a number of locations to contain useful values, thus:

```
STARTADDRESS 200
ONE:      1            ;Address 200 contains the number 1
MINUS1:   −1           ;Address 201 contains the number -1
          1756         ;Address 202 (unlabelled) contains
                       ;another number
```

The assembler will translate these decimal numbers into the form of bit-patterns which will be stored in the required memory locations. Within the store, of course, they become indistinguishable from other bit-patterns which have been created as a result of translating mnemonic assembly-language instructions. As we saw in Chapter 2, the Papyrus instruction ADD A, 65 has the binary machine-code form 0000100101000001, which is the same bit-pattern as would be used to represent the decimal number 2369; so we could, in fact, have used this numeric representation as a way of writing the instruction in a program. Of course, this is not something that we are likely to want to do; we mention the possibility only to underline the fact that the processor does not recognize the difference between program **instructions** and numeric **data** values. Within the store, all appear as bit-patterns that can be either executed as instructions or used in other ways.

Another consequence of this is that, when we define a memory location to contain a value in this way, the value that is stored does not necessarily remain unchanged once the program begins to execute instructions. If the program performs the instruction:

$$STORE \quad A, ONE$$

the result will be to change the value stored in the location labelled 'ONE', so that it may no longer contain the number 1 which was stored there when the program was assembled. We sometimes say that the declaration:

$$ONE: \quad 1$$

causes the labelled location to be **preset** with the value 1, but this can only define an **initial** value to be stored there.

Immediate operands

Presetting the value stored in a location, in the way described above, gives us one way of introducing particular numeric values for use in a program. As we have explained, however, the fact that a location has a preset value does not guarantee that this value will remain unchanged: it is not a **constant**. The effect of a constant *is* obtained, however, if the operand value we require is bound into the coding of the instruction itself rather than fetched from a separate memory location.

In Papyrus, when we write an instruction in the form:

ADD   A, 28

this is interpreted as meaning 'Add into the A register the value obtained from memory location number 28'. This is an example of what we call a **memory reference instruction** because it makes reference to a specific location, address 28, in the memory (Figure 3.5).

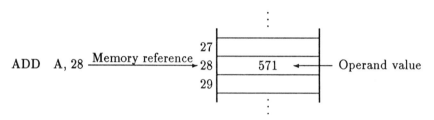

Figure 3.5   A memory reference instruction

If, however, we write the instruction:

ADD   A, #25

this will be interpreted as meaning 'Add into the A register the numeric value 25'. The presence of the 'hash' symbol (#) in front of the operand is taken to mean that this value itself is to be used as the actual operand, without any further reference to the memory. We call this sort of operand an **immediate** operand, because its value is obtained 'immediately' from the instruction itself rather than from an addressed memory location. Another name sometimes used is a 'literal' operand.

An instruction with an 'immediate' operand, such as ADD A, #25, is not a 'memory reference instruction' because it does not require to perform an 'operand fetch' from the memory in its cycle of execution. Naturally, this means that the binary coding of the instruction must be different from that used for a memory reference instruction, so that the Papyrus processor can distinguish the two kinds of instruction and carry out the cycle of instruction execution correctly. The Papyrus memory reference instruction 'ADD A' was given the **function code** 00001001. The equivalent 'immediate operand' form of the ADD A instruction will have a different function code.

Fortunately, of course, we will not have to remember these different codes. The PASS assembler, when it encounters an instruction whose operand is preceded by the 'hash' symbol, will automatically recognize this as an immediate-operand instruction and will create the appropriate bit-pattern within the object program.

3.2   Program control instructions

We saw in Chapter 2 how a high-level language statement of the form (for example):

$$result := p+q-r$$

can be carried out, at the primitive machine level, by a sequence of simple instructions. Indeed, we know that this must be so, because any program we write in any high-level language will, after having been **compiled**, be represented within the computer in the form of a machine-code 'object' program. Since every high-level language program has to be translated into a machine-code form before it can be executed, it is clear that everything that can be done using the high-level language is also possible at the primitive machine level.

The simple programs we have discussed so far take the form of **sequences** of simple assignments and other statements. When we write a program in this form, there is an implied sequence of execution that follows the sequence in which the statements are written; that is to say, when we write two consecutive statements such as:

$$a \quad := \quad b+c;$$
$$d \quad := \quad a*2;$$

we expect the second assignment to take place after the first. As we have seen, the same pattern of **sequential** execution applies also to the execution of machine instructions. In this case, **control** of the sequence of execution is determined by the changing value of the program counter register. The value of PC determines the address of the next instruction to be executed, and, as we described in Section 2.2, PC is normally incremented during the execution of the instruction so that the next instruction will be fetched in sequence from the next address in memory.

For all but the most simple programs, however, this simple pattern of sequential execution is inadequate. In order to write more useful programs, we need to be able to define sequences of computation that are both **conditional** (that is to say, they are carried out in some circumstances but not in others) and **repetitive**. These more complex execution patterns require, at the primitive machine level, **control instructions** to alter the sequence of execution.

Jump instructions

In high-level languages, the simplest variation from the normal pattern of sequential execution of statements in their written order is brought about by a GOTO statement. For example, in BASIC, we might write, as part of a program:

$$100 \quad GOTO\ 50$$
$$110 \quad X = 5$$

When this program is performed, execution of the statement on line 100 will cause a **change of control**, so that the next statement to be executed will be that on line 50, rather than the one on line 110 which follows 100 in the written sequence. Thereafter, execution of succeeding statements will proceed in order from line 50 (until another change of control is effected).

At the machine-instruction level, the equivalent of a GOTO statement is provided in the form of a **jump** instruction. In a Papyrus assembly-language program, we could write, for example, the instruction:

$$JMP \quad 115$$

The effect of this instruction being executed will be to bring about a change of control to the **address**, 115, specified as the operand of the instruction. Suppose, for example, the 'JMP 115' instruction is contained in location number 55. In the normal sequence of execution, the *next* instruction to be executed would be that stored at address 56; the consequence of the jump instruction, however, is to change this so that the next instruction obeyed will be found in the location whose address is 115. A possible consequent execution sequence is illustrated in Figure 3.6.

How is this 'change of control' brought about? Remember that, in Papyrus and other von Neumann-type computers, the **program counter** register defines the address from which the next instruction to be executed will be fetched. In the cycle of instruction execution described in Section 2.2, we saw that the value of PC is incremented after an instruction is fetched, so that the next instruction will be fetched from the succeeding memory

Sequence of control

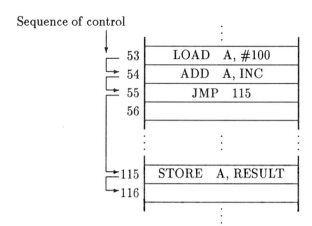

Figure 3.6   Change of control through a jump

address. The effect of the 'JMP' instruction, however, is to bring about a further change in the value of PC. In the 'execute instruction' stage of the cycle, the value of the operand (115 in our example) is transferred into PC, so that by the end of the cycle, this becomes the address defined for the next 'instruction fetch'. A 'jump' instruction, thus, is essentially a LOAD instruction into the PC register; the consequent change in the execution sequence arises from this because of the special role of PC.

Conditional jumps

All high-level languages (or, at least, all those of the type that we have been considering) possess some form of **conditional statement**. For example, in Pascal, we can write a statement such as:

$$if\ p >= q\ then\ max := p\ else\ max := q\ ;$$

The interpretation of this statement is that, if the value of the variable p is greater than or equal to that of q, then the assignment $max := p$ is performed; otherwise, the assignment performed is $max := q$. We know already that each of these assignments will be performed by carrying out a sequence of one or more instructions at the primitive level; for example, in Papyrus machine code, the first assignment could be effected by the instructions:

$$LOAD \quad A, \ P$$
$$STORE \quad A, \ MAX$$

A similar pair of instructions can be used to perform the second assignment. In order to achieve the effect of the Pascal conditional statement, however, we need a mechanism that will bring about the execution of one, and only one, of these instruction sequences. This mechanism is the **conditional jump** instruction.

As we have seen, a jump instruction brings about a change in the sequence of **control** of the program's execution, i.e. instead of the next instruction in memory being performed in sequence, the value of the program counter is changed to select some other instruction for execution. A **conditional** jump instruction performs this 'change of control' only when some specific condition is satisfied.

An example of a conditional jump instruction is the Papyrus JNEG instruction, 'jump if negative'. An example of this in a program might be:

$$JNEG \quad 75 \qquad ; \ jump \ to \ address \ 75 \ if \ result \ is \ negative$$

The effect of this instruction is, when the required condition is satisfied, a 'jump', or change of control, takes place to address 75. If the condition is *not* satisfied, the instruction has no effect, and PC will be incremented in the normal way so that execution continues from the next address in memory.

How is the 'condition' to be defined which determines whether the jump will be performed? As we described in Section 3.1, when an arithmetic operation is performed, one or more **status bits** in the status register, SR, may be set to record conditions that arise as a result of the operation. In particular, if an arithmetic instruction such as ADD or SUB has a negative result, the 'sign' bit in SR will be set. The effect of the JNEG instruction is to change the value of PC, bringing about a jump, if and only if this particular status bit is set. Other Papyrus instructions JZERO, JOVR, and JC will 'jump' on the state of the zero, overflow, and carry status bits, respectively. The JPOS instruction 'jump if positive', is a little more complicated, as it must produce a jump only if *neither* the 'sign' nor the 'zero' status bits are set in SR.

An example

Now it is possible to see how a Pascal-type conditional statement can be effected at the machine-instruction level. Consider, again, our example in Pascal:

if p>=q then max := p else max := q ;

Figure 3.7 shows a sequence of Papyrus assembly-language instructions which would achieve a similar effect. This breaks down into three parts:

```
          LOAD   A, P
          SUB    A, Q        ;P-Q : Status bits set in SR
          JNEG   ELSE        ;Sign bit of SR shows negative result
;If not negative, execution continues - the 'THEN' part
          LOAD   A, P
          STORE A, MAX       ;MAX := P
          JMP    ENDCOND     ;Jump to 'ENDCOND', skip over
                             ;'ELSE' part

ELSE:     LOAD   A, Q
          STORE A, MAX       ;MAX := Q
ENDCOND:                     ; (continue : - end of conditional)
```

Figure 3.7   A 'conditional statement' in Papyrus assembly language

first, an operation is performed (subtracting *q* from *p*) which will set the **status bits** in SR; then, depending on the result of this, one or other of two simple assignment sequences is performed. The 'THEN' sequence follows on from the testing of the condition if no jump is performed; otherwise, a jump to the **label** ELSE causes a different sequence to be performed. Notice, however, that at the end of the 'THEN' assignment there is a further jump, JMP ENDCOND, to the end of the entire sequence; this is required because the normal incrementing of the program counter would otherwise cause execution to continue in sequence into the 'ELSE' part.

Notice also that in writing the 'JMP' and 'JNEG' instructions in assembly language, the operands of the instructions—the 'jump destinations'—were written not as numeric addresses but in symbolic form, as **labels**. This is for just the same reason as we use symbolic **identifiers** such as P, Q, and MAX to refer to program variables. In assembly language, both variable-names (identifiers) and program-instruction labels have exactly the same significance; in both cases, we are using a symbolic name, or label, as a substitute for the numeric address of a memory location. In the case of, for example, the label ELSE which occurs in Figure 3.7, the location

referred to contains a machine instruction, whereas an identifier such as
MAX will label a location that is being used to store a program variable.
Essentially, however, the two kinds of label are just the same, and, in Papyrus assembly language, both instructions and data-words are labelled in
exactly the same way. The assembler will, of course, translate all references
to both variable-names and other labels into the appropriate location addresses. So, for example, if in Figure 3.7 the instruction labelled 'ELSE'
is stored in location number 60, then PASS will translate the instruction
JNEG ELSE into the machine-code equivalent of JNEG 60.

Program loops

In high-level languages, the other simple departure from the normal pattern
of statements being executed in their written order occurs when a program
loop is performed. In Pascal, execution of the loop statement:

> *for i:=1 to 10 do*
> *begin*
>   *read(nextnum);*
>   *total := total+nextnum*
> *end;*

will cause the sequence between *begin* and *end* to be repeated 10 times. The
effect is that 10 numbers will be read and their sum accumulated in *total.*

We can reproduce this effect in assembly language using only those
machine instructions we have so far encountered. Observe that we could
write the Pascal loop in a rather cruder form, as follows:

> *i := 1;*
> *100:*   *if i > 10 then goto 200;*
>   *read(nextnum);*
>   *total := total+nextnum;*
>   *i := i+1;*
>   *goto 100;*
>
> *200:*

To write a loop in this way would not, of course, make good use of the Pascal
language, nor would it lead to a well-structured program. In assembly
language, however, we have much more limited language facilities at our
disposal, and this is essentially the form in which our loops must be written.
It follows, also, that even the well-constructed Pascal loop with which we
began will, after compilation, appear in machine code in this more basic
form.

The clumsier form of the Pascal loop can be translated quite directly, line by line, into Papyrus assembly language (Figure 3.8). Notice the use

---

```
            LOAD  A, #1        ;A := 1
            STORE A, I         ;I := 1
STARTLOOP:  SUB   A, #10       ;A := I-10
            JPOS  ENDLOOP      ;if result > 0, goto endloop
            read_integer       ;A := next number (NEXTNUM)
            ADD   A, TOTAL     ;A := TOTAL+NEXTNUM
            STORE A, TOTAL     ;TOTAL := A
            LOAD  A, I
            ADD   A, #1        ;A := I+1
            STORE A, I         ;I := A
            JMP   STARTLOOP

ENDLOOP:
```

Figure 3.8   A simple loop in Papyrus assembly language

of the **immediate** operands, #1 and #10, to incorporate these **constant** values into the program; for program **variables**, conversely, such as I and TOTAL, **memory reference instructions** are required.

It is easy to see that Figure 3.8 offers a general framework for the programming of many simple forms of loop in assembly language. Other kinds of loop structure, such as the Pascal 'while' and 'repeat' forms, are equally easy to represent. In each case, the assembly-language (and hence machine-code) form of the loop consists of a sequence of instructions, the execution of which is repeated as a result of a 'jump' instruction which returns control to the start of the loop (the JMP STARTLOOP in Figure 3.8). Repetition of the loop is terminated by a **conditional jump** instruction which tests the condition required to end the loop.

3.3   Programs in execution

We have, so far, described only a handful of simple types of instructions which can be written in the PASS assembly language and executed by the Papyrus processor. We shall be introducing some further instructions in later chapters; already, however, we have seen that even a very limited set of instructions is sufficient to enable us to reproduce many of the effects of more complex high-level language constructs. The **arithmetic** instructions, ADD and SUB, coupled with the LOAD and STORE instructions, allow us to build up sequences to perform the equivalent of **assignment** statements involving the evaluation of arithmetic expressions. These sequences can be organized into **conditional** and **loop** structures using only the simple **jump** instructions which we have defined.

This limited repertoire of instructions, in contrast to the richness of form found in high-level languages, is characteristic of the 'primitive level' programming interface. The consequence is, as we have already begun to see, that when a high-level language program is translated into machine code, quite lengthy and sometimes complex instruction sequences are sometimes required to achieve the required effects. For example, if we wish to perform a multiplication operation, using only the simple instructions we have described so far, we would have to write a sequence in which a loop was used to perform a repeated addition operation for the necessary number of times.

The construction of these sequences of simple instructions to achieve higher-level functions is the essence of assembly-language programming. More importantly, of course, creation of these instruction sequences to carry out high-level language program forms is central to the operation of a high-level language compiler. Both in order to write assembly-language programs successfully, and to understand how high-level language programs are performed in their object-code form, we need to study and understand what is happening within the computer when these instruction sequences are executed.

Machine states

Let us consider, again, the effects of an instruction such as ADD A, #25 being executed by the Papyrus processor. There are three such effects:

1. The value contained in the 'A' register is changed (specifically, the number 25 is added to it).

2. The **status bits** in SR are changed to record the conditions of carry, overflow, sign, and zero which may arise as a result of the addition.

3. The **program counter**, PC, is incremented to contain the address of the next instruction in sequence.

No other 'visible' parts of the machine are altered in any way; we need not here concern ourselves with any changes to invisible registers such as the instruction register, IR. We can say, therefore, that the execution of this instruction has brought about a change in the (visible) **state** of Papyrus, the details of which are as described above. We can think of every instruction as having this effect: of changing the **state** of the machine in some defined way.

What are the constituents of the machine 'state'? They are precisely those parts of the machine architecture that can be affected by the execution of instructions, i.e. the locations of the **memory**, and the set of visible processor **registers**. If we consider each register, like each memory location, as being a form of **word** which at any time contains a particular bit-pattern, then the complete set of bit-patterns, or values, of all these words defines a particular **state** of the machine.

This idea of machine 'state' is useful in two ways. First, it allows us to describe at any time, precisely and completely, all the details of the condition of the machine which are relevant to the execution of programs. Secondly, it provides us with a way of defining the precise effect of each machine instruction, in terms of the 'change of state' brought about by the instruction. We can think of any sequence of instructions being executed as bringing about a series of changes of machine state, starting with some **initial state** and concluding with some **final state**. Studying the successive states which arise in the course of this execution sequence allows us to examine in complete detail what effects are being produced by the instructions being performed.

Program tracing

Pursuing this idea of an instruction bringing about a change of state in the machine, we can examine the complete **execution history** of a sequence of instructions, or a complete program, if we have a record of all the machine states that have arisen in the course of its execution. Such a complete record would, of course, involve a great deal of information: we would need to record, at the start of the sequence and again after every instruction was executed, all the values contained in all the locations of memory and all the processor registers. Fortunately, however, for most purposes a much more limited examination of the machine state will be sufficient to tell us all we need to know. If we assume that the only locations in the memory whose values are liable to change are those that are **referenced** by instructions in the program, then a sufficient description of the machine state at any time will be obtained by examining these locations only, in addition to the processor registers.

The series of changes to program variables and register values brought about by the execution of successive instructions is sometimes called a **trace** of the program's execution: a 'complete' trace, including all registers and relevant memory locations, is equivalent to an 'execution history'. In the case of the simple Papyrus programs and execution sequences which we have studied so far, a complete trace would need to include only the values of PC, A, and SR, as well as any memory locations used as variables.

Consider, for example, the simple Papyrus program shown in Figure 3.9. This program reads as data an integer number and stores its value, n, say, in the location labelled N. It then performs a loop to read a further n numbers whose sum is accumulated and stored in the location labelled TOTAL.

For this program, the machine **state** can be described sufficiently at any time by the values of the processor registers PC, A, and SR, and of the memory locations 200 and 201 which are being used for the variables N and TOTAL. The **trace** of changes to these values brought about by the execution of the program will give us a complete **execution history** of the program.

This execution history is shown in Figure 3.10. Each line of this describes the state of the machine immediately *before* the execution of an instruction. The instruction to be executed will, of course, be that obtained from the memory location whose address is the value of the PC register; for clarity, we have shown this instruction in symbolic form as part of the 'trace', at the end of the line. Thus, the trace commences with a description of the machine state just as the program is about to begin its execution. The computer will be put into this **initial state** when the object program created by the PASS assembler is **loaded** into the memory in readiness for its execution. At this point, the program counter has been given the initial value 100, and both the A register and SR have been set to zero (although it is not, in general, safe to assume that this will be so). Because we are interested in the values of individual bits in SR, its value is shown as a bit-pattern rather than as an integer. However, the only status bits we need consider are those that represent the sign, overflow, carry, and zero conditions, so all the other bit-values of SR are not shown, and are represented in the bit-pattern as dots.

The other significant components of the machine 'state' are the values of the variables N and TOTAL used in the program. The variable N is equivalent to the memory location 200, and was declared using the 'WORDS   1' directive. Because no initial value for this location was specified, its value is undefined, and we see from the first line of the trace in Figure 3.10 that this value is in fact the number 127. In some systems, the software that **loads** the object program into the memory will also set the values of all undefined memory locations to zero; but again, as with initial register values, it is not in general safe to assume that this will be so. In the case of the other program variable, TOTAL, however, its equivalent memory location (201) *has* been set to the initial value of zero. This is because the declaration of TOTAL, in the program of Figure 3.9, gave it this **preset** value.

The first 'instruction' performed when the program begins its execution will be the *read_integer* function, the code for which is stored at address 100. The principal effect of performing this system function is to read a numeric value which will be typed on the machine keyboard as data, and to place this value (in its binary representation) in the 'A' register. The other, incidental, effect is that (as for all non-jump instructions) the program counter is incremented to prepare for the next instruction to be fetched.

The change in the machine state brought about by the execution of this system function is shown in the next line of the 'trace' of execution. The value of PC has increased by 1, so that it now has the value 101. The 'A' register now contains the value 3, which we assume to be the number that was typed in as data on the keyboard. No other elements of the state have changed. The *next* instruction to be executed will be the one stored in location 101, as indicated by the new value of PC; this is the second instruction of the program. In the source program of Figure 3.9 this instruction was written as:

$$STORE \quad A, N$$

but in the program trace we have shown this as:

$$STORE \quad A, 200$$

to show that this **memory reference instruction** will **reference** the location whose address is 200. The effect of this instruction is shown on the following line of the trace: we see that now the irrelevant initial value of the variable N has been replaced by the value 3.

We can follow the execution of the program in Figure 3.9 by examining the program trace, line by line, observing the state changes brought about by each instruction being executed in turn. The sequence of instructions executed follows the written program sequence until the first JPOS instruction is encountered; at this point, execution continues from address 101, representing the label LOOP. The sequence of instructions 101–107 is repeated three times in all, representing the three **iterations** of the loop which starts at the label LOOP and continues to the JPOS LOOP instruction in the source program. The third time the sequence is repeated, however, the SUB A, #1 instruction at address 106 reduces the value in A to zero, and the **zero status** bit in SR (the rightmost bit) is set to 1 accordingly. In consequence, the succeeding JPOS instruction does *not* bring

---

PROGRAM   ADD_NUMBERS

;This program reads as data a number, n, then reads
;and sums a further n numbers

STARTADDRESS   100
             read_integer   *;read the value of n into A*

;now the main loop
LOOP: STORE   A, N   *;store into N number of loops left*
             read_integer   *;read the next number*
             ADD   A, TOTAL   *;add to total*
             STORE   A, TOTAL   *;and save in the memory location*
             LOAD   A, N   *;look at the 'loop counter' variable*
             SUB   A, #1   *;decrement it*
             JPOS   LOOP   *;if not yet zero, continue the loop*
;end of the loop: print the results
             LOAD   A, TOTAL
             print_integer
             stop   *;end of program*

STARTADDRESS   200
N: WORDS   1
TOTAL: 0   *;preset to value 0*

END

Figure 3.9   PASS program to add a sequence of numbers

PC	A	SR	N(200)	TOTAL(201)	Instruction	
100	0	0...........000	127	0	read_integer	
101	3	0...........000	127	0	STORE	A, 200
102	3	0...........000	3	0	read_integer	
103	68	0...........000	3	0	ADD	A, 201
104	68	0...........000	3	0	STORE	A, 201
105	68	0...........000	3	68	LOAD	A, 200
106	3	0...........000	3	68	SUB	A, #1
107	2	0...........000	3	68	JPOS	101
101	2	0...........000	3	68	STORE	A, 200
102	2	0...........000	2	68	read_integer	
103	700	0...........000	2	68	ADD	A, 201
104	768	0...........000	2	68	STORE	A, 201
105	768	0...........000	2	768	LOAD	A, 200
106	2	0...........000	2	768	SUB	A, #1
107	1	0...........000	2	768	JPOS	101
101	1	0...........000	2	768	STORE	A, 200
102	1	0...........000	1	768	read_integer	
103	32 000	0...........000	1	768	ADD	A, 201
104	−32 768	1...........100	1	768	STORE	A, 201
105	−32 768	1...........100	1	−32 768	LOAD	A, 200
106	1	0...........000	1	−32 768	SUB	A, #1
107	0	0...........001	1	−32 768	JPOS	101
108	0	0...........001	1	−32 768	LOAD	A, 201
109	−32 768	1...........000	1	−32 768	print_integer	
110	−32 768	1...........000	1	−32 768	stop	

Figure 3.10   Execution history of the program of Figure 3.9

about a jump; execution continues to the instruction at address 108, and hence to the end of the program.

Notice also what happens when the third number read was added to the total. The addition being performed is 768+32 000, but because this is too large to be stored as a positive number in a 16-bit word, there is an **overflow** into the sign bit. The result is that the value in A is recorded as −32 768, and both the **sign** and **overflow** bits in SR are set. In a more complete program, we might have tested the overflow condition at this point and taken some appropriate action; as it is, however, we have ignored the possibility of overflow (and, as a result, the answer obtained is incorrect). The next LOAD instruction changes the condition of the status register, and the conditions arising as a result of the ADD are lost.

Not all computers behave in exactly the same way in their treatment of status conditions. In some, an overflow condition will remain set in the status register until it is explicitly examined and reset. In others, a LOAD instruction does not affect the status bits. In Papyrus, however, LOAD is treated as if it were an **arithmetic** instruction which causes status bits to be set to record its result, while the various 'Jump' instructions do not change the value of SR.

Execution monitoring and dry-running

Figure 3.10 showed a complete execution history for a program obtained by tracing the changes of the program variables and processor registers as it was performed. To obtain this kind of information from a program executing on a real machine, we need to be able to **monitor** its execution, instruction by instruction.

On most microcomputer systems, various **software tools** will be available to assist in program monitoring. It is important to be able to study the execution of a program in this detailed manner in order to identify any errors that may arise. In the example in Figures 3.9 and 3.10, a program to add three positive numbers produced a clearly incorrect answer, a negative number. The reason for this error emerges when, from a study of its execution history, we observe that an overflow condition has occurred that was not allowed for.

This process of detecting and correcting errors that arise in a program's execution is often called **debugging**, involving the removal of **bugs**, i.e. program errors. This kind of debugging has a much larger role in assembly-language programming than in programming using a high-level language. The reason for this is that modern high-level languages such as Pascal enforce many constraints on the ways in which programs can be written, to prevent many kinds of errors occurring. For example, in most high-level languages it is impossible to change the actual **statements** of the program while it is executing. At the primitive level, however, there is nothing to prevent a program from performing a STORE instruction which will change the value stored in *any* memory location—including locations used for program instructions.

Because of the importance of this 'debugging' activity, the software tools used for monitoring program execution are often called **debuggers**. Their use, however, need not be confined to the detection of program errors: it is equally important to be able to trace program execution as a way of studying the characteristics of a particular computer, especially when we are first learning about it. The program monitoring facilities offered by different debuggers will vary. In some, we may be able to trace machine registers and memory locations to produce an instruction-by-instruction execution history like that of Figure 3.10. Alternatively, we may be able to execute the program in **single-step** mode; in this case, execution of the program is suspended after each instruction is performed, allowing us (through commands to the debugger) to inspect values of memory locations and other details of the machine state.

Another useful feature, often provided in software debuggers, allows us to define a **breakpoint** in a program. The simplest kind of breakpoint specifies an instruction address at which program execution will be suspended. For example, in the program of Figure 3.9 we might have 'set' a breakpoint at the STORE A, TOTAL instruction in the main loop. The effect of this would be that, whenever the address of this instruction (104) is reached in the program execution sequence, the program would pause temporarily. Again, this allows us to inspect the state of the suspended program at our leisure. The advantage of using breakpoints, as opposed to single-stepping or obtaining a complete trace of the program's execution, is that we can identify in advance the particular points in the program sequence at which we wish to inspect the machine state.

Even if no software tools are available to assist us in monitoring the execution of programs, the idea of an 'execution history' is still a useful one. It is possible, although laborious, to trace the execution of a program manually, by working out and writing down what we *expect* to be the outcome of each instruction being executed in turn. We can write this in the tabular form of Figure 3.10, in which each line represents a machine state reached, including values of registers and variables. We call this kind of manual tracing of the program's execution a **dry run**.

Of course, as well as being laborious to produce, a 'dry run' execution history depends on our knowing the effects of each instruction being executed, and on writing these down correctly. Although it cannot tell us anything we did not already know about the way the computer works, it *does* often help us to understand what is happening when a program is performed. The reason for an unexpected program result is often immediately made clear by the painstaking exercise of 'dry-running' the program until we understand the cause of our original misconception.

Hexadecimal notation

Most of the examples we have used so far of programs and instructions in execution have involved simple arithmetic on integer values. When we describe the operations involved, and when we write the statements and declarations of the programs to perform them, we usually refer to the numbers involved by expressing them in the **decimal** notation of everyday use. We know, however, that when these numbers are represented within words of the store or processor registers, this representation is in the form of (twos complement) **binary** notation.

When we are monitoring the progress of a program in execution, we need to be able to inspect the values of memory locations and registers. If these values were to appear in binary notation, as bit-patterns, then we would find great difficulty in interpreting them correctly. One long string of '1' and '0' symbols looks, at a glance, much like any other, and we need to inspect a bit-pattern quite closely to decide even, for example, roughly how large a number it represents.

For this reason, most 'debuggers' and other software tools for inspecting the machine state and monitoring program execution will present the contents of registers and program variables in the more familiar and readable decimal form. If the locations thus displayed *are* being used to contain numeric-type values, then this is, of course, exactly the form in which we would wish to inspect them. Sometimes, however, this is not the case, and the presentation of a bit-pattern in the form of a decimal number may then be unhelpful. For example, if we wish to inspect a location containing the code for the instruction ADD   A, 65, we will not find it very useful to have this bit-pattern presented in the form of the decimal number 2369. Equally, if we examine the state of the status register, it is not easy to interpret the decimal number $-32\,764$ as meaning that the 'sign' and 'overflow' status bits are both set.

We can, of course, use the binary notation as a way of representing these kinds of values. Very often, however, we find it convenient to make use of a representation which is neither binary nor decimal: the **hexadecimal** notation. The hexadecimal form, like binary and decimal, is a **positional** notation. Whereas in binary notation each bit-position represents a power of 2, and in decimal notation each digit-position represents a power of 10, a number in hexadecimal notation is expressed as a sum of powers of 16. Thus

Decimal	Binary	Hexadecimal
1	1	1
2	10	2
3	11	3
4	100	4
5	101	5
6	110	6
7	111	7
8	1000	8
9	1001	9
10	1010	A
11	1011	B
12	1100	C
13	1101	D
14	1110	E
15	1111	F
16	10000	10
32	100000	20
255	11111111	FF
256	100000000	100
−1	1111111111111111	FFFF
	(16-bit twos complement binary)	(16-bit hexadecimal)

Figure 3.11 Decimal, binary, and hexadecimal numbers

the hexadecimal number 129 is interpreted as $1 \times 16^2 + 2 \times 16^1 + 9 \times 16^0$, that is, $256 + 32 + 9 = 297$ in decimal notation.

We can express any integer in binary notation, as a sum of powers of 2, using only the **binary digits** 0 and 1. In **decimal** notation, we require the 10 decimal digits 0,1,...,9. In **hexadecimal** notation, we will require **16** different 'hexadecimal digits' in order to represent any integer in powers of 16. The convention we use is that these 16 digits are written as 0,1,2,3,4,5,6,7,8,9,A,B,C,D,E, and F. Thus the hexadecimal number which we write as AB is equivalent in decimal notation to $10 \times 16^1 + 11 \times 16^0 = 171$. Figure 3.11 tabulates some hexadecimal numbers in comparison with their binary and decimal equivalents.

Why is this representation useful? The reason is that the **base** 16, unlike the decimal base 10, is itself a power of 2. The consequence of this is that there is a very simple relationship between the binary and hexadecimal forms of a number. Each hexadecimal digit represents a number in the range 0–15, which can be expressed in binary form using exactly 4 bits. This means that translation from hexadecimal into binary form is a simple matter of taking each digit in turn and expressing it as a 4-bit pattern. The reverse conversion is equally easy: each group of 4 bits in the binary representation is translated into a hexadecimal digit (Figure 3.12).

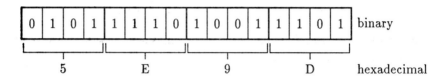

Figure 3.12   A binary-coded word and its hexadecimal value

This simple relationship between the two forms, and the ease with which we can convert each to the other, makes hexadecimal notation a convenient 'shorthand' for expressing binary numbers. Numbers in hexadecimal form are more 'manageable' than when written in binary: they are easier to write down and we are less likely to make mistakes in writing them or interpreting their values. Whenever we need to do so, we can quickly and easily convert them into the form of a bit-pattern. For these reasons, many debuggers will, perhaps as an option, allow the contents of memory locations and registers to be displayed in hexadecimal form, and many assemblers allow program constants and presets to be represented in this notation.

3.4   *Arithmetic and control on the 68000

Byte and longword operations

The 68000 ADD and SUB instructions which we described in Chapter 2 were used, in our examples, to perform **twos complement** arithmetic on signed numbers of size one word (16 bits). As we have mentioned, however, the 68000 data registers are in fact each of size 32 bits, and the 68000 processor has the capability to perform operations on values of size one byte (8 bits) and of size **longword** (32 bits) as well as one-word values. Recall from the machine-code form of the ADD instruction (Figure 2.12 in Section 2.4), that a 2-bit field in the bit-pattern was used to define the size of the operands of the instruction. In fact, most of the 68000 instructions which perform operations using the data registers, D0–D7, are present in different forms, to allow the operands referenced to be of any of the three sizes, byte, word, or longword. Longword arithmetic is useful, of course, when the numbers we are dealing with are too large to be contained in 16-bit words. Some of the advantages of being able to perform operations on single bytes will become clear in the next chapter.

In the 68000 assembly language, we write instructions to deal with operands of different sizes by attaching the qualifier .B, .W, or .L to the function mnemonic. For example the instruction written as:

$$ADD.L \quad D7,D6 \qquad * \ D6 := D6+D7$$

would perform an addition between 32-bit (**longword**) values contained in the registers D7 and D6. The instruction:

$$MOVE.B \quad BYTE1,BYTE2$$

would have the effect of copying a single **byte** value from the location labelled BYTE1 into the location BYTE2. The forms ADD.W, MOVE.W, and so on, are identical to the unqualified ADD and MOVE instructions, defining operations on **word** values.

As we know, an address in a 68000 computer refers to a location of size one byte. A word occupies two consecutive byte locations, starting at an even-numbered byte address. When we refer to a **longword** contained in the memory, this will occupy two consecutive words of store, or four byte locations. The instruction:

$$MOVE.L \quad 30,D3$$

would copy into register D3 the values contained in the four bytes with addresses 30, 31, 32, and 33. In all cases, the address of the word or longword referenced is the address of its first byte, which is the 'leftmost' or **most significant** byte of the value stored (Figure 3.13).

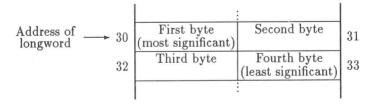

Figure 3.13 A longword stored in four bytes of memory

Some care must be taken when writing programs in which instructions are included to operate on values of different sizes. For example, the instruction:

$$ADD.B \quad D1, D2$$

will add together one-byte values obtained from the registers D1 and D2, leaving the result in D2. In all such cases, only the lowest (least significant) byte of each register is used or altered. In this example, any bit-pattern contained in the higher-order bytes of D2, perhaps as a result of a previous word-length operation, will remain unchanged. This will be so even if the result of the addition is too large to be contained in a single byte; an **overflow** condition will then arise, but there will be no effective 'carry' into the higher part of D2. An example of this effect is shown as Figure 3.14.

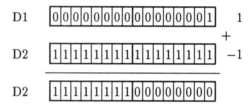

Figure 3.14   Result of performing a **byte**-length addition into D2

Extending values

Sometimes it is useful to **extend** a one-byte value contained in a register so that it occupies a full word, or to extend a word into a longword. If the value being extended is positive, then this simply means that the more significant byte or bytes of the register must be 'cleared', i.e. set to zero. We cannot extend a *negative* value in this way, however. The value −1 is represented in a single byte, in twos complement notation, by the bit-pattern 11111111. In order to extend this number to occupy a full word, without changing its value, it is necessary to create the bit-pattern 1111111111111111 which is the twos complement representation of −1 in 16 bits. In general, therefore, **extending** a number requires its **sign bit** (1 or 0) to be **propagated**, i.e. copied, into all the bits of the extension. There are two special instructions to perform this sort of extension within 68000 registers:

$$EXT.W \quad D0$$

will extend the low-order byte of D0 to occupy a full word; and:

$$EXT.L \quad D5$$

extends a word in D5 to longword size, occupying the full 32 bits of the register. These instructions operate only on the data registers, D0–D7; a value stored in a memory location cannot be extended in this way.

Other arithmetic instructions

On many processors, addition and subtraction are essentially the only *arithmetic* operations that can be performed by single instructions, so that multiplication, for example, has to be carried out by writing a program loop to perform repeated addition. The 68000 processor, however, is more powerful than many; there are 68000 instructions to perform both multiplication and division on binary-coded integers.

The MULS instruction multiplies together two **signed** 16-bit numbers (expressed in twos complement form) to create a product which is represented as a signed 32-bit number, i.e. as a **longword**. This extension into longword form is necessary because otherwise we would only be able to multiply quite small numbers without overflow arising. Unlike ADD and SUB, the MULS instruction can be performed in one 'direction' only; its **destination** must be one of the data registers, D0–D7. For example:

$$MULS \quad FACTOR, D4 \qquad * D4 := D4 * FACTOR$$

This instruction will multiply the value contained in the lower 16 bits of D4 (interpreting this as a twos complement signed number) by the value contained in the memory word labelled FACTOR. Any bits set in the high-order half of D4 will not influence the operation. The result of the instruction will appear as a signed 32-bit value in register D4.

The DIVS instruction works in the opposite way: it divides a longword value held in a register by a one-word divisor, leaving the result in the register. The result, or **quotient**, is expected to be small enough to be expressed in one word, contained in the lower half of the register; if this is not so, an overflow condition will arise. The upper (high-order) half of the destination register will, after the instruction is complete, contain the **remainder** of the division. For example, consider the instruction:

$$DIVS \quad FOUR, D7 \qquad * D7 := D7 \div FOUR$$

where FOUR is the identifier of a memory location containing the number 4, that is binary 100. Figure 3.15 shows the value of register D7 before and after this instruction. The operation performed was $14 \div 4$, giving a quotient 3, stored in the lower half of D7, and a remainder 2, held in the upper half. We can, of course, ignore the remainder if we wish by simply treating the result as being of size one word. The instruction:

$$MOVE.W \quad D7, QUOTIENT$$

would have the effect of copying only the lower half of the register into the memory.

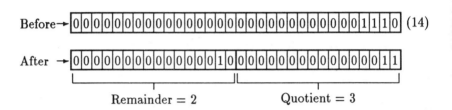

Figure 3.15   Result of performing the division 14÷4

MULS and DIVS are the appropriate instructions to use if we wish to perform arithmetic on signed twos complement numbers. Sometimes, however, it is useful to be able to perform these operations on 16-bit and 32-bit patterns which are interpreted as **unsigned** numbers, i.e. as positive binary values. In this case, the equivalent instructions we use are MULU and DIVU. Their effects are similar to those described above, except that in every case the numbers concerned are dealt with as positive, and the most significant bit of each is *not* interpreted as a sign. The difference is clear if we consider the case of a one-word pattern of 16 bits each of which is 1. As an **unsigned** binary number, its value is interpreted as $2^{16} - 1$, or 65 535. In **signed** twos complement notation, conversely, a bit pattern containing all 'ones' has the value −1. If we multiply this number by 1, using the 'signed' multiplication instruction MULS, we would expect the answer to be −1, which in longword form is expressed as a pattern of 32 ones. In this case, the negative sign of the number has been **propagated** into the high-order extension of the register. In unsigned arithmetic, however, the result of multiplying 65 535 by 1 will still be 65 535, so the high-order half of the longword result will be zero.

Two other simple instructions may be mentioned at this point. The NEG instruction will **negate** its operand, which may be in a register or memory location, and of any of the three permitted sizes. For example, if the register D0 contains the value 18, then:

$$NEG \quad D0$$

will leave it containing the 16-bit twos complement representation of −18. If the byte of memory labelled UNIT contains the bit pattern 11111111, representing the value −1 in 8 bits, then:

$$NEG.B \quad UNIT$$

will leave UNIT containing the value 1.

The CLR instruction is used to **clear**, i.e. to set to zero, a register or memory location. Again, the operand may be of size byte, word, or longword. Thus:

$$CLR.L \quad MEMLOC \qquad * MEMLOC := 0$$

will set the longword labelled MEMLOC to zero.

The status register and condition codes

Some equivalent of the Papyrus status register, which was described in Section 3.1, is invariably found in computers of the von Neumann type. In the 68000, this register is also referred to as SR, and is again of size 16 bits (Figure 3.16). The 'high' byte of this register, however, is for normal program purposes inaccessible, i.e. none of these bits is affected by the operation of normal program instructions. The use of this half of the register, known as the **system byte**, will be explained in Chapter 6 when we come to examine more closely how data input and output operations are performed by the 68000.

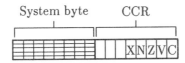

Figure 3.16   The 68000 status register

The low-order byte of the 68000 status register is also referred to as the **condition code register**, or CCR. Within this register, five individual status bits, or 'condition codes' may be set as a consequence of the execution of instructions such as ADD or NEG. Four of these, the N(negative, or sign) condition bit, Z(zero), V(overflow), and C(carry), have exactly the same meaning and function as the four Papyrus status bits we described in Section 3.1, and are set each time an arithmetic instruction is obeyed to record the status of the result of the operation. In this respect, the MOVE instruction is also treated as if it were an 'arithmetic' instruction, so that the zero and negative conditions are set according to the value 'moved'. No overflow or carry condition can arise as a result of the MOVE instruction, so its effect will always be to set the V and C bits to 0. Similarly, the CLR instruction will always set the Z bit to 1, and the N, V, and C bits to 0.

The fifth condition code, X, also records a 'carry' condition, but is not set by all the instructions that can affect C. Its purpose will be explained when we come to discuss how to perform arithmetic on numbers too large to be contained in single registers.

Immediate operands

For the 68000, as for Papyrus, we can write instructions whose operands are constants, obtained **immediately** from the coding of the instruction itself. Generally, any instruction that uses an 'effective address' to refer to its operand can be written in a form such that this operand is a constant. The 68000 assembly language uses the same convention as PASS for this, immediate operands being written preceded by a 'hash' (#) symbol. Examples of instructions using immediate operands include:

```
ADD       #2, D1            * D1 := D1+2
MOVE      #10, TEMP         * TEMP := 10
MULS      #4, D7            * D7 := D7*4
MOVE.L    #$7FFFFFFF, D2    * D2 := (HEX)7FFFFFFF
```

The last example illustrates another convention used in the 68000 assembler. We can write a numeric value in **hexadecimal** notation if we precede this with the 'dollar' character ($). In this example we have used the hexadecimal form to define a longword value in which all the bits except the sign bit are 1, so that the value expressed is the largest positive number which can be contained in 32 bits using twos complement notation.

The 68000 also has a number of special instructions for dealing only with immediate operands. Notice that the usual form of the ADD instruction allows us to add the value obtained from a location whose **effective address** is given, into a register (or vice versa). In the 'immediate' form of this instruction, the 'effective address' is replaced by a constant, so that we can add a numeric value into a register. If we want to add a constant value directly into a memory location, we need a different instruction:

```
ADDI   #1, COUNTER     * COUNTER := COUNTER+1
```

The 'add immediate' instruction can be written in byte, word, or longword forms. There is also a special version for dealing with the very common cases of operands that are *small* numeric constants:

*ADDQ   #1, COUNTER   * COUNTER := COUNTER+1*

This 'add quick' instruction has exactly the same effect as the ADDI instruction quoted above, but can be used only to add a constant in the range
1–8. In the binary machine code for the ADDI instruction, the immediate
operand occupies the word (or in the case of a longword operand, two
words) following the instruction word. In the case of the ADDQ instruction, however, the small constant is encoded in three bits of the instruction
word itself (Figure 3.17). This not only means that the instruction occupies

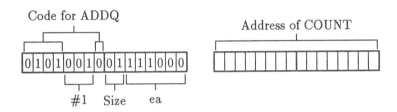

Figure 3.17   Machine code for ADDQ   #1, COUNT

less memory, but also that its execution will be quicker because fewer words
have to be fetched from memory in performing the instruction-execution
cycle.

The Subtract instruction is also available in 'immediate' and 'quick'
forms, SUBI and SUBQ. The MOVEQ instruction is rather different from
ADDQ and SUBQ: it can be used only to move a constant value into a
register, and the range of values of the constant is −128 to +127. This
allows the whole of the instruction to be executed in a single instruction
word (Figure 3.18). Note that the constant value is **extended** to fill the
full 32 bits of the destination register when the instruction is executed.

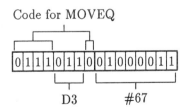

Figure 3.18   Machine code for MOVEQ   #67, D3

Presets and constants

In the 68000 assembly language, numeric values may be **preset** into memory locations using the DC (define constant) directive:

FIFTY:	*DC*	*50*	* *word labelled 'FIFTY' given value 50*
BYTEA:	*DC.B*	*2*	* *preset into a single-byte location*
	DC.B	*$FF*	* *another, using hexadecimal notation*

Notice the use of forms DC.B (and also DC.L) to define different sizes of preset values. The DS directive, which we met in Chapter 2, can also be written in DS.B and DS.L forms to declare a number of bytes or longwords as data locations. Some care must be taken when using DS.B and DC.B; since every word or longword declared must start at an *even* byte-address, it is usually a good practice to declare an even number of bytes each time.

Despite its name, the 'define constant' directive does not really define a **constant**, of course, since the value preset in the memory location may be altered subsequently by, for example, a MOVE instruction to that destination. We can, however, define a true constant using the EQU directive, thus:

*SIZE: EQU   100   * SIZE=100*

This **declaration** does not (unlike DC) set aside a memory location to contain the value 100; rather, it defines the identifier SIZE to be identically **equivalent** to the number 100. The effect is like that of a CONST declaration in Pascal; whenever the identifier SIZE is used in the program, it will be equivalent to using the number 100. Examples of this use might be:

LIMIT:	*DC*	*SIZE*	* *preset the value SIZE (i.e. 100) into memory*
	ADDI	*#SIZE, TOTAL*	* *TOTAL := TOTAL+100*

Notice that in the latter case we still require the # symbol to precede the identifier SIZE to show that we mean the numeric *value* 100 rather than the memory location whose *address* is 100.

Jump and branch instructions

The simple 'jump' instruction has on the 68000 the same form as for Papyrus:

*JMP   LAB   * 'GOTO LAB'*

where LAB is the label of a location. In fact, the operand of the 68000 JMP instruction can be any general **effective address**: the possible forms that this can lead to will be explained in the next chapter. Usually, however, we want the destination of a jump to be, as in this example, an address **label**. In these cases, we can use a less general form of jump instruction, called (in 68000 terminology) a **branch**.

The instruction:

$$BRA \quad LAB \quad * \text{'}GOTO \text{ } LAB\text{'}$$

has exactly the same effect as JMP LAB. Apart from the fact that the only form of operand possible for a BRA instruction is a simple label, the only difference between this and JMP is in the way the operand is expressed in machine-code form. In the case of JMP, the numeric address that corresponds to the label LAB is encoded as the operand of the instruction, in the word following the instruction word. In the machine-code form of BRA, however, the 'branch address' is expressed as a numeric difference, or **displacement**, from the value of the program counter when the instruction is obeyed. This is a **relative** address (relative, in this case, to the value in PC) as opposed to an **absolute** address (which is the form used in all the **memory reference** instructions discussed so far). We will return to consider these terms in the next chapter, when we examine in more detail how operands of instructions can be defined.

The advantage of using this form of 'relative address' for the destination of a branch instruction is that in most cases, jumps, or branches, do not go very far, so that the 'destination address' of the branch is quite near to the address at which the branch is located. This means that the displacement, or relative address, is quite small, so that the BRA instruction can (quite often) be encoded as a single word. Once again, these calculations can almost always be left safely to the assembler, which will generate the correct object code; we will not normally need to know how many words are required for each instruction, or how large the displacement of a branch is.

Conditional branches

Conditional jumps, for the 68000, are all of the 'branch' type, the branch being taken depending on the value of one or more of the condition code bits in the status register. The simplest of these depends on a single condition code only; for example:

```
BEQ   DEST   * GOTO DEST IF 'ZERO' STATUS = 1
BNE   DEST   * GOTO DEST IF Z = 0
```

Similarly, BCS and BCC ('carry set' and 'carry clear') depend on whether C=1 or C=0; BVS and BVC depend on the value of the overflow bit, V; and BMI (branch if minus) and BPL (branch if plus) depend on the N(negative) bit in SR.

The 'true' result of an arithmetic operation cannot always be determined by examining a single status bit, however, because of the possibility of **overflow** leading to an incorrect-signed result. To help with this, the 68000 has a number of conditional branch instructions which will branch depending on the result of an arithmetic operation, taking into account the overflow cases:

BGT	Branch if result > 0
BLE	Branch if result ≤ 0
BLT	Branch if result < 0
BGE	Branch if result ≥ 0

These instructions are appropriate for use when we are performing normal (twos complement) arithmetic on signed numbers; the branch is performed depending on the combination of N, Z, and V conditions arising as a result of the operation we are testing. Occasionally, however, we wish to perform arithmetic in which each word (or longword, etc.) is treated as an unsigned, positive number, with no special consideration being given to the sign bit. In these cases, the **carry** condition, rather than overflow, informs us when the result has gone 'out of range'. Two special branch instructions allow us to test the result of **unsigned** arithmetic, taking proper account of carry conditions:

BHI	Branch if result is 'higher' than zero
BLS	Branch if result is 'less than or same as' zero

Test, decrement, and branch

A final group of 68000 branch instructions is intended to help particularly with the programming of **loops**: these are the 'test, decrement, and branch' instructions. As an example, consider the instruction:

$$DBEQ \quad D5, LOOPSTART$$

Three possibilities arise from this:

1. The condition tested (in this case 'EQ', or Z=1) is **true**: in this case *no* branch is performed and execution continues to the next instruction;

2. The condition is false; in this case the register D5 is **decremented**. If this leads to D5 becoming negative, then again, no branch is performed.

3. If, after decrementing D5, its result is not −1, then a branch to the label LOOPSTART is made.

The assumption made in the design of this rather complex instruction is that it will be written as the *final* instruction of a loop in which the register specified (D5 in this case) is being used to contain a 'loop counter'. The instruction advances this counter (downwards), and terminates the loop when it becomes negative; the condition tested (EQ in this case) allows for another terminating condition. A flowchart representation of the sequence involved is shown as Figure 3.19. 'Test, decrement, and branch' instructions are defined corresponding to each of the conditional branch instructions described above. There is also an unconditional form of the instruction:

$$DBF \quad D3, LOOP \qquad * \; D3 := D3-1; \; GOTO \; LOOP \; IF \; D3 \neq -1$$

Note that the Bcc (Branch on condition code) and DBcc groups of instructions, which depend on the condition code bits set in SR, do not themselves change these bits. This is so even if the DBcc instruction decrements a register to zero, for example; the Z status bit will continue to record the status of the previous arithmetic operation.

COMPARE instruction

The usual way in which condition codes are set is as a result of an arithmetic operation such as ADD. Sometimes, however, it is convenient to be able to **compare** the values of variables without actually performing any operation. The CMP instruction has this effect; for example:

$$CMP \quad OP, D1$$

will set the condition codes according to the result of the operation D1-OP, but without changing the value in D1. The general form of this instruction is:

$$CMP \quad (ea), Dn$$

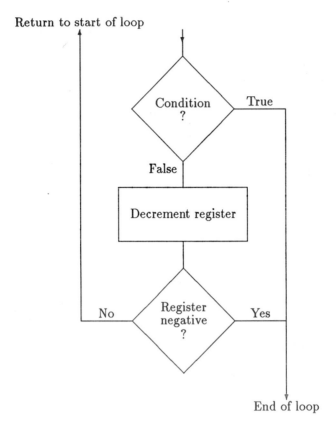

Figure 3.19 A DBcc instruction concluding a loop sequence

i.e. it can compare any register value with another value obtained from a register or from memory. There is also a 'compare immediate' instruction;

$$CMPI \quad \#5, DATAWORD \qquad * \, Result \, of \, DATAWORD - 5$$

Both CMP and CMPI can be used in byte, word, or longword forms.

A program example

To end this chapter, let us consider a program written in 68000 assembler that includes many of the instructions and program forms we have been discussing. The program of Figure 3.20 calculates the average of n integers which are read as data (using, again, our presumed system function

```
TTL     AVERAGE
* Program to find the mean of n numbers

ORG  $1000                      * hexadecimal starting address
                                * for machine code
N:  EQU  100                    * define a constant value for N

* Initialize total and loop counter variables
        CLR.L   D1              * D1 := 0
        MOVE    #N, D2          * D2 := N

* Now the main loop to sum n numbers
LOOP:  read_integer             * read next number into D0
        EXT.L   D0              * extend it to fill 32 bits
        ADD.L   D0, D1          * D1 (TOTAL) := D1+D0
        SUBQ    #1, D2          * D2 (COUNTER) := D2-1
        BGT     LOOP            * continue until counter reduced to 0

* Finally calculate the average
        DIVS    #N, D1          * D1 :=D1/N
        MOVE.L  D1, ANSWER      * move remainder and quotient
                                * into memory
        MOVE.W  D1, D0          * D0 := 'quotient' part of result
        print_integer           * print quotient
        MOVE.W  ANSWER, D0      * D0 := 'remainder' taken
                                * from memory

        print_integer

        TRAP    #0              * end of program instructions

ANSWER:  DS.L  1

END
```

Figure 3.20   Program to average n numbers

read_integer). The value of n has been defined as a constant, 100, using the EQU directive; the other references to N in the program are all of the form #N, showing that its **immediate** value (100) is being used in each case.

The program has at its heart a **loop** to read and sum the n numbers. Notice that both the total, and the loop counter, are contained throughout the loop in **registers**; here we are taking advantage of the presence in the 68000 of several data registers to avoid the use of memory locations for these variables. To allow for the possibility that the total will become too large to be contained in 16 bits, the summation is performed using a **longword** (ADD.L) instruction. We have assumed, however, that the read_integer function places the value read into the lower 16 bits of register D0, so we have used the EXT.L instruction to extend this to 32 bits before the addition is performed.

After completing the summation, the total obtained is divided by N to obtain the average. As we know, the effect of the DIVS instruction is to leave the *quotient* of the division in the lower-order word of the register, while the *remainder* occupies the high-order 16 bits. In the program, both remainder and quotient are placed in memory using a single MOVE.L instruction to store them in the longword labelled ANSWER. The 'quotient' part of the result is printed after moving the lower-order word of the result register into D0. To extract the remainder, we have moved a **word** from the address labelled ANSWER into D0. This will be, of course, the first (or high-order) word of the longword stored there, i.e. the word containing the remainder of the division.

3.5 Exercises

1. Express the decimal number 73 (a) in binary form, and (b) in hexadecimal notation.

2. Examine the bit-pattern for the instruction ADD   D5, D3 (Figure 2.13). Express this (a) in hexadecimal form, (b) as an **unsigned** decimal number, and (c) as a signed decimal number, interpreting the pattern as twos complement binary.

3. Write the decimal number 19 as an 8-bit binary pattern. Form the ones complement of this pattern. Add 1 to this to form the twos complement. Verify that the bit pattern resulting is the same as that obtained by performing the subtraction 0–19 in 8-bit binary.

4. Write a sequence of 68000 instructions to perform the equivalent of the Pascal conditional statement:
    if a < b + 1 then result := a else result := 0

5. Write a sequence of 68000 instructions to perform the equivalent of the Pascal loop:
    while a > 0 do
    begin
        read(a);
        if a > 0 then sum := sum + a
    end

6. Consider the following 68000 instruction-sequence:

```
         MOVE   NUM, D0
LOOP:    SUBQ   #1, NUM
         BEQ    FINISH
         MULS   NUM, D0
         JMP    LOOP
FINISH:  MOVE   D0, ANSWER
```

(a) Perform a **dry run** of this sequence, recording the values of D0, NUM, ANSWER and the ZERO condition bit after each instruction, for an initial value NUM = 5.

(b) Write a 68000 program to contain this sequence, and find out how to obtain an **execution history** for it on the system you are using. Execute it in this way, tracing the same registers and locations as in your dry run, and compare the results.

7. Write a 68000 program that will multiply two positive integers, each held in a single word, by performing a simple repeated addition loop. The program should check that its answer is correct by comparing this with the result of a MULS operation.

Chapter 4

Data types and addressing

4.1 Simple data types

The fundamental mode of operation of a von Neumann computer is the sequential cycle of instruction execution, described in Chapter 2, in which both instructions and the values on which they operate are held as bit patterns in the computer's memory. We have concentrated up to now on the form and function of the **instructions** involved in this cycle, and the ways in which they are organized into characteristic program structures such as loops. The operands, or data values, of the instructions we have used for illustration have all been simple integers, and we have seen how both positive and negative numbers can be represented within the memory of the computer using twos complement binary notation.

The data values manipulated by high-level language programs, of course, are not only simple integers. A language such as Pascal allows us to **declare** variables of different **type**, and to use these variables in expressions and other program constructs. The type of a variable defines what set of values it can assume, and, implicitly, what kinds of operations are possible using these values. Simple variable types which can be used in Pascal and most other high-level languages include not only **integer**, but also **real**, **character**, and **boolean** types.

To repeat, once again: every program feature that is present in high-level languages must have an equivalent at the primitive machine level. It follows that each high-level data type must be represented in the form of bit patterns within words of the store. In this chapter we will study the form of these representations, and the instructions and other machine features that are required to perform operations using values of different types.

Real numbers

Most arithmetic in programs involves not only integer values, but **real** numbers which may have fractional values. One common way of writing a real number is to use an extension of the **positional** notation used for integers, in which the integer and fractional parts of the number are separated by a decimal point. In this case, digits to the right of the decimal point are associated with a **negative** 'positional power'. For example, the number 24.75 is a representation for $2\times10^1 + 4\times10^0 + 7\times10^{-1} + 5\times10^{-2}$.

Again, we can adapt this notation to provide a means of representing non-integer numbers in the form of bit patterns. A real number in binary notation is written using a **binary** point to separate the integer and fractional parts of the representation. Thus, the decimal number 24.75 is written, in binary notation, 11000.11, which is evaluated as $1\times2^4 + 1\times2^3 + 0\times2^2 + 0\times2^1 + 0\times2^0 + 1\times2^{-1} + 1\times2^{-2}$, i.e. $16+8+0+0+0+\frac{1}{2}+\frac{1}{4} = 24.75$. Notice that in this case, figures to the right of the point are associated with a negative power of **two**. As another example, the binary number written as 0.1011 is evaluated as $1\times2^{-1} + 0\times2^{-2} + 1\times2^{-3} + 1\times2^{-4} = 0.5 + 0 + 0.125 + 0.0625 = 0.6875$.

A number expressed in this form can be represented within a word of memory as a bit-pattern in which some bit-positions carry an implied negative power of two, or fractional bit-value. For example, we could represent the binary number 11000.11 (decimal 24.75) in a 16-bit word, using the high-order byte to contain the integer part, and the lower byte the fractional part of the number (Figure 4.1). In this case, the position of the

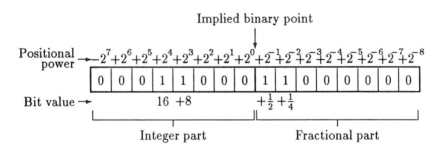

Figure 4.1   A binary fraction in a 16-bit word

binary point lies, by implication, between the two bytes of the word; there is no need for any *explicit* representation of the point within the bit-pattern. Notice also that the most significant bit of the word is still being used to contain the **sign** of the number, which is being represented in a **twos complement** form.

This method of expressing real numbers in binary words is called a **fixed-point** representation, because the position of the implied binary point is fixed within the bit-pattern to give each bit-position a defined positional power. There is no need for the point to be fixed in the middle of the word, as in Figure 4.1; we might equally well have decided to place it so that the first 12 bits of the word contain the integer part of the number, leaving 4 bits only for the fractional part. However, just as in decimal notation the number of **decimal places** used in writing a number determines the accuracy, or **precision**, with which the number can be expressed, so too in binary notation the number of bits used for the fractional part will determine the degree of accuracy possible in the representation. In decimal notation, the number 3.1415927 might be written as 3.1416 correct to four decimal places. Similarly, in binary fixed-point notation, it will often be necessary to 'round' a binary fraction so that it is expressed as accurately as possible within the number of binary places available.

In everyday decimal notation, the rules for adding and subtracting fractional numbers are exactly the same as for integers, provided we remember to 'line up' the decimal points in all numbers before performing the calculations. Similarly, the twos complement ADD and SUB instructions we have studied for performing integer arithmetic in the computer will serve equally well for performing operations on fixed-point real numbers, provided that we are consistent in our choice of a position for the implied binary point within each bit-pattern. We need, therefore, no special instructions or other hardware features to deal in simple ways with real numbers. The fixed-point binary fraction representation is another **abstraction**, i.e. a different way of interpreting a bit pattern which, in the computer, is treated no differently from an integer representation.

Floating-point representation

Fixed-point number forms are sometimes used to perform real-arithmetic calculations in computer programs, and the numeric data types of some high-level languages (for example, COBOL) are represented in this way in the object program. More often, however, fixed-point representation does not give the flexibility we require when performing real-arithmetic calculations. The problem may be seen from a consideration of the representation used in Figure 4.1. The 8 bits used to contain the integer part of the number allow us to represent numbers in the range −128 to +127 only, while the 8 bits available for the fractional part allow this to be represented correctly only to the nearest $\frac{1}{256}$, i.e. to an accuracy of less than three decimal places.

We could, of course, increase both the maximum **magnitude** of the representation and its **precision** by increasing the number of bits used for the integer and fractional parts. For example, we might use a whole 16-bit word for each part, allowing us to represent numbers in the range $\pm 32\,768$ to an accuracy of about five decimal places. The problem remains, however, because in numerical computation we often want to deal in numbers which are either very large (like 8.2 thousand million) or very small (like 0.00000001) and fixed-point representations are always liable to be found wanting.

We can overcome the problem by observing that any real number can be expressed in the form $m \times 2^e$, where m is a positive or negative fraction, such that $0.5 \leq |m| < 1$, and e is a positive or negative integer. This form of expression is analogous to the way in which we sometimes write decimal numbers in the form 0.82×10^{10} or 0.1×10^{-7}. Because we are deriving a **binary** form of representation, however, the **exponent** e will represent a power of 2, and the **mantissa** m will be a pure binary fraction (with no leading zeros). We call this a **floating-point** form of representation because the magnitude of a number is indicated not by its position relative to the decimal or binary point, but by the power expressed in the exponent.

A number expressed in this form can be stored in the memory of the computer by, for example, using one word to contain the mantissa m and another for the exponent e. Consider, for example, the decimal number 3.5. We can express this in the required form by writing it as 0.875×2^2, i.e. the mantissa is 0.875, which is a number between $\frac{1}{2}$ and 1, and the exponent is 2. Figure 4.2 shows how this could be represented in two words of store. Notice that the exponent is a simple integer, encoded in twos complement binary form. The mantissa is a signed fixed-point binary fraction, evaluated as $0.5+0.25+0.125 = 0.875$. In this case, the position of the implied binary point is immediately following the sign bit of the word. The sign bit itself carries the power -2^0, or the value -1; thus, for example, the number -0.75 would be represented in the form $-1+0.25$.

At first sight, the example of Figure 4.2 seems to show a very roundabout way of representing a number which could have been expressed very simply in fixed-point form. Floating-point notation, however, allows us to represent numbers whose **magnitude** is very much greater than would be possible in a fixed-point representation. For example, using the format of Figure 4.2, we can represent an exponent in the range $-32\,768$ to $+32\,767$: thus the largest positive number we can represent has the value of (nearly) $2^{32\,767}$, and the smallest (non-zero) positive number which can

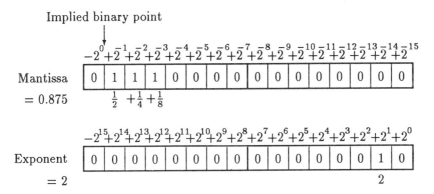

Figure 4.2   A floating-point representation of the number 3.5

be represented exactly is $0.5 \times 2^{-32\,768}$. Whatever the magnitude of the number expressed, the same number of **significant figures** of accuracy is maintained. Because of the constraint that the mantissa must be in the range 0.5–1, all the leading zeros of the fractional part are eliminated, allowing the full 15 bits of the mantissa word (excluding the sign bit) to be used effectively. Thus all numbers are represented to a constant precision equivalent to 15 significant binary figures, or about five significant decimal figures. In 15 bits of a fixed-point representation, conversely, a number is expressed to about five decimal places, which may in the case of very small fractions include no **significant** figures at all.

Some form of floating-point representation is almost always used when real-number values in high-level language programs are translated into their primitive-level object program form. The number of bits used for the exponent and mantissa, and sometimes other minor details of the representation, may vary depending on the language and computer in use, so that, for example, the accuracy of a real-arithmetic calculation is not always the same for two different systems. Whatever the details of the representation, it is clear that arithmetic involving floating point numbers will be more complicated than is the case for either integers or fixed-point fractions. For example, multiplication of two floating point numbers requires that the mantissa fractions are multiplied, and the exponent values are added, i.e. $(a \times 2^b) \times (c \times 2^d) = (a \times c) \times 2^{b+d}$. Even this does not complete the calculation, however, since some further adjustments will be needed to ensure that the mantissa of the result is kept in the required range of 0.5–1.

Many powerful computers have special instructions for performing real-arithmetic operations (add, subtract, multiply, and divide) using some de-

fined floating-point number representation. In most present-day microprocessors, however, there are no such instructions, and floating-point arithmetic has to be carried out using sequences of integer operations on expo-
nents and mantissae separately. These program sequences are quite complex, and require some instruction types which we have not yet dealt with
in this book. Fortunately, however, we are rarely called upon to write programs to perform real-arithmetic calculations in assembly language; almost
always, high-level languages are more appropriate for this kind of computation.

Characters

When, in a high-level language program, we declare a variable that is of
character type, the values which can be assigned to that variable may be
any of the character symbols that can be typed, for example, by pressing
a single key on a VDU keyboard. Variables of this type allow us to write
programs that will read textual characters as data, store, compare, and
manipulate them within the program, and write them for display on the
VDU screen or a printer.

Not all keyboards are exactly identical, but most allow us to type a
nearly standard set of characters including upper- and lower-case letters,
punctuation marks, numeric digits and arithmetic symbols, and a number
of other special symbols. If we include also several non-printing characters
such as SPACE and RETURN, there are in all 128 characters in this universal set. For reference purposes, each character is given a numeric code, in
the range 0–127, so that, for example, the upper-case letter 'A' is given the
numeric value 65; the digit '1' is coded 49; and the SPACE character has
the code 32. This allocation of numeric codes to character symbols is an in-
ternationally accepted standard, the International Standards Organization
(ISO) character code. For historical reasons, however, it is more commonly
referred to as the **American Standard Code for Information Interchange,**
or **ASCII code.**

The fact that there are just 128 characters in this standard set is not
an accident. The set of character-code values, 0–127, is precisely that set
of values which can be expressed in binary notation using just 7 bits. This
allows us to store the ASCII code for any character, as a positive integer,
in a single **byte** of memory. A byte contains, of course, 8 bits, so that in
storing the character code we need not make use of the most significant
bit, thus avoiding any complications that might arise through the interpretation of this bit as a sign. In fact, because the ASCII code is used as a
standard representation of characters for **transmission** between computers
and other devices, the topmost bit *is* often made use of. In the commonest

case, it is given the value 1 or 0 in order to make the total number of '1' bits in the byte an *even* number. This **even parity** coding, an example of which is shown as Figure 4.3, provides for an elementary measure of checking against the possibility of bits becoming 'lost' in transmission through equipment error. When storing the character code internally within the

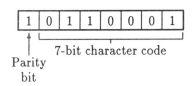

Figure 4.3 ASCII code for character '1' (49) stored with even parity

memory of the computer, however, it is usually more convenient to omit this **parity bit**, using 7 bits of the byte only to contain the character value.

The representation of character symbols using the ASCII code, and their storage in the form of bit-patterns within bytes of memory, is an almost universal convention within all kinds of computers and programming languages. When, as with Papyrus, the memory words addressed by the computer are two or more bytes in length, then two forms of storage may be used. In **unpacked** storage, each character variable occupies the lowest byte of a whole word of memory. In **packed** storage, conversely, a 16-bit word is used to contain the codes for two characters, one in each byte. Packed storage is, of course, more economical in its use of memory, which may be important when large numbers of characters are being stored, but for single variables of character type it may be easier and more convenient to use a whole word for each.

Operations on characters

In Pascal and many other high-level languages, the kinds of operation that are possible on variables of type 'character' are quite limited. We can read, write, and compare characters, but, not unreasonably, we are not allowed to add or multiply character variables as if they were integers. We say that Pascal is a **strongly typed** language because the **type** of a variable defines quite strictly what sorts of operations can be performed on it. In other languages, BASIC for example, the rules are less strict; we call these languages **weakly typed**.

At the primitive machine level, both integers and characters, and indeed other types of variable, are stored in the memory in the same forms, i.e. as bit-patterns within bytes and words of store. Because there is nothing to distinguish a bit-pattern that represents the **character** 'A' (ASCII code 65) from one that represents the **integer** 65, it follows that the operations that are possible on character variables are the same as those that are used to perform integer arithmetic. To compare two characters, for example, we can use the SUB instruction to subtract their ASCII values, and then test the status of the result. We can also, however, *add* the ASCII values of two characters, even though the result of this operation is unlikely to have any sensible meaning.

This is another example of the contrast between high-level languages, whose rules are intended to limit the scope for introducing errors to programs, and machine-level languages which in general allow us to do whatever the machine permits, sometimes with absurd or even disastrous consequences. Most assembly languages are inherently **untyped**, in that all their variables are simply 'words' with no intrinsically different characteristics. The **typing** rules of a language like Pascal are enforced at a higher level, when the program is checked for errors as it is compiled.

Logic values and operations

In high-level language programs we often use variables whose purpose is to record whether some condition has, or has not, arisen in the execution of the program. In Pascal, we would define such a variable to be of **boolean** type. The only values that can be assigned to a boolean variable are the **logic** values, TRUE and FALSE.

Because only two values are possible for this kind of variable, a single **bit** is sufficient to represent it. We have been using the two 'states' of a bit to represent the binary digit values 0 and 1 in the binary representations of numbers. We know, however, that this is an **abstraction**, and there is no reason why we should not attach some other significance to each bit-state. In this case, the two bit-states are used to represent the boolean, or logic values FALSE and TRUE. Conventionally, the bit-value 0 is used to signify FALSE, and the bit-value 1 is TRUE.

In the machine-code form of a high-level language program, it is often most convenient to use a whole word to store each program variable. In this case, it is usual to represent a boolean variable with the value TRUE by a word in which every bit is set to 1 (the equivalent of the value -1 in twos complement integer form) while FALSE is represented by a zero word. We could, however, in a 16-bit word, store 16 different logic values, each represented by a different bit. In effect, this is the way in which the processor **status register** is used; each bit in the register represents a different machine condition, whose status (logic value) is set (1, or TRUE) or **unset** (0, or FALSE). The two forms are shown in Figure 4.4.

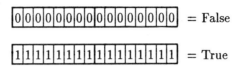

(a) In 16-bit words

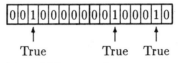

(b) As single bits within a word

Figure 4.4   Alternative representations of boolean values

Operations on logic values, stored as single bits, are particularly significant to an understanding of how computers work. This is because the **bit**
is the basic unit of information storage in the computer, and, as we have
seen, all different kinds of information are represented in the memory as
bit-patterns. It follows that all the machine instructions to perform arithmetic and other operations will, when carried out by the processor, involve
more elementary operations performed on the individual bits of the words
involved. These **elementary logic operations**, in fact, form the basis on
which the operation of digital computers is built.

Truth tables

Because a bit can have only two values, there are only a very limited number
of *distinct* elementary logic operations which are possible on pairs of bits,
and furthermore, it is quite easy to define the result of such an operation
completely. One way of doing this is to use a **truth table**, an example of
which is shown as Figure 4.5. The table describes the result of a particular

A	B	Result
false	false	false
false	true	false
true	false	false
true	true	true

Figure 4.5   Example of a truth table

logic operation applied to two logic variables (or **bits**), A and B. The first two columns of the table itemize all the possible combinations of values for A and B, and the final column shows the result of the operation in each case. In the example of Figure 4.5, the result value is **true** only when both **A and B are true**; so we say that this truth table defines the logical AND operation.

In Figure 4.5, the 'logic values' of A, B, and the result of the operation are written as **true** or **false**. Since, however, we know that we shall be applying logic operations to bit-patterns held in computer words, it will be more convenient to use the representations 1 and 0 for bit-values. Figure 4.6 shows the truth table for the AND operation using this notation. Figures 4.5 and 4.6 describe exactly the same elementary logic operation;

A	B	A AND B
0	0	0
0	1	0
1	0	0
1	1	1

Figure 4.6   Binary truth table for the AND operation

the use of binary digit representations for the logic values simply gives us a consistent way of describing the contents of a memory bit or word.

The operation A AND B has the result **true**, or 1, if and only if both A is 1 (**true**) and B is 1 (**true**). Some other elementary logic operations are tabulated in Figure 4.7. The first of these, the OR operation, has the

A	B	A OR B		A	B	A XOR B		A	B	A = B
0	0	0		0	0	0		0	0	1
0	1	1		0	1	1		0	1	0
1	0	1		1	0	1		1	0	0
1	1	1		1	1	0		1	1	1
		(i)				(ii)				(iii)

Figure 4.7   Truth tables for (i) OR, (ii) Exclusive-OR, (iii) Equals

result 1 if *either* of its operands, A or B, has the value 1: 'result is true if A is true **or** B is true'. This is an **inclusive**-OR; the second truth table in Figure 4.7 defines an **exclusive**-OR operation (often written as XOR), the result of which is true if one, but not both, of A and B are true. The third table shows the result of comparing two logic values (or boolean variables) for equality; the result is true if A and B are either both true (1) or both false (0).

Notice that the result of the 'equals' operation is exactly the opposite of the XOR operation. We could have described the latter as a 'not equals' operation, since A XOR B is true only when the values of A and B are different. Another way of saying this would be to write:

$$A \, XOR \, B \equiv NOT(A = B)$$

'NOT' is another elementary logic operation, which takes only a single operand. The result of NOT A is to **invert** the logic value of A, i.e. NOT $1 = 0$, and NOT $0 = 1$.

Logical instructions

Elementary logic operations are fundamental to the way in which a digital computer functions, at a level *below* that of the 'primitive interface' at which we have been working. However, most computers also allow us to perform logical operations at the machine-instruction level, using **logical instructions** which operate on bit-patterns held in memory words and registers.

In Papyrus, the instruction:

$$AND \quad A, PATTERN$$

will perform a set of logical AND operations between the bits contained in the A register and those contained in the memory word labelled 'PATTERN'. The operations are performed bit-by-bit on the two words, leaving the result in the A register, i.e. if A_i is the ith bit of register A, and P_i the ith bit of the word stored as PATTERN, then the result of the operation is:

$$A_i := A_i \, AND \, P_i \qquad (0 \leq i \leq 15)$$

Figure 4.8 illustrates an example of the effect of an AND instruction. The Papyrus OR instruction works in a similar way; again the operation takes effect on pairs of corresponding bits in the two bit-patterns. The NOT instruction, however, is **monadic**, taking only one operand, which (in the Papyrus machine) must be a register. Thus the instruction:

$$NOT \, A$$

has the effect of **inverting** (or **complementing**) each separate bit of the A register.

As we have said, variables of **boolean** type are often implemented, at the machine level, as words in which every bit is set to 0 to represent

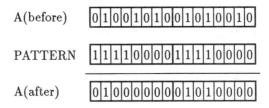

Figure 4.8 Result of the instruction AND   A, PATTERN

the value **false**, or 1 to represent the value **true**. In this case, the AND,
OR, and NOT instructions will operate with the same effect on every bit,
preserving the convention in the result: it is easy to verify, for example,
that A AND B will have the result 'all ones', or **true**, only if both A and
B contain the representation of **true**.

In other cases, these instructions may be used to examine and change
the values of individual bits in a representation. Suppose, for example, we
wish to know the state of bit 3, say, in the A register. The instruction:

$$AND \quad A, \#8$$

will have the effect of setting to zero every bit in A with the (possible)
exception of bit 3. This is because the binary representation of the number 8
has a zero in every bit position except bit 3, and an AND operation between
a zero-valued bit, and either a 1 or 0, will have the result 0 (Figure 4.9).
Bit 3, however, will remain unaltered by the instruction, because (as the

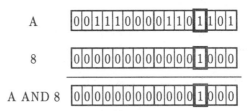

Figure 4.9 Using an AND operation to mask out unwanted bits

truth table of Figure 4.6 tells us) 0 AND 1 = 0, and 1 AND 1 = 1. Hence
the effect of the instruction is to leave A = 0 if bit 3 *was* zero, or A ≠ 0 if
bit 3 was 1.

This is an example of the use of a **mask** to isolate a particular bit (or
bits) in a word. In this case the value 8 is being used to 'mask out' all the

bits in A except the single bit 3 in which we are interested. Combinations of logical instructions can be used to set, clear, or invert particular bits in a word as required. For example, the sequence:

```
LOAD    A, BITS
AND     A, #16
NOT     A
STORE   A, TEMP
LOAD    A, BITS
OR      A, #16
AND     A, TEMP
STORE   A, BITS
```

will have the effect of **inverting** bit 4 of the word in BITS, while leaving all other bits unchanged. You may like to try to confirm this by 'dry-running' this sequence of instructions using the truth tables for AND and OR.

Shift operations

We have seen how it is possible to use logical instructions to isolate a particular bit in a word. Unfortunately, the result is to leave the required bit set (or clear, as the case may be) somewhere in the middle of the word; in Figure 4.9, for example, the bit we are interested in is left as bit 3 of a otherwise empty A register. This is particularly inconvenient if we wish to compare the values of bits placed in different positions in their respective words. In these and other cases, it is useful to be able to move bits around *within* a bit-pattern, so as, for example, to place a bit we wish to inspect in bit position 0 of the word. This kind of movement of bits can be performed using a **shift** instruction.

In the simplest kind of shift operation, the values of all the bits of a word are transferred to bit-positions displaced by one or more places from their original position. This is called a **logical** shift, and may take place in either direction along the word. For example, the Papyrus instruction:

$$SLL \quad A, \#3$$

will **S**hift the bits of A **L**ogically **L**eft by 3 bit-positions. This is easiest to see using an illustration (Figure 4.10). In this example, the bits in the A register are all relocated three places to the left within the word. Bits 'shifted out' of the left of the register are lost, but notice that the *last* bit shifted out changes the state of the **carry** bit in the status register. The register is filled up with three zero-value bits at the right of the bit-pattern.

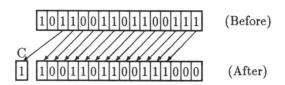

Figure 4.10   Effect of a logical left shift on the A register

A logical *right* shift works in just the same way, except that the displacement of bits is towards the right of the word; again, the last bit shifted out becomes the value of the carry status bit, and zeros are shifted in to the bit-positions vacated at the left of the word. Logical shift operations are useful because they can be used (like logical masking operations) to clear particular bit-positions in the word, and also to relocate the remaining bits as required. For example, suppose the memory locations TWOCHARS contains the ASCII codes for two characters, stored in **packed** format, one in each byte of the word. The instructions:

```
LOAD    A, TWOCHARS
SLR     A, #8            ; shift right 8 places
STORE   A, CHAR1
LOAD    A, TWOCHARS      ; get the two characters again
SLL     A, #8            ; shift the top byte out of the word
SLR     A, #8            ; and shift the lower byte back again
STORE   A, CHAR2
```

will **unpack** the two characters and place them in the bottom bytes of two separate memory locations.

In a **logical** shift operation, bits that are 'shifted out' of the end of a word are lost. In an alternative kind of shift, the **circular** shift or **rotate** operation, bits shifted out of one end of the word reappear to fill the vacated bit positions at the other end. Figure 4.11 illustrates this for a circular shift right by one position. Notice that whereas bit 1 of the original pattern is shifted into bit position 0, bit 0 is shifted round to reappear in bit position 15. A circular shift of more than one place is effected as a sequence of one place shifts. Notice also that in this illustration, the **carry** status bit is again set to show the value of the (last) bit shifted round. This is the effect of the Papyrus shift instructions; not all processors work in exactly the same way in this respect.

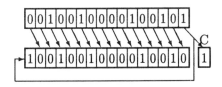

Figure 4.11   A circular right shift of one position

Arithmetic shifts

Both logical shift instructions and **circular** shift instructions operate on 'untyped' values, i.e. on arbitrary bit-patterns within the register being shifted. In another kind of shift operation, this bit-pattern is treated as a **signed** value in twos complement binary notation; this is an **arithmetic** shift. In an arithmetic shift operation, the sign of the value operated upon is not changed as a result of the shift.

Again, some of the minor details of the way this kind of shift takes place may vary between different computers. In Papyrus, the arithmetic *left* shift instruction leaves the sign bit (bit 15 of the word) unchanged, while shifting the other bits in the same way as for a logical shift operation (Figure 4.12). Again, the carry status bit is set to show the last bit shifted out from the

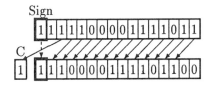

Figure 4.12   An arithmetic left shift by two places

word. As this is an **arithmetic** shift, however, the **overflow** status bit may also be set, if the value of the bit shifted out is different from that of the sign. The effect of an arithmetic left shift by n binary places, if no overflow condition arises, is equivalent to a multiplication of the signed value in the word by 2^n. This will not be true, of course, if a '1' bit is shifted out of the left of a positive number, or a '0' bit from a negative number, so in these cases the overflow status will be set.

An arithmetic *right* shift is equivalent to a *division* by 2^n. To achieve this, the value of the sign bit is **propagated** in the shift to retain the correct sign and to produce the expected twos complement binary result

(Figure 4.13). An arithmetic right shift of a positive number has the same

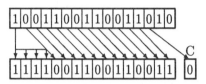

Figure 4.13   An arithmetic right shift, showing propagation of sign

effect as a logical right shift. The effect of division by 2^n, of course, will only be approximate if '1' bits are shifted out at the right.

4.2   Arrays and memory reference

All the data types that we have considered so far have been *single* valued: simple integers, real numbers, characters, and logic values. In many programs, however, we need to deal in *multiple* values: arrays, tables, and other **data structures**.

Because, as we have seen, a single value of any particular type is represented within (usually) a single word of memory, it is easy to see that we can represent multiple values within an appropriate number of words. Consider, for example, a Pascal **array** declared in the form:

counts: array[1..10] of integer;

For readers who are not fully familiar with Pascal, this declaration defines an array, or ordered set, of variables each of type integer. The array as a whole is given the identifier *counts*, and the individual **elements** of the array are numbered from 1 to 10 for reference.

It is clear that we will require at least 10 words of memory to represent this array. Figure 4.14 shows the simplest way of doing this, using 10 consecutive memory locations, starting, in the example, at address 150. Notice that each array element has its own memory location with a unique address; for example, the element which we would refer to in the Pascal program as *counts[5]* occupies location number 154. Again, we have a correspondence between each **identifier** used in the high-level language program, and an **address** at the primitive level. It is usual to use the address of the first element of the array as the address of the array itself, i.e. we would say that the address of the array *counts* was 150.

Clearly, the simple scheme illustrated provides a way of representing arrays, the elements of which could be integers, real numbers, or of any

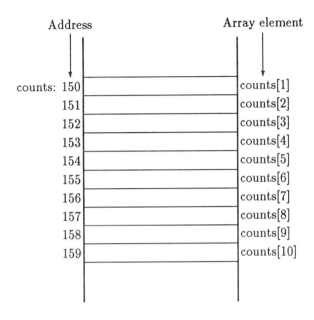

Figure 4.14   A Pascal array in the memory

other simple type. What happens, however, when we wish to refer to an element within the array? We can see that the Pascal assignment:

$$counts[5] := 17$$

requires that the value 17 be placed as the contents of location number 154. In Papyrus machine code, this could be effected by a pair of instructions of the form:

$$LOAD \quad A, \#17$$
$$STORE \quad A, 154$$

It is not so easy, though, to see how a Pascal statement of the form:

$$counts[n] := 17$$

could be carried out, when the value of n will not be known when the program is written and compiled into machine code. We will also find it difficult or impossible to write machine-code instructions to reproduce the effect of a simple loop such as:

$$for\ i := 1\ to\ 10\ do\ counts[i] := 0;$$

To deal with these cases, we will need the machine code to include, not different instructions, but ways of referencing the memory that are different from those that we have so far encountered. These different forms of memory reference are the **addressing modes** available in the computer.

Indexed addressing

In order to deal with arrays, and in particular with the referencing of elements within arrays, we require a primitive-level equivalent of the **indexing** operation implied when we write, in Pascal, a statement of the form:

$$counts[n] := 1;$$

We can achieve this effect with the use of a **register** to contain the value of the **index** required (n, in this example). Papyrus has a special **index register**, B, intended for this purpose. In most respects, the B register appears as an identical second 'accumulator', like the A register; for example, we can LOAD a value into it, or perform arithmetic in it, using equivalent instructions to those used for A. Thus:

```
LOAD   B, NUMBER   ; B := number
ADD    B, #5       ; B := B+5
```

In one important respect, however, the B register is different. Because it is designated as an **index register**, it can be referred to in the *operand* field of an instruction when an indexing operation is required.

A typical instruction of this type might take the form:

$$STORE \quad A, COUNTS(B)$$

in the PASS assembly language. The effect of this instruction, as with other 'STORE A' instructions, is to copy the value contained in the A register into a memory location. In this case, however, the memory location referenced will not be simply the word labelled 'COUNTS', but will be obtained by adding the value obtained from the B register to the address of COUNTS. The B register here is being used as an **index** to the **base address** given by the label COUNTS. This **indexing** operation is illustrated in Figure 4.15.

Consider again the storage of the array COUNTS in memory, illustrated in Figure 4.14. In the PASS assembly language, we might **declare** such an array with a directive of the form:

$$COUNTS : WORDS \ 10$$

which sets aside 10 words of memory, the first of which is labelled COUNTS. If this location, as in Figure 4.14, is address 150, then the instruction:

$$STORE \quad A, COUNTS(B)$$

is equivalent to writing:

$$STORE \quad A, 150(B)$$

i.e. the **base address** of the array is the address, 150, of its first element. If the B register contains the value 4, then the address referenced by the instruction will be 150+4 = 154, and it is this word that will receive the value stored from the A register.

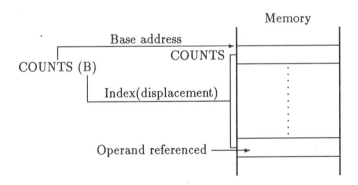

Figure 4.15 An indexed addressing operation

The advantage of this mechanism is that we are now no longer constrained to referencing locations the addresses of which are known when the program is written. The problem of performing *counts[n] := 17* is solved—we would write:

```
LOAD    A, #17        ; A := 17
LOAD    B, N          ; B := n(index to array)
STORE   A, COUNTS(B)  ; counts(B) := A
```

Likewise, the loop to clear all elements of an array is straightforward:

```
              LOAD    A, #0           ; value to store in array
              LOAD    B, #0           ; array index
CLRLOOP:      STORE   A, COUNTS(B)    ; counts(B) := A(=0)
              ADD     B, #1           ; increment index
              SUB     B, #10          ; test for end of loop
              JZERO   FINISHED
              ADD     B, #10          ; restore index value
              JMP     CLRLOOP
FINISHED:
```

This is not necessarily the shortest or best way to achieve this result, but is written in this way so that the steps involved may be seen clearly. The important point, again, is that the value of the **index**, in the B register, is changed by the action of the program, so that the actual address referenced by the instruction:

$$STORE \quad A, COUNTS(B)$$

is different each time the instruction is performed (Figure 4.16).

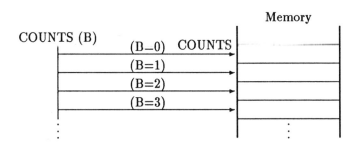

Figure 4.16   Indexing through the elements of an array

Addressing modes

The Papyrus ADD A instruction, which we have used for many of our simple examples, has now appeared in three different forms, corresponding to different ways of obtaining the value of its operand. In the first case, the instruction:

$$ADD \quad A, MEMLOC$$

adds into the A register the value obtained from the memory location whose label is MEMLOC. If this location has the address 80, say, then the instruction will appear in the memory in a form equivalent to:

$$ADD \quad A, 80$$

i.e. the **label** (or **identifier**) MEMLOC and the **address** 80 are equivalent. In the machine-code form of the instruction, the numeric value of the address is encoded as the 'operand' **field** of the instruction word (Figure 4.17).

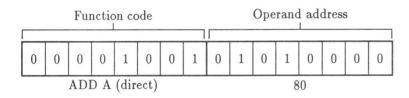

Figure 4.17 Papyrus machine code for ADD   A, 80

In the second form of the ADD A instruction that we have encountered, the value of the operand is obtained **immediately** from the instruction word without any further memory reference. In PASS, we would write this instruction as, for example:

$$ADD \quad A, \#34 \quad ; A := A + 34$$

which would appear in the memory encoded as in Figure 4.18.

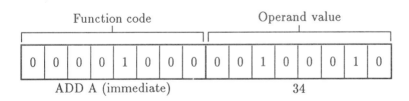

Figure 4.18 Papyrus machine code for ADD   A, #34

Notice the similarity between the two instruction codings shown in Figures 4.17 and 4.18. In both cases, the operand of the instruction is represented in binary form in an 8-bit field of the instruction word. There is nothing about this bit-pattern to show that in one case the operand is a memory **address**, while in the other it is an immediate operand **value**. The only difference between the two instructions is in the coding of the ADD A function in the top byte of the instruction word. Both of these codes are recognized by the Papyrus processor as being forms of the ADD A instruction, but the different versions allow it to distinguish between the two different ways in which the operand of the instruction is to be obtained. We refer to these as being two different **addressing modes** of the ADD A instruction.

The introduction of a third way of referencing an operand, using the index register B, requires another addressing mode. The PASS instruction:

$$ADD \quad A, MEMLOC(B)$$

would appear in Papyrus machine code in the form shown in Figure 4.19. Again, the operand field of the instruction contains a binary representation

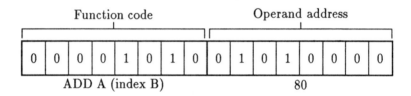

Figure 4.19   Papyrus machine code for ADD   A, 80(B)

of the address MEMLOC; but in this case, unlike that of Figure 4.17, the value of the index obtained from the B register is added to this **base address** before the memory reference is made. The Papyrus processor is able to interpret the instruction in this way because the coding of the ADD A instruction in the top byte of the word is different from either of the other two cases we have examined.

In fact, a closer examination of the different function codes used for the three versions of the ADD A instruction reveals a pattern. In each case, the coding of the top five bits is the same, i.e. 00001, while the lower three bits are coded as:

000   (immediate operand)
001   (operand directly addressed)
010   (operand addressed with indexing)

This regular pattern illustrates the way in which Papyrus instructions are encoded. The Papyrus instruction set is **orthogonal**, which is a way of saying that the general form of the encoding, the breakdown of the instruction into fields, and the interpretation of each field is the same for each type of instruction. In each case, the first five bits of the function code defines the operation to be performed (in this case, ADD A) while the remaining three bits define the addressing mode to be used when determining the operand of the instruction (Figure 4.20).

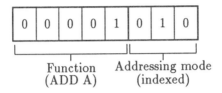

Function   Addressing mode
(ADD A)   (indexed)

Figure 4.20   Encoding of the function-code byte of a Papyrus instruction

This way of encoding instructions is particular to Papyrus; other computer processors have quite different instruction forms which may be less regular. The difficulty faced by the designer of a computer instruction set is in trying to represent all the different types of instruction and addressing modes in a simple, clear, and orthogonal way, when only a limited number of bits are available for the encoding. In Papyrus, since we are cheating by not attempting to define a complete instruction set, we are not required to confront these problems. For example, most of the illustrations we have used have defined operands that can be represented within the lower byte of the instruction word, but, as was mentioned in Section 2.3, all Papyrus instructions are present in versions for both 'short' operands of this form, and 'long' operands which make use of the following word of memory for their representation. Distinguishing between short and long instruction forms will require the use of another bit in the function code. We will not, however, attempt to pursue this and other questions any further: an attempt to define a complete instruction set and to encode it in the pattern we have described is likely to expose problems that we will find difficult to resolve!

Absolute and relative addressing

Two of the three addressing modes introduced so far define different forms of **memory reference** instructions. In the case of an instruction such as:

ADD   A, MEMLOC

we say that the memory reference is **direct**: the operand is **directly addressed** by the address (label) MEMLOC. The address identified by the label MEMLOC defines a unique location in the memory which is referenced by the instruction: we call this the **absolute address** of the operand.

Consider, now, the second form of memory reference instruction:

$$ADD \quad A, MEMLOC(B)$$

In this case, the **direct address** that is referred to (MEMLOC) is **indexed** by the value of B before the memory reference is made. The address identified by MEMLOC (80, say) no longer defines an **absolute** location in memory referenced by the instruction; the reference is **relative**, depending on the value of B.

There are two ways of thinking about this form of addressing. If we pursue the idea that the register B contains an index, then we would say that the value of B defines an address which is **relative** to the **base address** MEMLOC. Alternatively, we might think of the register B as containing a (variable) **base address**: in this case, the identifier MEMLOC defines a **relative address**, or **offset**, which is interpreted as a displacement from this base. Figure 4.15 illustrated the first interpretation; the second is shown in Figure 4.21.

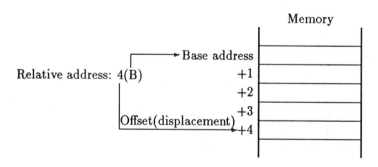

Figure 4.21   Relative addressing

The significance of instructions that address memory relatively is that the locations thus referenced are not fixed when the instructions are written or compiled into machine code. The instruction ADD A, MEMLOC will, once it has been compiled, *always* refer to the same memory location MEMLOC, with the absolute address 80. ADD A, MEMLOC(B), however, can be made to refer to different locations by changing the value of the base address in B.

One advantage of this is that it enables programs to be written that are not constrained to make use of any particular area of memory for their variables. The usefulness of this will become more apparent when, in Chapter 5, we look at how subroutines and local variables can be dealt with at the primitive level.

For similar reasons, on many computers jump instructions refer to a jump destination address that is not absolute, but relative to the address of the instruction itself (defined by the current value of the program counter register). The advantage of a relative jump of this kind is that the piece of program containing the instruction is not tied to a particular part of the memory: it is **relocatable**, and will work in the same way wherever it is placed in the store. This enables a high-level language compiler, for example, to generate an object program the machine code of which is position independent, and can be loaded into any available area of memory.

Indirect addressing

Let us examine further the use of the B register to define a base address for relative addressing. A particular case of this arises when we write an instruction such as:

$$LOAD \quad A, 0(B)$$

In this instance, the instruction defines a zero-valued offset to the base address in B, so that the B register in fact contains the **absolute** address of the memory location referenced.

We have previously stressed the distinction that must be made between the **address** of a memory location and the value of its **contents**. On this occasion, however, the **value** contained in B is in fact the **address** of some memory location. What is more, we can manipulate this address-value just like any other bit-pattern; for example, we can add to it, or we can store it in another location in memory.

Suppose, for example, the declaration:

$$BASE : WORDS \; 100$$

has been used to set aside an area of memory for some purpose in our program. We can obtain the value that is the absolute address of this area by the instruction:

$$LOAD \quad B, \#BASE$$

Notice the use of the **immediate** form of addressing in this instruction. This means that, if the address of BASE is, let us say, 85, then the machine-code form of this instruction will be the equivalent of:

$$LOAD \quad B, \#85 \quad ; B := 85$$

which will have the effect of loading the address of BASE (i.e. the number 85) into the B register. We could then go on to store this number elsewhere; for example, the subsequent instruction:

$$STORE \quad B, INDADDR$$

would have the effect of leaving the location labelled INDADDR containing the address of BASE.

In order to avoid the confusion of terminology that can arise when dealing with addresses in this way, we often use the term **pointer** to mean a value that is itself a location address. Figure 4.22 illustrates the significance of this term, for the example we have been discussing. Suppose that

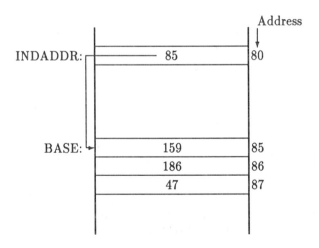

Figure 4.22   A pointer in the store

the location labelled INDADDR has the address 80. We have placed in this location the value 85, which is a pointer to the location labelled BASE whose address is 85. We would say that 80 was the **direct address** of the location INDADDR, or the **indirect address** of the location BASE.

In Papyrus machine language, further addressing modes are available for referencing memory locations in this **indirect** way. The instruction:

$$LOAD \quad A, INDADDR$$

is, as we know, an example making use of **direct** memory addressing; its effect will be to load into the A register the contents of location 80, i.e. the value 85. The instruction:

$$LOAD \quad A, (INDADDR)$$

however, uses an **indirect** addressing mode. In this case, the value loaded into A will be the **contents** of the location whose **address** is contained in location 80. Location 80 (INDADDR) contains the pointer value 85, so the value loaded by this instruction will be the value contained in location 85, i.e. (from Figure 4.22), the value 159.

The convention we have used in PASS to signify an **indirectly** addressed instruction operand is common, although not universal. Use of the identifier INDADDR in an instruction implies that the operand is to be obtained **directly** from the location thus labelled. When the label is enclosed in brackets, however, the interpretation is that the location referenced contains the address of the final operand location. The PASS assembler will, of course, translate the two different instruction forms into machine-code instructions within which different **addressing modes** are encoded.

Using pointer structures

The ability to store and manipulate pointer values, and to use them to refer to memory locations indirectly, enables many more complex forms of data organization to be used in programs. Suppose, for example, we want a program to print one of five different lines of text, perhaps to deal with five different cases arising in answer to a question asked of the user. The program in Pascal might take the form:

```
case answer of
        1: writeln('Much too small!');
        2: writeln('Much too large!');
        3: writeln('Too small.');
        4: writeln('Too large.');
        5: writeln('Correct! Well done.');
    end;
```

Here the integer variable *answer* is used to select one of five text strings to be displayed.

How could the textual data used in this program be organized within the store? Clearly, each line of text could be stored as a kind of **array**, using a number of consecutive memory locations. Because the lines are not all of the same length, we might use a special value such as −1 to mark the end of each line. In this way, all the text required can be stored in an area of memory of size 74 words (using **unpacked** character storage). Figure 4.23 illustrates this: for brevity, we have pictured the memory as being organized in rows of 10 words, although this does not, of course, represent any physical memory organization. We have also shown the contents of each word as

		0	1	2	3	4	5	6	7	8	9
TEXT:	140	M	u	c	h		t	o	o		s
	150	m	a	l	l	!	−1	M	u	c	h
	160		t	o	o		l	a	r	g	e
	170	!	−1	T	o	o		s	m	a	l
	180	l	.	−1	T	o	o		l	a	r
	190	g	e	.	−1	C	o	r	r	e	c
	200	t	!		W	e	l	l		d	o
	210	n	e	.	−1						

Figure 4.23   A block of text in the memory

being a character symbol, rather than writing the ASCII code value which will actually be used to represent this in the memory.

		0	1	2	3	4	5	6	7	8	9
POINTERS:	100	140	156	172	183	194					

		0	1	2	3	4	5	6	7	8	9
TEXT:	140	M	u	c	h		t	o	o		s
	150	m	a	l	l	!	−1	M	u	c	h
	160		t	o	o		l	a	r	g	e
	170	!	−1	T	o	o		s	m	a	l
	180	l	.	−1	T	o	o		l	a	r
	190	g	e	.	−1	C	o	r	r	e	c
	200	t	!		W	e	l	l		d	o
	210	n	e	.	−1						

Figure 4.24   An array of pointers to text strings

In this organization, the first line of text is stored in 15 words of memory starting at address 140, the second line starts at address 156, and so on. In our program, we would need to identify the starting address of each line, in order to select the correct text for each of the five cases required. To help us do this, we might set up an array of **pointers** to the five lines of text.

Figure 4.24 shows this arrangement. The array POINTERS contains five address-values, stored here in locations 100–104. The first word contains the address of (**points** to) the first line of text, stored starting at address 140. The second word of the pointer array contains the value 156 which is the address of the second line of text, and so on.

In a PASS assembly language program, we could now write instructions to reproduce the effect of the Pascal program statements written above, as follows:

```
LOAD    B, ANSWER      ; ANSWER is a number, 1-5
SUB     B, #1          ; obtain an index, value 0-4
LOAD    B, POINTERS(B) ; B := pointer to line of text
```

```
; now print the line of text whose address is in B
PRINTLOOP: LOAD A, 0(B)    ; A := next character
    JNEG     ENDLOOP        ; -1 marks end of text
    print_character         ; print the character in A
    ADD      B, #1          ; increment B to point to next char.
    JMP      PRINTLOOP
```

ENDLOOP:

In this piece of program, we have assumed the existence of a system function *print_character*, analogous to the *print_integer* function used in earlier examples, which will display the text character whose ASCII value is in the A register. The B register is used to contain a pointer to the location containing the next character to be printed; each time the loop is traversed, 1 is added to this value, so that it will refer to successive locations in the memory.

Suppose, for example, the value of ANSWER is 3. This is reduced by 1 to give an **index** to the pointer array in the range 0–4, so that, in this case, the instruction:

$$LOAD \quad B, POINTERS(B)$$

will lead to B being given the value of POINTERS(2), i.e. 172 (from Figure 4.24). The first subsequent instruction:

$$LOAD \quad A, 0(B)$$

will, therefore, load A with the character stored at address 172, which is the first character of the required line of text. The next time the loop is performed, B will have the value 173, so that the character stored at this address will be loaded, and so on until the −1 word is encountered.

Two-dimensional arrays

In the programming of the example above, the B register was used to contain the address of a memory location to be referenced, using the **indexed** addressing mode. The example, however, illustrates an organization of data which is very widely used, and in some cases it may be more convenient to use **indirect** addressing modes to refer to elements of the data structure. A similar method is often employed when arrays of two (or more) dimensions used in high-level language programs are represented in the memory. Consider, for example, the Pascal declaration

matrix: array[0..2] of array[0..3] of integer;

which defines an array of three rows (numbered 0–2), each of which contains four integers.

This might be stored in the memory in the form shown in Figure 4.25. The actual elements of the array are stored as three groups of four num-

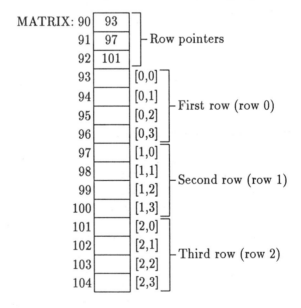

Figure 4.25 A two-dimensional array stored with row-pointers

bers in the locations 93–104, but the representation is preceded by three locations containing **pointers** to these three groups, or rows of the matrix.

Suppose we wish to refer to the element *matrix[i,j]*, i.e. element number *j* in row number *i*. The Papyrus instructions to obtain this element could be:

```
LOAD    B, I              ; B := row index
LOAD    A, MATRIX(B)      ; A := row pointer
STORE   A, ROWADDR        ; store in memory
LOAD    B, J              ; B := element number in row
LOAD    A, (ROWADDR)(B)   ; obtain element by indexing indirectly
```

The final instruction of this sequence uses an addressing mode that is both **indirect** and **indexed**. The location ROWADDR has been set up to contain the address of row *i* of the matrix, and this address is indexed by the element number, *j*, to obtain the final element address.

Suppose, for example, *i* has the value 1 and *j* the value 2. Then the instruction:

$$LOAD \quad A, MATRIX(B)$$

will refer to the location whose address is MATRIX(90)+B(1): location 91, which contains the pointer-value 97. This value is stored in the location labelled ROWADDR. The instruction:

$$LOAD \quad A, (ROWADDR)(B)$$

will obtain the value 97 from ROWADDR, add to it the value 2 contained in B, and use the resulting address (99) to fetch the required element [1,2] of the array.

Summary of addressing modes

The addressing modes described for Papyrus illustrate some of the possible forms that may be found in real computers. In detail, different kinds of computers will vary both in the addressing modes offered and in the precise way in which address calculations are performed. It is possible, however, to categorize the principal types that may be encountered, using the classification of operands as immediate, direct or indirect, which has been introduced in this chapter.

In this summary, we will assume the presence of an index register B (which may, of course, be given a different register name in other computers) and will use the symbol D to denote the numeric value of the 'operand' field obtained from an instruction. In different cases, and in different computers, D may be contained in part of the instruction word, or in the following word of memory, or both. Possible ways in which D can be used to obtain the final operand value include:

Immediate—#D The value of D is itself the operand. A term sometimes also used for this kind of operand is **literal** constant.

Direct—D D is the address of a memory location which contains the operand.

Indexed—D(B) The value in the register B is added to D to obtain the operand address. This addressing mode can also be described as **relative**, using D as a **displacement** from the **base address** contained in B.

Indirect—(D) The address of the location **directly** referenced is D. The value obtained from this location is the address of the final operand. Thus, the **direct** or **primary** address P = D; the **indirect** or **secondary** address S = (P), i.e. the contents of location P.

Pre-indexed indirect—(D(B)) In this case the **primary** address P is obtained by indexing D with the value contained in B. Thus:

$$P = D+(B) \quad \text{(as for indexed direct addressing)}$$
$$S = (P) \quad \text{(address of final operand)}$$

Post-indexed indirect—(D)(B) Here the indexing is applied to the secondary address:

$$P = D$$
$$S = (P)+(B)$$

A pictorial representation of these modes is also given in Figure 4.26, in which the location of the final operand value is in each case shown in bold. Papyrus instructions generally operate between a register and a value obtained using the operand field value, D. In other machines there may be instruction forms in which both operands are obtained from the memory, for example, or in which both operands are obtained using registers. The latter case introduces some further possible addressing modes:

Register direct—B The operand value is obtained directly from the register (B, in this case).

Register indirect—(B) The value in register B defines the address of the operand. This is equivalent to the **indexed** mode used with D = 0.

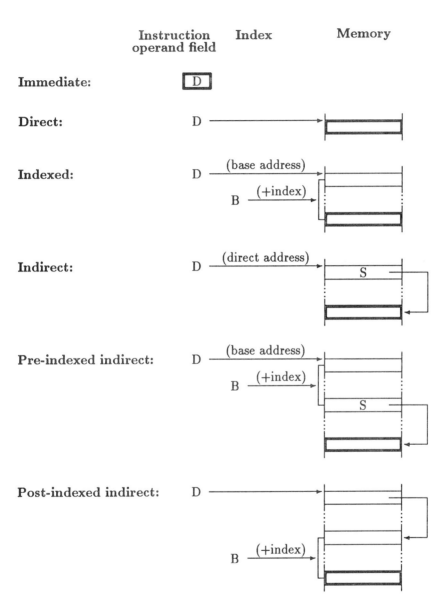

Figure 4.26 Forms of addressing

Few kinds of computer will offer all of these modes; some will offer variants involving different combinations of indexing, indirection, and use of registers. Fortunately, it is usually possible to find several different ways of achieving the same effect, using different forms of indirect or indexed addressing, so no one mode is indispensable.

4.3   *Addressing in the 68000

Address registers

Apart from the simple direct and immediate modes that have been used in earlier chapters, most of the addressing modes available for the 68000 processor make use of a set of eight **address registers**, A0–A7. One of these, A7, has some special properties and is used in a different way, which will be described in the next chapter. The other address registers are all identical, and fulfil a similar role to that of the Papyrus B register, i.e. they are used to contain a base address, or address index.

The address registers are all 32 bits long, and values moved into address registers are automatically sign-extended to this size. Using the full 32 bits means that all the memory which may be available on a 68000 system can be referred to using an address register, without the risk of encountering 'address overflow' problems. The value in an address register is **signed** because it may express either an address (pointer) value, which must be positive, or an index which may be positive or negative.

The instructions that can be used to load and change the value in an address register are broadly similar to those that refer to the data registers, although there are fewer of them. MOVEA, ADDA, SUBA, and CMPA are analogous to the MOVE, ADD, SUB, and CMP instructions which have been described in earlier chapters, but all refer to an address register as their destination. For example:

MOVEA	*POINTER, A3*	**A3 := contents of POINTER*
ADDA	*#2, A5*	**A5 := A5+2*
CMPA	*LIMIT, A1*	**Set condition codes for result of A1-LIMIT*

MOVEA is, in fact, really just a special case of MOVE with an address register as its destination, and not all assemblers recognize MOVEA as a separate instruction. The CMPA instruction may be used, as in this example, to compare the values of two addresses for equality or inequality, and will set condition bits in the status register accordingly. The other address-register operations, however, MOVEA, ADDA, and SUBA, differ from MOVE, ADD, and SUB in that they do *not* affect the condition of the status register. Another difference is that all of these address-register operations may be used with operands of size word or longword, but not of size byte. As was mentioned above, operands of size word are automatically sign-extended to longword (32 bits) size when these instructions are performed.

One other instruction that is used to load an address register is rather different from any of those which refer to a data register. This is the load effective address (LEA) instruction. An example would be:

$$LEA \quad PLACE, A2 \qquad * A2 := address \ of \ location \ PLACE$$

The LEA instruction loads the value of the **address** of the location referenced into the address register, rather than its contents. In this respect, it is like an immediate instruction; for example, the instruction:

$$MOVE \quad \#PLACE, D3 \qquad * D3 := address \ of \ PLACE$$

would also move the address of PLACE into a register, because the 'immediate' operand referred to is the address contained in the instruction itself. The LEA instruction, however, can be applied in ways which achieve effects that could not be possible using immediate-mode addressing, as we shall see in the next sections.

Effective addresses

In Section 2.4, the term **effective address** was used to describe some of the ways in which 68000 instructions refer to their operands. The ADD instruction, for example, operates on two values, one of which is contained in a data register, and the other of which is obtained using the effective address defined in the instruction code. In earlier chapters, we have seen examples in which this effective address is used to refer to a register, a memory location, or an immediate operand; thus:

ADD	*D3, D5*	* *effective address is D3*
MULS	*TERM, D4*	* *effective address is memory location*
CMP	*#1, D0*	* *effective address is immediate*

In fact, as we shall describe, an effective address can define many other ways of obtaining operands using different **addressing modes**.

Most 68000 instructions, like ADD, use an effective address for only *one* of their operands; the MOVE instruction is unique in that it refers to two effective addresses, making it possible to MOVE values from one memory

location to another without using a register. For all those instructions that
use an effective address, the machine-code instruction representation includes a 6-bit field in which the effective address is defined. Some examples
of this were given in Chapter 2, Figures 2.12 and 2.13.

The 6-bit 'effective address' field in an instruction allows 2^6, or 64 different possibilities to be encoded. However, many of these possible addressing
modes involve use of a register, so that this field must also be used to
identify which register this is. Generally, therefore, we think of the 6-bit
effective address as comprising two 3-bit subfields: one to define the addressing **mode** of the instruction, and the other, (usually) defining which
of eight registers is involved.

Figure 4.27 tabulates the possible combinations that arise from this encoding. They represent the various forms of **addressing** used in the 68000
family of computers, i.e. the 68000 versions of some of the addressing modes
which were described, in general terms, in Section 4.2. In a completely or-
thogonal instruction set, each addressing mode would be available for use
with every instruction type. As we have already seen, this is not the case for
the 68000; for example, the operand of a 'Branch' instruction is restricted
to be a simple label (encoded as a memory address relative to PC) rather
than a general effective address. In fact, the 68000 instruction set is even
less orthogonal than appears at first sight. Even when an instruction refers
to an effective address that is encoded in the instruction word in the form
shown in Figure 4.27, it is not always the case that every addressing mode
can be used. Some of the restrictions are self-evident: for example, it is
clearly meaningless to use an 'immediate' operand as the destination of
an instruction, just as the statement $3 := n$ would be meaningless in a language such as Pascal. There are, however, other less obvious special cases,
many concerning the use of address registers as operands. Some of these
will be mentioned in the following section, and a complete summary of the
addressing modes available for each instruction is given in Appendix A.

Addressing modes

The table in Figure 4.27 summarizes the 68000 addressing modes as defined
by the 'effective address' field encoded within the machine code of an instruction. When writing programs, of course, it is not usually necessary to
be aware of the details of this coding; so in this section we will describe the
different addressing modes using the assembly-language forms of instructions for illustration. Rather than following the machine-code ordering of
Figure 4.27, we will begin with the simple addressing modes that have been
introduced in earlier chapters.

Effective address				
Mode	Reg	Form	Operand	Notes
000	Dn	Data Reg. Direct	Dn	Contents of reg.
001	An	Addr. Reg. Direct	An	Contents of reg.
010	An	Addr. Reg. Indirect	(An)	Pointer in An
011	An	Addr. Reg. Indirect with post-increment	(An)	followed by: An:=An+S
100	An	Addr. Reg. Indirect with pre-decrement	(An)	An:=An−S: then
101	An	Addr. Reg. Indirect plus 16-bit displ.	(An+d)	Indexed pointer to memory
110	An	Addr. Reg. Indirect + index + 8-bit displ.	(An+Rm +d)	Double indexing
111	000	Abs. Short (16 bits)	(d)	Memory direct
111	001	Abs. Long (32 bits)	(d)	Memory direct
111	010	PC + 16-bit displ.	(PC+d)	PC-relative
111	011	PC + index + 8-bit displ.	(PC+Rm +d)	Indexed PC-relative
111	100	Immediate	d	Literal operand

Key

Dn = data register
An = address register
Rm = data/address register
S   = operand size (1, 2, 3, or 4 bytes)
d   = operand field in instruction code

Figure 4.27 68000 addressing modes

Immediate Operand obtained from instruction code.

An immediate operand is a 'literal', whose value is contained in the word or longword following the instruction word itself. Examples:

```
ADD      #5, D3          * D3 := D3+5
MOVEA    #POS, A4        * operand is address of POS
CMP.L    #$7FAFBC0, D0   * using longword constant
```

Note that instructions such as MOVEQ and ADDI are special cases since, although they make use of immediate operands, these are obtained from particular instruction codes rather than using a general 'effective address' form.

Absolute short and **absolute long** Operand address obtained from instruction code.

These are the 68000 simple **direct** addressing modes. The operand address is contained in the word or longword following the instruction word. Examples:

```
MOVE    SOURCE, DESTINATION * two direct addresses used
ADD.B   DATA, D5    * address may refer to byte, word or longword
ADD     350, D3     * numeric absolute address
```

The instruction mnemonics used are the same for both absolute 'short' and 'long' modes; the **assembler** will determine which mode is required from the magnitude of the absolute address referred to. The instruction qualifier (.B, .W, or .L) refers to the size of the final operand referenced, not to the size of the address used to locate it.

Data register direct Operand contained in data register.

Most 68000 instructions require one of their operands to be one of the data registers, D0–D7. When this mode is used, both operands are obtained directly from registers; thus:

$$ADD \quad D3, D5 \quad * D5 := D5+D3$$

Address register direct Operand contained in address register.

In principle, this mode is analogous to the previous one, with the operand referred to being obtained from an address register, A0–A7, rather than a data register. In practice, there are a number of special features concerning the use of address registers as direct operands. As we have mentioned, the value in an address register is always taken to be a **long-word** of 32 bits, and any arithmetic operation with an address register as its destination will make use of the full 32 bits:

$ADDA.W\ ADDWORD,\ A3\ *\ A3(32\ bits) := A3+ADDWORD(16\ bits)$

To allow this sort of operation, a word-sized operand is always sign-extended to 32 bits before the operation takes place. Operands of size byte, however, are not permitted in address-register operations.

Apart from the special address-register operations MOVEA, ADDA, SUBA, CMPA, and LEA, and a few special cases which will be mentioned later in the book, the only instructions that can be used with an address register as their destination operand are the 'quick' operations ADDQ and SUBQ. There is also a restricted set of instructions that may use the 'address register direct' mode for their source operand; these are: ADD, ADDA, SUB, SUBA, MOVE, MOVEA, CMP, and CMPA. Examples:

$ADD.L\quad A2, D5\qquad * D5 := D5+A2$
$ADDQ\quad \#1, A3\qquad\quad * A3 := A3+1$
$MOVE\quad A3, POINTER\quad * POINTER(16\ BITS) := A3$

Address register indirect Operand address held in address register.

This is the simplest of a number of modes making use of address registers to contain an address or address index. For example:

$LEA\quad PLACE, A3\quad * A3 := address\ of\ PLACE$
$CLR\quad (A3)\qquad\quad\ * then, PLACE := 0$

Address register indirect with displacement Address register used as index.

Although in 68000 terminology this is described as an 'indirect' mode, it is probably more helpful to think of it as an indexed form of addressing. Again, as was the case for the Papyrus equivalent, we can think of the register as containing either a 'base address' to which a displacement obtained from the instruction code is added, or an index to the base address defined in the instruction. An example of the first might be:

$ADD\quad 3(A2), D2\qquad * D2 := D2+(A2+3)$

Here, the register A2 is being used, perhaps, to contain the address of an array, and the operand 3(A2) defines the address of element 3 of this. Conversely:

$$ADD \quad BASE(A2), D4 \qquad * \ D4 := D4 + (\#BASE + A2)$$

uses the label BASE in the operand field of the instruction to define the start address of an area of memory, with the value in A2 as an index (displacement) into this. Note that the operand address field, or displacement, in the instruction is 16 bits long, so there is a restriction on the range of addresses which can be specified in this way.

Address register indirect with index and displacement   The assumption of this more complex form is that the address register is being used to contain a base address, to which a displacement may be added using an 8-bit field of the instruction. The address thus calculated is further indexed by a value which is contained in either an address register or a data register. Both the 8-bit displacement and the specification of the additional index register required are encoded within the word following the instruction word.

For example, the instruction:

$$ADDI \quad \#100, \ 2(A4, D2)$$

will add 100 to the value contained in the memory location whose address is calculated as the sum of 2 + contents of A4 + contents of D2 (Figure 4.28). In this case, only the lower word of D2 is used in the address calculation;

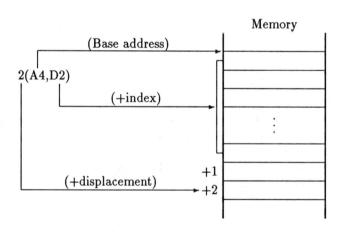

Figure 4.28   Address register indirect with index and displacement mode

to use all 32 bits of D2, we would have written 2(A4, D2.L).

Note also that we can write:

$$LEA \quad ITEM(A3, \; A2.L), \; A0$$

which will load into register A0 the **effective address** calculated from ITEM(A3, A2.L). Thus, if ITEM has been declared to be equivalent to the number 120, then the value loaded will be 120 + contents of A3 + contents of A2. This is an example which shows the use of the LEA instruction to calculate an effective (absolute) address that can be used subsequently, for example, with the 'register indirect' mode.

Post-increment and Pre-decrement modes Both of these modes reference the memory in exactly the same way as the address register indirect mode, i.e. the contents of an address register are used as the address of the memory location referred to. The difference in using these modes is that there is a 'side-effect' of the instruction involving the incrementing or decrementing of the address register used. For example, the instruction:

$$CLR.B \quad (A1)+$$

will set to zero the byte whose address is contained in register A1, and will *then* add 1 to the contents of A1. The effect of this is that a sequence of such instructions, perhaps within a loop, will clear a succession of consecutive locations.

The *increment* to the register brought about by this mode is determined by the size of the operand referenced. In the example above, the increment for a byte-sized operand is 1. However, the instruction:

$$ADD \quad (A2)+, \; D3$$

has the same effect as the sequence:

```
ADD    (A2), D3    * D3 := D3+contents of location (A2)
ADDQ   #2, A2      * A2 := A2+2
```

Similarly, a longword instruction will increment the address register by 4. This ensures that in each case, after the instruction is complete, the address register **points** to the *next* byte, word, or longword in memory as required.

The post-increment mode is useful for stepping 'forwards' through an area of memory. The pre-decrement mode allows us to do this in reverse; thus:

$$ADD \quad -(A1), \; D2$$

is equivalent to:

```
SUBQ   #2, A1    * A1 := A1-2 (predecrement)
ADD    (A1), D2  * then D2 := D2+contents of address (A2)
```

These modes are obviously useful for manipulating successive elements of arrays and similar structures. We will see some examples of this later, and, in the next chapter, some further applications of the modes.

Program-counter relative modes Two addressing modes are present on the 68000 which make use of the program-counter register as a base address for **relative** addressing. These modes are similar to the address register indirect modes with displacement and indexing, except that PC is used in place of an address register. Thus:

$$MOVE \quad 10(PC), \ D2$$

would have the effect of moving into D2 the contents of the location whose address is obtained by adding 10 to the current value of PC.

This would not, of course, be a convenient way to use the mode in a program, since this form requires us to calculate an address as a 'displacement', or difference, from the program-counter value for the current instruction. Most assemblers, fortunately, will allow us to write, instead:

$$MOVE \quad CONSTANT(PC), \ D2$$

where CONSTANT is the label of a memory location. The *effect* of this instruction is exactly the same as if we had written:

$$MOVE \quad CONSTANT, \ D2$$

i.e. the contents of the location labelled CONSTANT are moved into register D2. The difference is that when the program-counter relative mode is used, the assembler will translate the label into a displacement, or **relative address**, with PC as the address base. The effect is that the instruction does not refer to an **absolute** address, and thus the piece of program including the instruction and the location CONSTANT is not fixed to any particular part of the memory—it is **relocatable**.

Recall that the assembler translates **branch** instructions in a similar way; the label that is the destination of a branch instruction is translated, in the machine-code form of the instruction, into a displacement from the current program-counter value. The 'addressing mode' implied in 68000 branch instructions is, in effect, a program-counter relative mode.

The other program-counter relative mode allows us to use an address or data register as an index to the address calculated; thus:

$$MOVE \quad TABLEBASE(PC,D3), \ D0$$

will, if D3 contains the number 3, reference element number 3 of the area of memory whose address (relative to PC) is TABLEBASE. Figure 4.29

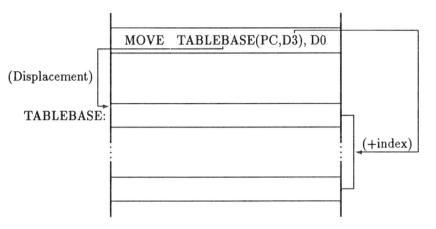

Figure 4.29   Indexed PC-relative addressing

illustrates this. Again, the use of PC as a base and the calculation of a relative displacement from this is 'invisible' to the programmer, for whom this mode is effectively a form of indexed direct addressing.

Both forms of PC-relative addressing are subject to a major restriction: they cannot be used to *alter* the contents of a memory location. This means, in effect, that the only values which can be referenced in this way (apart from jump destinations) are constants implanted in the program. This limitation, and the fact that the effects of these modes can be achieved using address-register indirect modes, mean that program-counter relative modes are not often used in everyday assembly-language programming. The real benefit of being able to construct pieces of program that are relocatable, or position-independent, emerges when writing software, such as operating systems and compilers, that is required to be used by many users, in various different contexts, and sometimes concurrently by a number of users sharing the same computer. We will return to this point in the next chapter, when we come to discuss **subroutines**.

A simple example

To end this section, we will illustrate the use of some of the modes described in a short and simple program. Figure 4.30 shows a program which displays a question, 'How many legs has a cow?', requiring the answer 1, 2, 3, or 4, and prints a suitable reply in response to the answer given. Perhaps it will not require too much imagination to see that this program could be

```
TTL     LEGS
* A (very) simple quiz program

ORG  $2000

* First ask the question
            LEA        QUESTION, A0      * A0 := Addr. of QUESTION
LOOPA: MOVE.B   (A0)+, D0                * D0 := character from string
            BEQ        OUTA               * end of loop if zero
            print_char                    * otherwise print char. in D0
            BRA        LOOPA              * and repeat loop

* Get the answer
OUTA:  read_integer                      * number read into D0
            MOVEA    D0, A0               * move it into the addr. registe
            SUBQ     #1, A0               * create index 0-3

* Now print the response
            MOVEA    POINTERS(A0), A1     * A1 := addr. of reply string
LOOPB: MOVE.B   (A1)+, D0                 * D0 := character from string
            BEQ        OUTB               * end of loop if zero
            print_char                    * print character in D0
            BRA        LOOPB              * and loop

OUTB:  TRAP     #0                       * end program

POINTERS:   DC     REPLY1, REPLY2,REPLY3,REPLY4
QUESTION:   DC.B   'How many legs has a cow? - 1,2 ,3 or 4? ',0
REPLY1:     DC.B   'Nowhere near!',0
REPLY2:     DC.B   'Twice as many!',0
REPLY3:     DC.B   'Quite close!',0
REPLY4:     DC.B   'Correct! Well Done!',0

END
```

Figure 4.30   A simple question and answer program

the framework for a rather more demanding quiz!

The **data structures** used in this program are essentially similar to those described in Section 4.2, when we considered this kind of program in a more general way (Figure 4.24). Look first at the text string QUESTION, and the four different replies. Each of these is declared as an array of bytes, occupying consecutive byte locations in the memory. The declaration DC.B, followed by a sequence of characters enclosed in quote symbols, has the effect of causing a sequence of consecutive locations to be **preset** with the ASCII values of the characters. Because we have used DC.B rather than DC.W, the characters are in this case stored in **packed** form. Each array (string) is terminated by a zero-valued byte; note that a declaration of the form:

$$DC.B \quad 'A', \$FF, 0$$

will cause three consecutive bytes to be preset with, respectively, the ASCII value of the character A, the hexadecimal number FF, and the number 0.

The **addresses** of the four 'reply' strings are preset in the array labelled POINTERS. Because the identifier REPLY1 is identically **equivalent** to the address of the location with this label, the declaration:

$$DC \quad REPLY1$$

will cause a location to be preset with the value of this address.

The first action in the program is to print out the 'QUESTION' string. For this purpose we have assumed a system function **print_char** which will display the character whose ASCII code is contained in register D0. To print the question, the address of the string QUESTION is first loaded into the A0 register, using the LEA instruction. The loop that follows uses the post-increment address-register indirect mode to obtain characters from successive bytes of the string, ending when the zero-valued byte is encountered.

The answer to the question is assumed to be a number in the range 1–4, from which 1 is subtracted to create an index in the range 0–3 into the POINTERS array. The instruction:

$$MOVEA \quad POINTERS(A0), A1$$

uses the 'address register indirect with displacement', or **indexed** mode, to obtain a pointer to the reply required. This is then used, in a loop similar to the first, to print out the text string.

Of course, it is impossible in a single short example to illustrate all the different modes of addressing available on the 68000, still less the various applications of these modes in using different kinds of data structures. Further ways of using the modes will emerge as we go on to illustrate other features of the 68000 and its application.

4.4   *68000 logical and shift instructions

Logical instructions

The 68000 instruction set includes instructions to perform the logical operations described in Section 4.1: AND, OR, NOT, and 'Exclusive-OR', which is given the assembler mnemonic EOR.

The AND instruction has similar forms to ADD; it can deliver its result into a data register, or into a general 'effective address', and can be used with operands of size byte, word, or longword. For example:

$$AND \quad MASK, \; D4$$

will leave in register D4 the result of performing a bit-by-bit AND operation between the lower 16 bits of D4 and the word contained in memory location MASK.

$$AND.B \quad D1, \; BITS$$

will 'logically-AND' the lower byte of D1 with the contents of the byte labelled BITS, leaving the result in the latter location.

There is also an 'AND-immediate' instruction:

$$ANDI \quad \#4, \; MEMBITS \qquad * \; MEMBITS := MEMBITS \; \text{and} \; 4$$

There is, however, no equivalent of the ADDQ instruction, nor is it possible to perform this operation on the contents of an address register.

The inclusive-OR instruction has exactly similar forms, with assembler mnemonics OR and ORI (OR-immediate). Exclusive-OR, however (Figure 4.7), is slightly more restricted, in that there is no general form which places the result of the operation in a register; thus, the *general* form of the instruction is:

$$EOR \quad Dn, \; (ea)$$

which performs the operation between the contents of the data register Dn and the contents of the effective address (ea) given, leaving the result in the latter location. There is also an immediate form:

$$EORI \quad \#12, \; MEMLOC$$

In both cases, of course, the destination 'effective address' may be a data register; there is, however, no form of the instruction that will perform the operation between a memory location and a register with the register as destination.

Finally, the NOT instruction has the general form:

$$NOT \quad (ea)$$

For example:

> NOT.B   DATABYTE   * invert bits of DATABYTE
> NOT.L   D2   * inverts 32 bits of D2

All the logical instructions will cause the N and Z bits in the status register to be set indicating a negative or zero result of the operation. Carry and overflow conditions cannot arise from these operations, so the V and C bits will always be set to 0 as a result.

Operations on single bits

As well as the logical instructions AND, OR, EOR, and NOT, which operate simultaneously on *all* bits of a byte, word, or longword, the 68000 has a number of instructions that can be used to examine and change the state of a *single* bit within a bit-pattern. The **bit test** (BTST) instruction sets the Zero Status(Z) bit in the status register to record whether a particular bit is 0 (Zero Status set) or 1; all other condition codes are unaffected. For example:

$$BTST \quad \#5, \, D3 \qquad * \text{ examine state of bit 5 of D3}$$

The bit-position to be examined may be specified literally, as in the above example, or be defined by the value of a data register. Thus, if D4 contains the value 2, the instruction:

$$BTST \quad D4, \, BITPATTERN$$

will test the state of bit 2 of the memory location BITPATTERN.

Although a general 'effective address' may be used to define the bit-pattern to be examined, the scope of the instruction is different depending on whether this is a register or memory location. When a data register is examined, the bit-number specified may be in the range 0–31, i.e. the full longword size of the register is available. When the effective address specified defines a memory location, however, this is assumed to be a single byte, and the bit-number should be in the range 0–7 (Figure 4.31).

Three other instructions all have the same form and effect as BTST, but also *change* the value of the bit examined. BSET will test the state of a specified bit, and change its state to 1; BCLR tests and sets to 0; and BCHG tests and **inverts** the state of the bit.

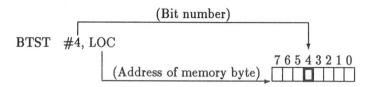

Figure 4.31   A bit test instruction

Shift instructions

Shift instructions on the 68000 generally operate on a data register, although there are restricted forms that will shift the contents of a word in memory, as we shall describe shortly. Consider first the instructions to perform a **logical** shift on a bit-pattern contained in a register. For example:

LSL.B   #3, D5

will shift the contents of D5 logically left by three bit-positions. Because the **size** of the operand in this case is 'byte' this instruction will shift only the lower 8 bits of D5, all the other bits of the register remaining unchanged. Bits shifted out of the high-order end of the byte are *not* shifted into the rest of the register; however, the last bit shifted out will change the state of the carry bit in SR.

The LSL and LSR (logical shift right) instructions are essentially the same as those described for Papyrus, in Section 4.1 and Figure 4.10. They do not affect the overflow (V) status, but will set Z and N to show the result state of the register. The number of places to be shifted may be specified literally, by a number in the range 1–8, or may be defined by the contents of a data register. In the latter case, the number of places specified may be in the range 0–63. If D7 contains the value 18, then:

LSR.L   D7, D1

will shift the longword in D1 18 places to the right. LSL and LSR (and the other 68000 shift instructions) can be used to shift a byte, word, or longword in a register.

The **arithmetic** shift instructions, ASL and ASR, have similar forms and restrictions. The ASR instruction has the same effect as that described in Section 4.1, Figure 4.13; the sign bit is propagated, the last bit shifted out is recorded as C, the overflow status is cleared, and the N and Z bits record the result sign and zero status. The ASL instruction, however, has a rather different effect from that described in Figure 4.12. The 68000 ASL instruction does *not* preserve the state of the sign bit, and in fact operates in exactly the same way as the logical left shift instruction LSL. The only difference is that if the ASL instruction causes the value in the sign bit to be changed at any time during the shift, the overflow status (V) will be set to record this. Thus, for all cases where no overflow occurs, a true arithmetic shift is performed.

The 68000 **circular** shifts are termed 'rotate' instructions with mnemonics ROL (rotate left) and ROR (rotate right). They function in exactly the same way as was described in Section 4.1 and Figure 4.11.

Logical, arithmetic, and circular shifts all have restricted forms which operate on a word in memory. In these cases, a general effective address may be specified for the operand, which must be of size **word**, but the instruction will cause the bit-pattern to be shifted by one place only. Thus:

ASR   MEMWORD   * contents of MEMWORD shifted right 1 place
ROL   (A3)   * rotate left one place location addressed by A3

Another example program

We will conclude this chapter with a rather more substantial program example to show the use of a number of the instructions and addressing modes that have been described. Figure 4.33 illustrates, in a limited way, an instance of a very common program application: to *search* for a particular entry in a **table**. In this case, the table consists of a list of names of people, each name being (for simplicity) assumed to be exactly 12 characters long (made up with spaces if necessary). Along with the name, each entry in the table contains some information about the person with that name. In the memory of the computer, each name is stored in 12 consecutive bytes, and the additional information in the two succeeding bytes. Each entry in the table is thus 14 bytes in length, and the declaration:

TABLE: DS.B   1400

has set aside enough space for 100 entries in the table.

The first byte of information simply contains the age in years of the person stored as an integer. The second byte, however, contains a **coded** representation of three pieces of information: the sex of the person, his or her marital status, and the number of children he or she has. The person's sex is represented by the setting of a single bit, bit 6 of this byte, 0 representing 'male', and 1 'female'. Bits 4 and 5 together have four possible values: 00, 01, 10, and 11, or in decimal: 0, 1, 2, and 3. This **field** of the byte is used to encode the person's marital status, as 'married', 'single', 'widowed', or 'divorced'. Finally, bits 0–3 of the byte contain the number of children of the person, expressed as an integer. The codings used are illustrated in Figure 4.32.

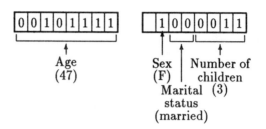

Figure 4.32   Coding information in memory bytes

We will assume that the table has been set up, to contain the names and other details of a number of people, in some earlier part of the program not shown in Figure 4.33. The purpose of the program as shown here is to find the entry in the table corresponding to a given name, and to print out the relevant information in textual form.

The program first reads in the 12-character name of the person whose entry is to be searched for (we assume a system function **read_char** to read a single character into D0). These characters are stored in the 12-byte array PERSON, whose address is placed in register A0 at the start of the loop. Register D1 is used as a 'loop counter' to ensure that exactly 12 characters are read. Notice that D1 is initialized with the number 11, rather than 12; this is because we have used the 'decrement counter and branch' instruction DBF, which continues to branch to the start of the loop until D1 becomes *negative* (refer to Section 3.4).

Once the name has been read, the program goes on to search the table, attempting to match the contents of the array PERSON with the 12-character name stored at each entry. Each comparison starts (at label CMPLP) with A0 containing the address of the array PERSON, and A1 the address of an entry in the table. D2 (initialized to 0) is used as an **index** into both names; thus, the addressing mode used is the 'address register indirect with index and displacement' form. In this case, the 'displacement' used is zero, so the two addresses referenced are A0+D2 (the address of a character in PERSON) and A1+D2 (the address of a corresponding character in an entry in the table).

The comparison of names proceeds character-by-character until a difference is found. In this case, a branch is made to label DIFF, which proceeds to move on to the next entry in the table. This involves adding 14 (the size of an entry) to the address in A1, so that A1 **points** to the succeeding

14-byte table entry. This, the *outer* loop of the program, terminates when the address register A1 reaches the LIMIT address of the end of the table, at which point the program halts, having failed to match the name read as data.

When a match *is* found, the program 'drops out' of the 'inner' comparison loop, and proceeds to print out the details of the person whose entry has been located. First the age of the person is printed as an integer. This value is contained in byte 12 following the start of the table entry; notice the use of the **equivalence** defining the identifier AGE to be identically equal to the number 12. Likewise, the equivalence DETAILS (=13) is used for the **displacement** of the final byte from the address of an entry. From this byte, the instruction:

$$AND \quad \#15, \quad D0$$

isolates bits 0–3 to allow the 'number of children' to be printed as an integer. To obtain the 'marital status' field, another **mask** is used to isolate bits 4 and 5, which are then shifted right four places to create a number in the range 0–3. This is then used as an index into the preset array MCHAR to print a character M, S, W, or D. Finally, the sex of the person is identified by testing bit 6 of the DETAILS byte, and the result used to select a character M or F to be printed.

In a real application, of course, a program of this type would certainly include a lot of detail that we have, for simplicity, omitted; for example, to print out the results in a sensible and clear fashion. This apart, the program is very typical of a very wide class, involving storage of information in tabular form, the use of application-specific binary encoding to represent details in a convenient and compact way, and the **searching** of the table to locate an entry required. This sort of program structure is found not only in many data-processing applications, but also in system programs such as compilers which are required to maintain tables of identifiers used in a program being translated.

```
TTL     FIND
* To find an entry in a table

ORG  $2000
AGE:       EQU 12
DETAILS: EQU 13

* (Assume that the table has previously been set up)
* Read the name of the person to be looked up
            LEA      PERSON, A0      * A0 := Address of 'person' arr
            MOVEQ    #11, D1         * D1 becomes loop counter
RDLP:       read_char                * read next character into D0
            MOVE.B   D0, (A0)+       * place into array
                                     * and increment pointer
            DBF      D1, RDLP        * loop until D1 becomes negativ

* Now search the table
            LEA      TABLE, A1       * A1 := addr. of first item in t
            LEA      PERSON, A0      * A0 := addr. of 'person' strin
SRCHLP:     CLR      D2              * use D2 as index into names
            MOVEQ    #11, D1         * and D1 as inner loop counter
CMPLP:      MOVE.B   0(A0, D2), D3   * fetch char. from 'PERSON'
            CMP.B    0(A1, D2), D3   * compare with entry in table
            BNE      DIFF            * escape from comparison
                                     * if different
            ADDQ     #1, D2          * otherwise increment index
            DBF      D1, CMPLP       * and continue comparison

* Dropping out of the loop indicates entry has been matched
            MOVE.B   AGE(A1), D0     * D0 := AGE entry from table
            EXT.W    D0              * extend to fill one word
            print_integer            * and print age of person
            MOVE.B   DETAILS(A1), D0 * D0 := details of person
            AND      #15, D0         * mask out all but bits 0-3
            print_integer            * print number of children
```

```
              MOVE.B   DETAILS(A1), D0    * get the details again
              AND      #48, D0            * isolate bits 4 and 5
              LSR      #4, D0             * shift to lower end of register
              MOVEA    D0, A2             * A2 is index in range 0-3
              MOVE.B   MCHAR(A2), D0      * get character: M/S/W/D
              print_char                  * and print it
              MOVE.B   MALE, D0           * D0 := 'M'
              BTST     #6, DETAILS(A1)    * Test bit 6 of details
              BEQ      LL                 * if zero, sex is 'M'
              MOVE.B   FEMALE, D0         * otherwise 'F'
LL:           print_char                  * print sex
              TRAP     #0                 * and finish

* end of main loop: entry not yet found
DIFF:         ADDA     #14, A1            * move on to next entry in table
              CMPA     #LIMIT, A1         * see if end of table
              BNE      SRCHLP             * if not, continue main loop
              TRAP     #0                 * then stop

MALE:         DC.B     'M'
FEMALE:       DC.B     'F'
MCHAR:        DC.B     'MSWD'
PERSON:       DS.B     12
TABLE:        DS.B     1400
LIMIT:        DS       1

END
```

Figure 4.33   Program to search a table

4.5   Exercises

1. How many bits are required to represent the mantissa of a floating-point number to an accuracy of nine significant (decimal) figures?

2. Outline a procedure for adding two real numbers that are represented in floating-point form, so that the result remains **normalized**, with a mantissa in the range 0.5–1. What kinds of instruction will be needed to write this procedure in 68000 machine language?

3. Draw a truth table to express the result of a logical operation on three bits A, B, and C, such that the result is 1 only if at least *two* of A, B, and C have the value 1. Write a **logical expression** equivalent to this truth table, using the logical operators AND and OR.

4. Write a piece of program in 68000 assembly language that will, for some ASCII 7-bit code contained in a byte in memory, count the number of bits set to 1 in the code. If this is an *odd* number, the program should then amend the byte to an 'even parity' coding.

5. Write sequences of 68000 instructions that will move a value from memory into a data register, in each of the following cases:

   (a) The **address** of the location to be referenced is contained in a location labelled PLACE

   (b) The location to be referenced is an element of an array, whose address is stored at location ARRAY, with the element number stored at location ITEM.

   What *general* forms of addressing are implied by these two cases? What particular addressing modes have been used in the instructions you have written?

6. Write a 68000 program that will read a paragraph of text, terminated with the symbol $, and count the occurrence of each of the upper-case letters A–Z in the text (ignoring all other characters). The results should finally be displayed in the form (e.g.):
   ```
   A   24
   B   14
   C   17
   ...etc.
   ```

7. Write a program that will read a sequence of numbers and print them out, sorted into ascending order.

Chapter 5

Subroutines and program structure

5.1 Subroutines

We have now described machine-level correspondences to almost all the common program forms found in typical high-level languages—including both **control** structures such as loops, and **data** structures such as arrays. The important exception is, of course, that all conventional high-level languages include some concept of a **subroutine**. Related terms sometimes used include **procedure, function, routine,** and **subprogram.** While distinctions can be made between these terms, all share a common core of meaning: they describe a section of program that is available to be made use of repeatedly at different points in the execution of the program within which it is contained.

A subroutine itself, whether written in a high-level or a low-level language, is not essentially different from any other piece of program. The 'body' of a Pascal procedure consists of a sequence of program statements, and likewise a subroutine at the machine level will appear as a sequence of instructions stored in some part of the computer's memory. What distinguishes a subroutine (or procedure) is that its execution may be brought about by a **call** from any part of the program. The 'call' involves a **change of control** (a jump) to the start of the subroutine. The end of the subroutine is marked by a **return** of control to the point in the program sequence following the point of call.

Figure 5.1 illustrates these changes of control. In this figure, M1, M2, ..., M10 represent steps in the execution of the main program sequence:

Main program sequence

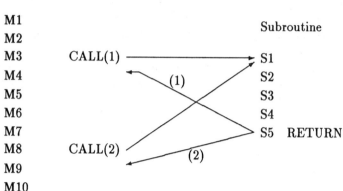

Figure 5.1   Subroutine calls and returns

these may correspond to statements in a high-level language program, or to instructions at the primitive machine level. S1, S2, ..., S5 represent the statements or instructions of a subroutine, which lie textually, and in the memory, outside the main program sequence. In this example, step M3 of the main program sequence invokes a **call** of the subroutine. This brings about a change of control, producing execution of the steps S1–S5 of the subroutine. At the end of the subroutine, there is a **return** of control to the point of call, so that M4 becomes the next step to be performed. Similarly, the call at step M8 produces an execution sequence of steps M8, S1, S2, S3, S4, S5, M9.

The characterization of Figure 5.1 can be applied to subroutines at any level of representation. In a high-level language there may be textual conventions and syntactic rules governing the ways in which subroutines are written. At the machine level, however, in general, *any* sequence of instructions can be performed as a subroutine if it is invoked by a suitable call and terminated by an instruction to produce a return of control. The essential means of implementation of subroutines, therefore, is the presence of **instructions** to provide these actions.

Call and return instructions

The call of, or **entry** to a subroutine, involves a change of control, i.e. the value of the program counter register is changed so that it **points**, not to the instruction following the point of call, but to the first instruction of the subroutine. When other 'change of control' instructions were introduced in Chapter 3, they were described as **jumps**. Although the terminology used varies between different computers, in Papyrus we will maintain this convention by describing the **call** instruction as a 'jump to subroutine', and giving it the mnemonic JSR.

The JSR instruction has a very similar form and effect to the simple jump instruction, JMP, described in Section 3.2. In the program sequence, execution of the instruction:

$$JSR \quad 100$$

will bring about a transfer of control to the subroutine whose first instruction is stored at location 100; or, more typically:

$$JSR \quad START$$

will bring about execution of the subroutine whose first instruction is labelled START. In either case, execution of the instruction:

$$RETURN$$

will reverse the change of control, causing execution to continue from the point following the JSR instruction.

As an example, consider the PASS program fragment of Figure 5.2. This piece of program includes a subroutine, the purpose of which is to read successive characters as data, ignoring any 'space' characters found. Each time the subroutine is performed, it returns with the next non-space character in the A register. In the program shown, the subroutine is being used to read two non-space characters, which are then printed out in reverse order (we have assumed the existence of system functions *read_char* and *print_char* which will read and print a single character, using the A register). There are, therefore, two **calls** of the subroutine, represented by two instructions written as JSR READNSCHAR.

Let us suppose that this piece of program is stored in successive memory locations starting at address 120, and that locations 150 and 200, respectively, are used for the variables SAVE and FIRST. Figure 5.3 shows a possible execution history for the program, in which we have **traced** the program counter and A register, the instruction executed, and the relevant memory locations. In this recorded history, the actual characters read were 'A' (ASCII code 65), 'space' (32,) and 'B' (66); the program has finally printed out the two non-space characters in reverse order, producing the output BA.

```
; piece of program to read two characters, ignoring spaces, and
; print them in reverse order.
          JSR     READNSCHAR    ; read a non-space character into A
          STORE A, FIRST        ; save it
          JSR     READNSCHAR    ; read another
          print_char            ; use system function to print it
          LOAD   A, FIRST       ; get the first character again
          print_char            ; print it
          stop                  ;end program execution

; subroutine to read characters, ignoring spaces, returning with a
; non-space character in the A register
READNSCHAR: read_char           ; use system function to read
                                ; character into A
          STORE A, SAVE         ; store it temporarily
          SUB    A, #32         ; compare with ASCII code
                                ; for 'space' character
          JZERO READNSCHAR      ; if space, loop to read another
          LOAD   A, SAVE        ; otherwise, get the character into A
          RETURN                ; and leave the subroutine
```

Figure 5.2   A PASS program including a subroutine

Return addresses

As the trace in Figure 5.3 shows, the *immediate* effect of a JSR instruction
is a simple transfer of control to the address specified as the operand of
the instruction. The RETURN instruction also brings about a change of
control. In this case, however, the destination address is not specified in
the coding of the RETURN instruction; instead, the transfer of control is
always to the address following that of the JSR from which the subroutine
was called. This **return address** may be different for each call of the
subroutine. Thus, the two executions of the single RETURN instruction
shown in Figure 5.3 effect changes of control to the return addresses 121
and 123, respectively.

How does the RETURN instruction 'know' which return address is required? Clearly, the information is not, and could not be, part of the coding

PC	A	Instruction		SAVE(150)	FIRST(200)
120	0	JSR	127	0	0
127	0	read_char		0	0
128	65	STORE	A, 150	0	0
129	65	SUB	A, #32	65	0
130	33	JZERO	127	65	0
131	33	LOAD	A, 150	65	0
132	65	RETURN		65	0
121	65	STORE	A, 200	65	0
122	65	JSR	127	65	65
127	65	read_char		65	65
128	32	STORE	A, 150	65	65
129	32	SUB	A, #32	32	65
130	0	JZERO	127	32	65
127	0	read_char		32	65
128	66	STORE	A, 150	32	65
129	66	SUB	A, #32	66	65
130	34	JZERO	127	66	65
131	34	LOAD	A, 150	66	65
132	66	RETURN		66	65
123	66	print_char		66	65
124	66	LOAD	A, 200	66	65
125	65	print_char		66	65
126	65	stop		66	65

Figure 5.3 Execution history of the program of Figure 5.2

of the instruction itself. The required return address can only be recorded at the point of **call** of the subroutine, when the JSR instruction is effected. It is this that distinguishes JSR from a simple jump; in addition to performing a change of control (changing the value of the program counter) the JSR instruction will record the current value of PC as the **return address** required for this call. Recall from Chapter 2 that, in the cycle of instruction execution, the value of PC is incremented to point to the *next* instruction before the current instruction is executed. In the case of a JSR instruction therefore, it is only necessary to save this value before PC is changed to point to the first instruction of the subroutine.

Different computers use different ways of recording the return address: in some, it is placed in a register; in Papyrus, as with most modern computers, the return address is stored in a memory location. The location used is not always the same one; its address is given by the value in a special register, SP. The RETURN instruction expects this register to contain a **pointer** to the location containing the return address. In effect, therefore, the RETURN instruction performs the equivalent of the assignment PC := (SP), i.e. PC is assigned the value obtained from the memory location whose address is in SP.

If the JSR and RETURN instructions had no other effects, then there would be a potential difficulty in dealing with programs in which subroutines are called from within other subroutines. Suppose, for example, the main program fragment of Figure 5.2 were to be written in the form of a subroutine, thus:

```
REVERSETWO:   JSR         READNSCHAR
              STORE       A, FIRST
              JSR         READNSCHAR
              print_char
              LOAD        A, FIRST
              print_char
              RETURN
```

Now, it becomes necessary to save two return addresses: one, the return address of the subroutine REVERSETWO, to which the RETURN instruction above will restore control and the other the return address of the subroutine READNSCHAR which is called from within REVERSETWO.

To enable this kind of **nesting** of subroutines, the JSR and RETURN instructions take steps to ensure that different memory locations are used to store the return addresses involved. Each time a JSR instruction is performed, the value (address pointer) in SP is decremented, and each time a RETURN instruction is performed, it is incremented. This means that if two JSR instructions are executed in sequence (without a RETURN in between), the two corresponding return addresses will be stored in two different (adjacent) memory locations. Thus, the complete effect of the JSR instruction can be described by the sequence:

(JSR SUBR)	*SP := SP-1*	*; decrement SP*
	(SP) := PC	*; save PC in address given by SP*
	PC := SUBR	*; jump to start of subroutine.*

The RETURN instruction reverses this effect, by *first* taking the return address from the location indicated by SP, and then incrementing SP:

(RETURN)	*returnaddress := (SP)*	*; get address from memory*
	SP := SP+1	*; increment SP*
	PC := returnaddress	*; jump to returnaddress*

This mechanism, illustrated in Figure 5.4, ensures that calls to, and returns from, subroutines are correctly matched— i.e. a RETURN instruction will always use the return address stored at its corresponding JSR.

Stacks

Let us examine further the consequences of the way in which Papyrus stores and retrieves return addresses for successive subroutine calls. Consider the following sequence of calls, in which the addresses of instructions are shown on the left of the mnemonics:

100		*JSR*	*SUBR1*	*; call subroutine SUBR1 (address 200)*
200	*SUBR1:*	*...*		*; first instruction of subroutine*
201		*...*		
202		*JSR*	*SUBR2*	*; call second subroutine (address 500)*
500	*SUBR2:*	*...*		*; start of second subroutine*
501		*...*		
502		*...*		
503		*JSR*	*SUBR3*	*; third nested call (address 600)*
600	*SUBR3:*	*...*		*; start of third subroutine*

Suppose that the value of the SP register, at the start of this sequence, is 1000. Then Figure 5.5 shows the succession of changes to its value, and the

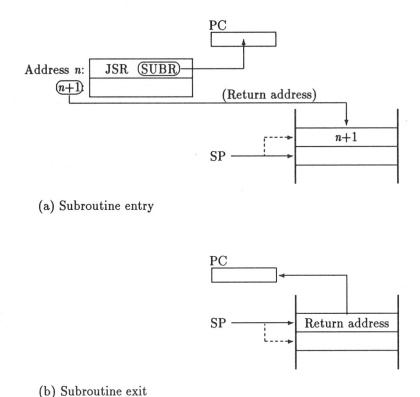

(a) Subroutine entry

(b) Subroutine exit

Figure 5.4   Subroutine entry and exit mechanisms

values of memory locations pointed to, brought about by the sequence of calls. At the start of the sequence (Figure 5.5a), SP has the value 1000, i.e. it **points** to memory location 1000. As a result of the first call instruction (JSR SUBR1, above) the value of SP will be decremented, and the location 999 to which it now points will be used to store the return address for the subroutine call. The JSR SUBR1 instruction is stored at location 100, so this return address is the address of the following instruction, 101 (Figure 5.5b).

The program proceeds to perform the instructions of the subroutine SUBR1, starting at address 200. When the instruction at address 202 is reached, another subroutine call is performed. SP is again decremented, so that the return address of this call, 203, is stored in location 998 (Figure 5.5c). Similarly, the continuation to the call of SUBR3 leads to the

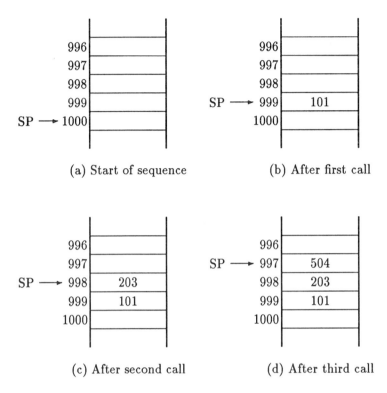

(a) Start of sequence   (b) After first call

(c) After second call   (d) After third call

Figure 5.5   Return addresses stored in a sequence of subroutine calls

state shown in Figure 5.5(d), in which three return addresses are stored in successive locations.

Notice that after each call, the value of SP points to the *last* return address. This means, in the example of Figure 5.5, that if a RETURN instruction is now executed, the return of control made will be to address 504, the return address of the call of SUBR3. This is what we would require, of course; the call of SUBR3 was made from within SUBR2, so we would expect the end of SUBR3 to lead to a return of control into SUBR2. Similarly, when SUBR2 terminates, control will return into SUBR1, and when a further RETURN instruction is executed, the final return address to which control will return will be 101, the instruction following the original call of SUBR1. At this point, the value of SP will again be 1000, as it was at the start of the sequence.

The picture we have of these events, illustrated in Figure 5.5, is of a series of return addresses being 'stacked', one on top of another, in a series of adjacent memory locations. When the time comes to retrieve these return addresses, they are taken off the 'stack', starting at the top, and working down until we reach the one at the 'bottom', i.e. the first return address stored. This is, of course, only a rather fanciful way of looking at the changes shown in Figure 5.5. The metaphor is sufficiently illuminating, however, for the term **stack** to be used generally to describe this kind of storage organization. It is for this reason that we gave the register the name SP, which stands for **stack pointer**.

A **stack** (in computing terminology) is an arrangement of memory which is such that values are retrieved from the memory in the reverse of the order in which they were stored. The term **LIFO** store, which stands for 'last in, first out', is sometimes used for this, as also are FILO (first in, last out) and 'pushdown stack'. We can see that the way in which the Papyrus JSR and RETURN instructions use the memory has this characteristic, so it is appropriate to say that the JSR instruction places its return address on a stack, from which it is retrieved by a corresponding RETURN instruction. The addresses are **stacked** and **unstacked** using memory locations determined according to the changing value of the stack pointer register, SP.

Strictly speaking, a stack can only be used in this way; the only value that is available at any time is the last one to be placed 'on' the stack. We call this element the 'top-of-stack' value, pointed to by SP. When the top of stack is retrieved, it is, in effect, 'removed' from the stack, exposing the adjacent element which becomes the new top of stack. Conversely, when an element is added to the stack, it becomes the new top-of-stack element, making the previous top of stack temporarily unavailable. Of course, when a 'stack' is formed within the ordinary memory of the computer, with the help of a register like SP, there is nothing to prevent other elements 'inside' the stack being accessed by referring to the memory addresses used to contain them.

There are in fact several ways in which a stack-like memory organization can be provided, and not all computers that make use of stacks implement them in precisely the way we have described. For example, it would be equally satisfactory for the SP register to be incremented by each JSR instruction, and decremented by a RETURN, rather than the other way round. The Papyrus method encourages us to 'start' the stack at the highest address available in memory. Each time a value is added to the stack, this will expand 'downwards' towards whatever other area of memory is in use; we will, of course, have to be sure that it does not expand *into* this area, or problems will arise (Figure 5.6)! To define the starting position, or base address, of the stack, we require to initialize the value in SP, for which purpose we can write an instruction such as:

LOAD   SP, #1000   ; SP := 1000

We will need to do this before any JSR instructions are executed, or unpredictable consequences will ensue.

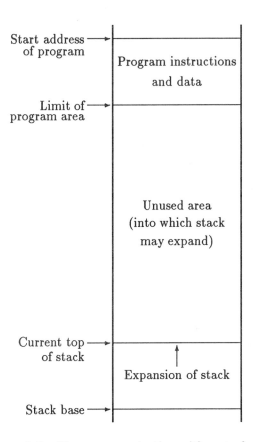

Figure 5.6   Memory organization with a stack

A stack is a convenient arrangement for storing and retrieving return addresses, because it enables us to allow subroutines to call each other in a nested sequence, without losing track of the corresponding sequence of returns we require. This is not, however, the only application of this memory structure, as we shall see later in this chapter.

System routines

Subroutines and procedures, in high-level or low-level languages, provide us with a convenient means to identify and represent parts of a program that are likely to be used repeatedly. For example, it is easy to imagine that the subroutine READNSCHAR, which we used as a simple example, might be called upon at various points in the execution of a large program. Being able to write the relevant instructions in the form of a subroutine saves us from the tedium of writing the same sequence of instructions repeatedly, and will also require less memory space to be used. Even more importantly, once we have written the instructions of a subroutine, we will need only to remember its **function**, and not the details of how it is written. It will be sufficient to remember that every time an instruction:

$$JSR \quad READNSCHAR$$

is performed, the result will be to place into the A register the ASCII code for the next non-space character input as data. This ability to organize programs so as to reduce the amount of detail that we have to remember is very important when we try to write large and complex programs without including errors; we will return to discuss this point further in Section 5.3.

Some subroutines provide functions which are so generally useful that they may be included in more than one program. This might, indeed, be so for the subroutine READNSCHAR which could be of value in very many kinds of program. In many systems, a **library** of useful subroutines is available, any of which may be selected for inclusion in a program as required. The most generally useful subroutines of all, however, are usually built in to the software of the computer system and retained permanently in the memory: these are the **system subroutines** or **system functions**.

We introduced the idea of a system function in Chapter 2, in order to enable programs to be written that perform input and output operations without going into the details of how these operations take place. This kind of **information hiding** is one of the great virtues of system functions, and indeed of all subroutines: they enable us to concentrate on the larger-scale problems of program design, without the need to worry about fine detail. In fact, the Papyrus system functions *read_integer*, *print_integer*, *read_char*, and *print_char*, which we have used so far, all take the form of subroutines that are stored somewhere in the memory of the computer. We need not, however, know anything about the instructions of these subroutines (although we will examine them more closely in the next chapter). In order to *use* them, we need only know what will be the effects of calling them.

In almost all computer systems there will be system functions to perform input and output operations, because these are some of the most generally useful program routines, and also because their program details can be complex. Other system functions may be provided for other purposes: for example, in computers that have no instructions to perform floating-point arithmetic, there may be system functions to carry out floating-point add, subtract, multiply, and divide operations. A list of the functions available will usually be provided in the description of the operating system for the computer; these functions are, of course, part of the software of the system rather than its hardware and may be different in different systems based on the same processor.

In most microcomputer systems, the principal system subroutines will be stored in Read Only Memory (ROM) to prevent any possibility of their instructions being accidentally overwritten, although this is not always the case in large-scale computers which have other ways of organizing memory to prevent such problems. In the simplest case, a system function can be used within a program by writing an instruction to call the subroutine at the memory address at which it is stored. For example, if we know that the system subroutine *read_char* is stored in a series of memory locations starting at address 10250, then the instruction:

$$JSR \quad 10250$$

will bring about execution of this function. We will not, however, want to have to remember a long list of routine addresses, so in most systems the assembler will provide some means to invoke system functions using **mnemonic** names. In PASS, as we have seen, a system function is called simply by writing its function name as an instruction; for example:

$$read\_char$$

will be translated by the PASS assembler into an appropriate JSR instruction.

5.2   Parameters

The simplest kind of subroutine performs an identical function each time it is called. For example, most high-level languages include some form of NEWLINE function, the purpose of which is to start a new line on the output device in use. A subroutine with this effect requires no further information to perform its task, which is the same in all circumstances. For most subroutines, however, this is not so. For example, the Papyrus system function *print_char* is used to print a single character on the output device. The character to be printed, however, is not always the same: its ASCII value is contained in the A register as a **parameter** of the subroutine.

A parameter, or **argument**, of a subroutine or function, is simply some further information that is required to enable the subroutine to carry out its defined task. The task of a NEWLINE subroutine is completely defined without the need for further information, whereas, clearly, *print_char* cannot proceed without knowing which character is to be printed. Another example would be a subroutine BIGGER, the purpose of which is to find which is the larger of two numbers. In this case the two numbers would have to be presented as parameters of the subroutine.

Parameters can take a number of forms, depending on the nature of the information required by the subroutine. In this section we will consider these various forms, and also the different ways in which parameters can be made available for use within a subroutine.

Simple value parameters

In many cases, the additional information required by a subroutine will be a simple **value** (or perhaps more than one value) of some type or types: for example, a numeric value, or the ASCII code value of a character. If you are familiar with Pascal, you will recognize this as a **value parameter**, as opposed to a **variable parameter**. In the examples we have seen so far, of system functions such as *print_integer* and *print_char*, the parameters have been of this nature, and have been presented to the subroutine by placing the required value in the A register prior to the subroutine call.

As another example, consider the subroutine BIGGER whose function was described above. A possible form of this subroutine in the PASS language is shown in Figure 5.7. In this case, we have made use of the Papyrus A and B registers to contain the values of the two parameters, i.e. of the two numbers whose values are to be compared. The subroutine will RETURN with the larger value in the A register. In order to make use of this subroutine, we might have in the main program a *calling sequence* such as:

```
LOAD    A, FIRST     ; A := first parameter
LOAD    B, SECOND    ; B := second parameter
JSR     BIGGER       ; call the subroutine
STORE   A, MAX       ; MAX := larger of two numbers.
```

Here, the two registers A and B are being used to pass the relevant information from the main program to the subroutine. This allows the subroutine to be written to perform a well-defined task: it compares the values in the A and B registers, and returns with the larger value in the A register. In the case of this particular calling sequence, the two values being compared are those of the variables FIRST and SECOND. This

```
; Subroutine to find the larger of two numbers
BIGGER: STORE   A, SAVEA   ; store the first number
        STORE   B, SAVEB   ; and the second number
        SUB     A, SAVEB   ; perform A-B for comparison
        JPOS    ABIG       ; jump if A bigger
        LOAD    A, SAVEB   ; otherwise, use value of B
        RETURN             ; and return with this in A register

ABIG:   LOAD    A, SAVEA   ; restore value of A
        RETURN             ; and return with it

SAVEA:  WORDS 1
SAVEB:  WORDS 1
```

Figure 5.7   A PASS subroutine with two parameters in registers

mirrors the distinction drawn, in languages such as Pascal, between the **formal** parameters of a procedure and its **actual** parameters. As far as the subroutine BIGGER is concerned, its task is defined as performing a comparison of the A and B registers; these are its **formal** parameters. In the main program, however, the values to be compared are contained in the variables FIRST and SECOND, which are thus the **actual** parameters for this call of the subroutine. The calling sequence effects an assignment of actual to formal parameters, in this case by loading the relevant registers. This kind of mapping between actual and formal parameters will also be required whenever a high-level language procedure is called; it will be for the compiler to implement an appropriate means of storing the information required to be passed to the procedure, perhaps, as in this case, using registers.

Two further points may be noted about the subroutine of Figure 5.7. The instructions make use of two variables, SAVEA and SAVEB, as temporary storage for its parameters. These may be thought of as **local** variables of the subroutine, in contrast to the **global** variables used throughout the program. Many assembly languages provide means for defining local variables so as to restrict their **scope**, i.e. to prevent their being used outside the subroutine for which they are declared. As there are a number of dif-

ferent ways in which this can be done, used in different assemblers, we will
not attempt to include this feature in PASS. Finally, note that the subroutine includes *two* RETURN instructions. The execution of the subroutine
will terminate, and control will return to the return address in the calling
sequence, whenever either of these instructions is executed. The RETURN
instruction is thus the **dynamic** end of the execution of the subroutine,
but not necessarily the **textual** end of its written instructions. Compare
this with the *stop* instruction which is the dynamic end of the execution of
a Papyrus program, whereas the textual end of a program written in the
PASS language is marked by the END directive.

Reference parameters

Consider, now, a simple subroutine the purpose of which is to exchange the
values of two variables. In Pascal, this might take the form of a procedure,
thus:

> *procedure swap (var p,q : integer):*
> *var temp : integer;*
> *begin temp := p;*
>   *p := q;*
>   *q := temp*
> *end;*

As with the subroutine BIGGER, this procedure has two parameters, given
the formal parameter-names *p* and *q*. We might call this procedure with a
statement of the form:

> *swap(one, another);*

which would have the effect of giving the **actual** parameter with the identifier 'one' the value previously assigned to 'another', and vice versa.

Notice, however, that in contrast to the subroutine BIGGER, it is not in
this case sufficient to pass the **values** of the parameters 'one' and 'another'
to the procedure. If we were to write this in PASS using the same method as
was used in BIGGER, with the values of the actual parameters contained
in the A and B registers, the only effect of the subroutine would be to
exchange the values in these registers, not in the memory locations used
for the variables concerned. In Pascal, this distinction is recognized by
the fact that the parameters *p* and *q* are *not* **value** parameters; they are,
instead, designated as **variable** (var) or **reference** parameters, with the
implication that their values may be altered by the effects of the procedure.

At the machine-instruction level, a **variable** corresponds to a **location** in the memory of the computer, and the **identifier** of the variable to the **address** of that location. Whenever an instruction changes the value of a variable, it must do so using its address. If, therefore, we wish to write a subroutine that will change the value of a variable that is specified as a parameter, the relevant information that must be passed to the subroutine is the **address** of this variable, *not* its **value**.

Figure 5.8 gives a possible form for the procedure swap, written as a PASS subroutine. The subroutine has been written, not in the simplest or

---

```
; Subroutine to exchange the values of two variables
; The addresses of the variables are passed in the A and B registers
SWAP:   STORE   A, ADDRP      ; save the first parameter-address
        STORE   B, ADDRQ      ; and the second parameter-address
        LOAD    A, (ADDRP)    ; obtain the value of P
        STORE   A, TEMP       ; and save it
        LOAD    A, (ADDRQ)    ; now get the value of Q
        STORE   A, (ADDRP)    ; P := Q
        LOAD    A, TEMP       ; previous value of P
        STORE   A, (ADDRQ)    ; Q := temp
        RETURN

ADDRP: WORDS  1               ; indirect address for P
ADDRQ: WORDS  1               ; indirect address for Q
TEMP:  WORDS  1
```

Figure 5.8   A PASS subroutine with reference parameters

most concise way possible, but rather to mirror the form of the equivalent Pascal procedure. The parameters of this subroutine are two variables, the **addresses** of which are contained in the A and B registers when the subroutine is called. The effect of the subroutine is to exchange the values in these two variables. Thus the calling sequence:

```
LOAD   A, #ONE        ; A := address of ONE
LOAD   B, #ANOTHER    ; B := address of ANOTHER
JSR    SWAP
```

will have the effect of storing the contents of the location labelled ONE in the variable ANOTHER, and the contents of ANOTHER in the location ONE.

Within the subroutine, the addresses of the actual parameters are stored in the locations ADDRP and ADDRQ respectively. Thus, if ONE is represented by address 500, then the value 500 will be the **actual** parameter passed in the A register, and stored in the location ADDRP. The instruction:

$$LOAD \quad A, \ (ADDRP)$$

uses an **indirect** addressing mode to reference this parameter; the value loaded will be obtained from the location whose address is stored at ADDRP. As this address is 500, the effect is to load the **value** of the actual parameter ONE. (Figure 5.9). Indirect addressing is subsequently used to

(Formal parameter)

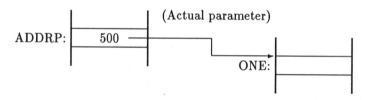

Figure 5.9   A reference parameter

obtain the value of ANOTHER, and to perform the assignment to ONE and ANOTHER.

This kind of **call by reference** (as opposed to **call by value**) is used in high-level languages such as Pascal whenever a procedure requires to change the value of a parameter. At the machine level (and hence in assembly-language programs) this is always equivalent to using the **address** of the variable concerned as an actual parameter. Some form of indirect addressing will then usually be employed to reference the actual locations corresponding to this variable.

Parameters in the store

The simple subroutines we have used for illustration have required only one or two parameters, and it has been most convenient to pass these parameters (in address or value form) using the general-purpose registers of the computer. Clearly, however, even though some computers will have more registers available for this purpose than does Papyrus, this method cannot be used in the most general case, to implement subroutines with an arbitrarily large number of parameters. The only alternative available to registers for storing the values, or addresses, of these parameters must be to contain them within the memory of the computer.

One possible method would be for the parameters to be always contained in the same nominated locations in the store. For example, we *could* have written the subroutine BIGGER in a form which meant that it always compared the values contained in two specific locations, labelled FIRST and SECOND. It would then be necessary for the calling sequence to ensure that these locations contained the relevant values to be considered.

While this method is occasionally useful, it is not in general very satisfactory. Strictly speaking, it does not involve the use of **parameters** at all; rather, the subroutine and the main program make common use of **global** variables to pass information. The disadvantages of this will be well-understood by those who have been introduced to the ideas of **structured programming**, or indeed to general principles of good programming practice in high-level languages. A subroutine that refers to a global variable by name is no longer self-contained; it is tied to a context within which this variable has been declared and assigned an appropriate value. It is also easy to forget exactly what **side-effects** a particular subroutine may have, in respect of alterations to global variables, so it becomes more difficult to use these subroutines in large programs without introducing errors. We will say a little more on this topic in Section 5.3.

One way to avoid the use of global variables within a subroutine is to place the actual parameters in a region of memory, the **address** of which is passed as a parameter. As an example, consider the subroutine BIGGEST in Figure 5.10, which finds the largest of three numbers. The numbers to be examined are contained in three consecutive memory locations, the address of the first being placed in the B register as a parameter for the subroutine. To use this subroutine, the calling sequence would be required to place the actual parameters in a suitable **parameter area**. Suppose, for example, the subroutine is to be used to determine *max(alpha, beta, 100)*, where *alpha* and *beta* are program variables. The calling sequence could be:

```
LOAD     A, #PARAMSPACE    ; address of parameter area
LOAD     A, ALPHA          ; first actual parameter
STORE    A, 0(B)           ; store in parameter area
LOAD     A, BETA           ; second actual parameter
STORE    A, 1(B)
LOAD     A, #100           ; third actual parameter
STORE    A, 2(B)
JSR      BIGGEST           ; call subroutine
STORE    A, MAX            ; returns with largest in A
```

Here, the program has first loaded the B register with the address of a block of (at least) three words of memory, which has been set aside by a declaration:

$$PARAMSPACE: \quad WORDS \quad 3$$

```
; Subroutine to find the largest of three numbers
BIGGEST:LOAD    A, 0(B)       ; fetch value of first parameter
        STORE   A, TEMP       ; store it locally
        SUB     A, 1(B)       ; compare first and second parameters
        JPOS    BIG1          ; first one is larger
        ·LOAD   A, 1(B)       ; get second parameter
        STORE   A, TEMP       ; TEMP := biggest so far
BIG1:   LOAD    A, 2(B)       ; get third parameter
        SUB     A, TEMP       ; compare with larger of two others
        JNEG    BIG2          ; TEMP is larger
        LOAD    A, 2(B)       ; third parameter is largest
        RETURN

BIG2:   LOAD    A, TEMP       ; contains largest-valued parameter
        RETURN

TEMP:   WORDS   1
```

Figure 5.10   Subroutine fetching parameters from memory

The values of the actual parameters are placed in these locations using an **indexed** addressing mode with the value in the B register (the address of the parameter area) as a **base address**. A similar mode is used within the subroutine to retrieve the parameters from the parameter area.

Note that, even though the actual parameters are referenced using an **address** passed in the B register, the subroutine in Figure 5.10 is still an example of call by **value** rather than call by **reference**. This is because it is the **values** of the actual parameters that are stored within the parameter area, so, for example, it is impossible for the subroutine to identify the memory location from which the parameter ALPHA was obtained. To implement call by reference, we would have to store the addresses of the actual parameters within the parameter area.

The advantage of this method of parameter passing is that it can be used for as many parameters as are required, and these parameters can be of any mixture of types, including, for example, **arrays**, which are most conveniently accessed by placing their base addresses in the parameter area. A variation sometimes employed, when the parameters for a particular call are fixed, is for these to be stored in the instruction sequence following the JSR instruction; for example:

```
JSR    SOMESUB
135              ; first actual parameter
-1               ; second actual parameter
...              ; instruction to which control returns
```

In this case, the subroutine SOMESUB must use the return address, which it can obtain from the stack, as the base address for referencing the parameters. It will also be necessary to increment the return address (twice) to ensure that when a RETURN is executed, control returns to the address following the location of the parameters.

Using the stack for parameters

Setting aside a designated area of memory for this purpose is a rather clumsy and inconvenient method of passing parameters. The alternative of implanting actual parameters in the instruction calling sequence is also less than ideal, since it is in principle preferable to avoid mixing instructions and other values in the same sequence of locations. We know that the processor is incapable of distinguishing instructions from other kinds of information stored in words, so a small miscalculation could result in parameter values being executed as if they were instructions, or instructions becoming overwritten.

The solution employed in most present-day computers is to use a stack to contain the values or addresses of parameters. This is convenient because it will of course be necessary to set aside an area of memory for use as a stack to contain the return addresses for subroutine calls; its further use for subroutine parameters is therefore a natural extension of this. The addresses of these parameters can be obtained via the stack pointer register, SP, so it will no longer be necessary to use a general-purpose register such as B for this purpose.

If we are to use the return-address stack for purposes other than the storing of return addresses, it will be useful to have some other kinds of instruction which make particular reference to the stack using the SP register. In Papyrus, there are in particular two special instructions that use the stack: PUSH and POP. The PUSH instruction places a value, taken from a register, 'on' the stack; thus:

$$PUSH \quad A$$

will cause the value in the A register to be left at the top-of-stack position determined by the current value of SP. The POP instruction reverses this effect; for example:

$$POP \quad B$$

would load B with the value taken from the top of stack.

The names PUSH and POP given to these instructions reflect the image of the stack as a kind of spring-powered store of values; new items added to the top 'push down' the stack, while items taken off cause the values beneath to 'pop up'. In fact, of course, the implementation of the stack mechanism is much more mundane. The effect of the PUSH A instruction is equivalent to this pair of instructions:

```
SUB     SP, #1    ; SP := SP-1
STORE   A, 0(SP)  ; Store A at address given by SP
```

Similarly for POP:

```
LOAD    A, 0(SP)  ; A := value from top of stack
ADD     SP, #1    ; increment stack pointer
```

Compare these with the way in which the JSR and RETURN instructions use the stack when a return address is stored and retrieved. We could say that the JSR instruction **pushes** its return address onto the stack, from which it is **popped** by a RETURN.

When a stack is also used for parameters of a subroutine, these can be pushed onto the stack in the calling sequence, and popped off the stack within the subroutine. As an example, Figure 5.11 gives an alternative programming of the subroutine BIGGER, this time using the stack for its parameters. The calling sequence for this might be as follows:

```
LOAD   A, FIRSTNUM      ; value of first parameter
PUSH   A                ; place it on the stack
LOAD   A, SECONDNUM     ; value of second parameter
PUSH   A                ; place it on the stack
JSR    BIGGER           ; call the subroutine
POP    A                ; larger number is found at top of stack
```

```
; Subroutine to find the larger of two numbers held on the stack
BIGGER:POP     A            ; A := return address from stack
       STORE   A, RETADD    ; save it locally
       POP     B            ; take second parameter from stack
       STORE   B, SAVE2
       POP     A            ; take first parameter from stack
       STORE   A, SAVE1
       SUB     A, SAVE2     ; compare the two values
       JPOS    BIG1         ; first parameter is bigger
       PUSH    B            ; push second parameter to stack
       JMP     (RETADD)     ; jump to addr. given in RETADD

BIG1:  LOAD    A, SAVE1     ; get first parameter again
       PUSH    A            ; and place it on the stack
       JMP     (RETADD)     ; return from subroutine

RETADD: WORDS  1
SAVE1:  WORDS  1
SAVE2:  WORDS  1
```

Figure 5.11   The BIGGER subroutine, using the stack for parameters

The effect of this calling sequence will be to enter the subroutine with the two actual parameters and the return address all stored in the stack, in the order shown in Figure 5.12(a). Because a stack is a LIFO (last-in, first-out) store, the subroutine must first POP the return address from the stack, storing it in a convenient memory location. The two actual parameters can then be referenced in turn; notice that they are obtained in the reverse order to that in which they were placed on the stack. In this form of the subroutine, the result (the value of the larger number) is

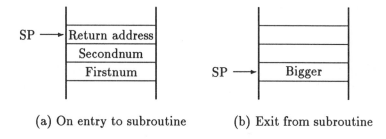

(a) On entry to subroutine   (b) Exit from subroutine

Figure 5.12   State of the stack before and after execution of subroutine

finally pushed onto the stack, so that the main program calling sequence will find this value at the top-of-stack position (Figure 5.12b). The return from the subroutine is not, in this case, made using a RETURN instruction, since the return address is no longer to be found on the stack. Instead, the indirect addressing mode is used to perform a jump to the location whose address is stored at RETADD, i.e. to the return address that was placed there at the start of the subroutine.

At first sight, this use of a stack mechanism to pass parameters (and, in this example, to return a result) seems to be much less convenient than making use of registers. The advantage, of course, is that the stack is effectively as large as we want it to be, so we can have as many parameters as are required. The use of a stack also provides a very well-defined and simple general structure which can be used in the same sort of way for many different kinds of subroutine. In particular, high-level language compilers often find it most convenient to use this method, not only when producing the machine-code versions of procedures in the source program, but also to produce simple machine code for the evaluation of arithmetic expressions. For example, the machine code produced for the evaluation of an expression such as:

$$x^*y+z$$

will often be of the form:

```
push    x
push    y
call    multiply    (result left on stack)
push    z
call    add
```

Compilers find it very easy to translate expressions into instruction sequences of this kind, using simple subroutines ('multiply', 'add', and so on) which each expect two parameters to be found on the stack, and leave a result in their place.

Recursion

Using a stack to contain parameters, rather than setting aside a designated parameter area in the store, has the advantage that the allocation of locations for parameters in a stack is, so to speak, automatic. Neither in the calling sequence nor within the subroutine is it necessary to know the particular addresses used for each parameter, nor need these be the same each time the subroutine is called. Both when placing parameters on the stack, and when referencing parameters within a subroutine, they are located, effectively, by their position **relative** to the current top-of-stack position. This has important consequences when dealing with **nested** subroutines which call each other, and especially when dealing with **recursive** subroutine calls.

A recursive subroutine, or procedure, is one that may in some circumstances call *itself* to perform some subsidiary task. In simple, concrete terms, a PASS subroutine SOMESUB will be recursive if it contains, somewhere within its text, an instruction:

$$JSR \quad SOMESUB$$

which brings about a further call of the same subroutine. Of course, this instruction must not be executed on every occasion on which the subroutine is performed, or the result will be an endless sequence of calls.

The usual example given of a recursive procedure is one to calculate the **factorial** of a number n, where:

$$\text{factorial } n = n*(n-1)*\ldots*2*1$$

We could define a **recursive function** to perform this calculation by identifying two cases:

1. factorial $1 = 1$
2. factorial $n = n * \text{factorial}(n-1)$

In Pascal, we could write this function as follows:

```
function factorial (n: integer): integer;
begin
     if n=1 then factorial := 1
     else factorial := n*factorial(n−1)
end;
```

A possible equivalent in PASS is shown in Figure 5.13. This subroutine,

---

```
; A recursive subroutine to calculate factorial n
FACTORIAL:PUSH    A            ; push the param. n onto the stack
         SUB      A, #1        ; A := n-1
         JZERO    OUT          ; if n=1, finish
         JSR      FACTORIAL    ; otherwise, calculate factorial n-1
         PUSH     A            ; push the result onto the stack
         JSR      MULTIPLY     ; multiply n by factorial n-1
         RETURN                ; return with result in A

OUT:     POP      A            ; take the param. from the stack
         RETURN                ; and return
```

Figure 5.13   A recursive subroutine in PASS

FACTORIAL, expects its parameter n to be passed in the A register, which is also used to return the result. Within the subroutine, however, the parameter is stored for future reference on the stack using a PUSH instruction. If $n=1$, an immediate exit from the subroutine is made, popping n (the value 1) from the stack, and returning with this value in the A register. In all other cases, the subroutine FACTORIAL is called **recursively**, with the value $n-1$ in the A register as a parameter.

The sequence of events will become clearer if we consider a simple example. Suppose the subroutine is invoked to calculate factorial 3, with the initial calling sequence:

$$LOAD \quad A, \#3$$
$$JSR \quad FACTORIAL$$

If this instruction is located at address 120, then the return address 121 will be placed on the stack and the subroutine FACTORIAL entered. The first instruction of this places the value of the parameter, 3, on the stack, which now has the state shown in Figure 5.14(a). Because n does not have the value 1, a *further* call of the subroutine FACTORIAL is now made. Suppose the address of the subroutine label FACTORIAL is 500; then the JSR FACTORIAL instruction *within* this subroutine is located at address 503. When this instruction is executed, the return address 504 will be

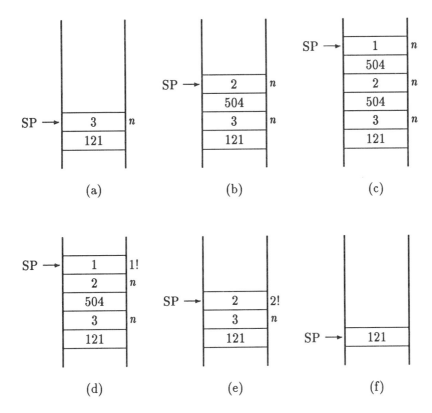

Figure 5.14   Sequence of stack changes while performing FACTORIAL

pushed onto the stack, and a new entry to the start of FACTORIAL made
with the value 2 in the A register. This is again immediately pushed onto
the stack, to leave the state shown in Figure 5.14(b). A similar sequence
leads to a third recursive call of FACTORIAL, following which three return
addresses and three values of n (3,2, and 1) are left on the stack (Figure
5.14c).

Notice at this point that there are, in effect, three different versions of
the parameter n, corresponding to the three separate calls of the subroutine, each of which is stored securely in a distinct location on the stack.
There was no need for the subroutine FACTORIAL, or its original calling
sequence, to organize this explicitly; the organization follows automatically
from the properties of the PUSH and POP instructions and the use of the
stack for return addresses.

On the third call of FACTORIAL, the parameter in the A register has the value 1, so execution proceeds via the label OUT to remove this value from the stack and RETURN, via the return address at the top of the stack, to address 504. This is the point immediately following the JSR FACTORIAL instruction *within* the subroutine, at which the value in the A register (1, in this case) is again placed on the stack. At this instant the state of the stack is shown in Figure 5.14(d). Comparing this with Figure 5.14(c), we see that the last return address (504) and the value $n=1$ have been removed from the stack, to be replaced by the value of factorial 1 (written in mathematical notation, 1!). The *third* call of FACTORIAL (the one with parameter $n=1$) has now completed, and the result of calculating FACTORIAL(1) is now at the top-of-stack position.

Execution of the *second* call of FACTORIAL now continues, and a subroutine MULTIPLY is called to multiply the factorial calculated so far (1!) by the *current* value of n. This is the value, 2, stored immediately above the return address for this call of FACTORIAL. We will assume that the subroutine MULTIPLY expects to find its two parameters on the stack, and that it will remove them and return with their product in the A register. The subroutine FACTORIAL can now terminate with a RETURN to address 504, and the value 2 in the A register.

The return to address 504, of course, transfers control again into the middle of the subroutine, and the value in A is again immediately placed on the stack. We are now back within the *first* invocation of FACTORIAL; the stack (Figure 5.14e) contains only the original return address (121) of the first call, the original parameter value $n=3$, and the value of 2! which has been calculated so far. All that remains is for 3*2! to be calculated, with a final call of MULTIPLY to leave this product in the A register. The stack (Figure 5.14f) now contains only the return address into the original calling sequence, which will be removed when the final RETURN is executed in FACTORIAL.

Stack-based store organization

The example of recursion may seem to be a rather esoteric use of the mechanism of a stack. In fact, the concept of recursion is quite important in computer science; its implementation always involves the use of a stack, and an examination of the concrete practicalities of this implementation can be helpful in understanding the abstract concept involved.

Even excluding the particular case of recursion, however, the generality and flexibility of a stack-based memory organization make it the most suitable for dealing with procedure parameters in most implementations of high-level languages. Many implementations of Pascal-like languages, indeed, go further in that they organise the whole of the memory space (excluding that part used for instructions) as a single stack.

Suppose, in some Pascal-like language, a program is written that declares **global** variables n and m, before calling a procedure FIRSTPROC, with parameter 100. FIRSTPROC in turn declares an array of five integers, and calls another procedure, SECONDPROC. Figure 5.15 shows the way in which the memory could be organized to administer this sequence. The al-

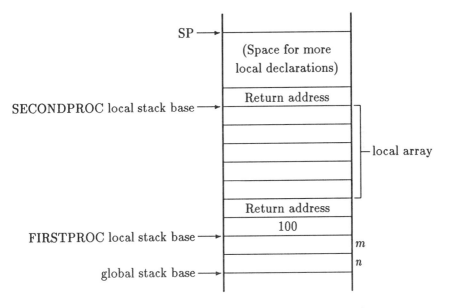

Figure 5.15   A stack-based memory organization

location of memory starts at a **global stack base**, and the variables n and m are allocated locations above this base. As this is done, the stack pointer is advanced so that when FIRSTPROC is called, its return address and parameter (100) will be stacked 'above' these locations. Within FIRST-PROC, the declaration of an array makes use of more space within the stack, and the subsequent call of SECONDPROC causes a further return address and, perhaps, further subsequent declarations to be added.

The advantage of this method of allocating space is that it allows declarations of variables to proceed dynamically as the program is executed. Each time a procedure is called, any memory space it requires for its local variables is allocated, starting at the current top-of-stack position. When the procedure terminates, the stack pointer is restored to the position it had at the start of the procedure, effectively wiping out all record of the local variables declared within; this of course conforms to the semantics of **block-structured** languages like Pascal.

Within a procedure, local variables may be referenced using some form of relative addressing with the **local stack base** as a base address. Each time a procedure is entered, a new local stack base is defined, with its value set to the current top of stack. It is helpful if the computer in use has a special register to define this **local address base**, and if there are special instructions to assist in performing the necessary adjustments to this and to the stack pointer value whenever a procedure is entered or terminates. Even with a simple machine like Papyrus, however, it is possible to implement this kind of memory organization, but to describe this in detail is really outside the scope of this book.

Macros

Within the topic of subroutines, it is relevant to discuss something that is not strictly part of this topic, but a related concept: the **macro**. Like a subroutine, a macro is a piece of program that may be used repeatedly, possibly with different parameters, at various points throughout a program. The instructions of a subroutine are stored in a unique set of locations to which control is transferred whenever the subroutine is invoked. In the case of a macro, conversely, the relevant instructions are replicated in the memory at each point of invocation. A macro, thus, is not a single piece of program to which a call can be made, but a defined sequence of instructions which may be repeated at various points within a program. The distinction is illustrated in Figure 5.16, for a sequence of two instructions.

Consider the example of the SWAP subroutine of Figure 5.8. Without using a subroutine, we might have written the following sequence of instructions to 'swap' the contents of locations P and Q:

$$
\begin{array}{ll}
LOAD & A, P \\
LOAD & B, Q \\
STORE & A, Q \\
STORE & B, P
\end{array}
$$

This is shorter, neater (and faster in execution) than the subroutine SWAP. However, if we were writing a program that required a SWAP operation to be performed perhaps tens or hundreds of times, we would find it very tedious to have to repeat the same sequence over and over again, and to do so would increase the risk of errors being introduced. In this case, we might find it useful to define the sequence of instructions as a **macro**.

In PASS, the *definition* of a macro is performed using the MACDEF **directive**. We could define a macro SWAP thus:

> *MACDEF SWAP (P,Q)*
>   *LOAD A, P*
>   *LOAD B, Q*
>   *STORE A, Q*
>   *STORE B, P*
> *ENDMAC*

This definition does not in itself cause any instructions to be stored in the memory. However, whenever within the program subsequently we write a **macro-instruction** of the form (for example):

SWAP FIRST, SECOND

the effect will be to create at that point in the object program a sequence of four instructions corresponding to the definition of SWAP, with the identifiers FIRST and SECOND replacing P and Q respectively.

Notice that, like a subroutine, this macro has **formal** parameters (in this case, P and Q) and **actual** parameters, FIRST and SECOND. In the case of a macro, there is no need for the actual parameters to be stored, on the stack or elsewhere, when the macro is 'called'. Instead, the assembler, when translating the SWAP FIRST, SECOND macro-instruction, will use the addresses of FIRST and SECOND as the effective addresses of P and Q when the instructions of the macro definition are translated into machine code. The **parameter substitution** in this case is **textual** rather than **dynamic**; it is performed by the assembler when the program is translated, so that, within the object program, each occurrence of a macro-instruction is no different from the code which would have been produced by writing the instructions directly.

Unlike subroutines, therefore, which have a clearly defined existence within the object program, a macro is a source-program construction which is no longer apparent at the machine-execution level. Strictly speaking, an **assembler** performs a one-to-one translation from mnemonic instructions into binary machine-code instructions for execution. Most modern assembly languages, however, are really **macro-assemblers** which provide some means for the definition of macros within a program, and hence for the translation of mnemonic macro-instructions into sequences of one or more machine-level instructions. The value of this is that it allows us to define higher-level 'instructions' than those provided by the computer processor itself, and even to introduce a measure of **machine-independence** into our programs by defining a set of macros to meet the requirements of the problem being solved. One application where this approach is sometimes used is in the implementation of compilers for high-level languages. A compiler

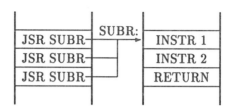

(a) Subroutine

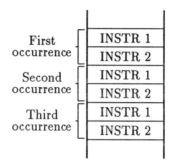

(b) Macro

Figure 5.16   Subroutines and macros

for a language such as Pascal can be written to translate the Pascal source
program, not directly into any particular machine code, but into an **inter-
mediate code** of instructions which are essentially machine-independent.
To complete the translation for any particular machine, it is only necessary to define a suitable set of macros for the translation of each of these
intermediate-level instructions (Figure 5.17).

5.3   Structure in machine-level programs

This is not a book principally about assembly-language *programming*; we
are, rather, using assembly language as a medium for describing the characteristics of hardware and software at the 'primitive' instruction level.
When we come to use computers for solving real problems, there are very
good reasons for avoiding the use of assembly language whenever possible.
There remain, however, occasions when the use of this level of programming

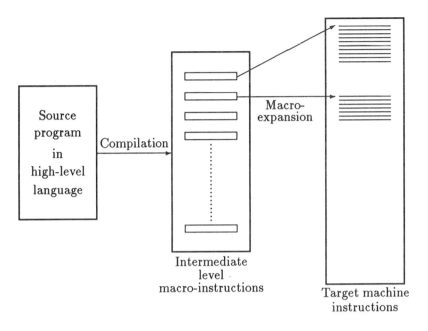

Figure 5.17 Two-stage compiling using macros

is appropriate, or, sometimes, inescapable; for example, when writing some of the system routines which will support the operation of a particular computer. In so far as we may be required to write programs in assembly language, therefore, it will be important to approach the task with the same professional discipline as we would apply to writing programs at other levels.

If your study of high-level language programming has progressed beyond a very preliminary stage, it is likely that you will have encountered some of the ideas of what has come to be known as **structured programming**. It is outside the scope of this book to discuss this topic in depth, but a brief and informal summary may be appropriate.

The central premise from which these ideas derive is that not even the most skilled programmer can consistently write large and complex programs that are error-free, unless some methodology is applied to organize and simplify the task in a systematic way. The methodology of structured programming, and of related methods of program development, involves the breaking down of a complex problem into a collection of simple parts, each of which is sufficiently small and well-understood to enable us to write it in the form of a program that we can realistically hope to be a correct implementation of the task it is required to perform.

Two approaches are possible. In a **top-down** style of development, the overall problem to be solved is first examined, and broken down into a small number of well-defined parts: for example, reading and organizing the data, performing the main program task, and producing the results. Each of these parts is then subjected to the same kind of analysis and refinement. This process continues until the parts that emerge are defined in sufficient detail to allow them to be written as parts of the program.

Figure 5.18 is a pictorial representation of a top-down problem analysis. In the alternative, **bottom-up**, approach, individual program parts

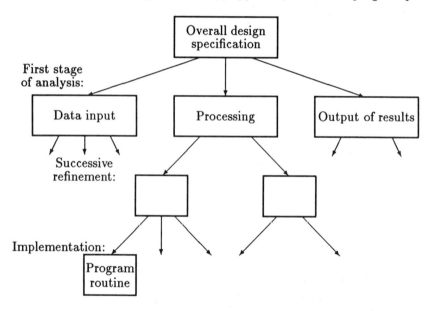

Figure 5.18 A top-down program design analysis

which are expected to contribute to the solution of the problem are identified and implemented, probably as program subroutines. These routines are then used as building blocks to create more complex program modules, the process continuing until a complete program is constructed. In principle, this is a less satisfactory approach than top-down design, since it does not demand a clear overall definition of the problem to be solved. In practice, however, many programmers make use of a mixture of top-down and bottom-up styles in working towards an implementation of a complex problem.

Both subroutines and macros may be used to implement the parts from which the final program is constructed. It may not be sufficient, however, simply to organize a program as a collection of arbitrary subroutines. If the relationship between these subroutines, and the ways in which they interact in the execution of the program, is unduly complicated, then the advantage of this kind of program structure will be lost. Each individual routine may be error-free, but major errors may emerge in the way they combine and communicate within the program.

If we are to avoid these problems, it is important to apply some general rules of good design to the way in which subroutines are written. We begin by recognizing that a subroutine, if it is to be used effectively as a program building block, must be **self-contained**, and must perform some well-defined and clearly understood task. Some consequent design guidelines are summarized here.

1. **Single entry and exit points** In high-level languages, it is usually impossible to enter a subroutine or procedure at any point other than at its start. At the machine instruction level, however, a JSR instruction may be executed with any destination address, so subroutines can be written in a way that allows for their execution to commence at any of several different points in their instruction sequence. Use of this device is likely to undermine the integrity of the subroutine as a simple and well-defined program component, and should generally be avoided.

The corresponding stricture, demanding a single point of departure from the subroutine, is perhaps less firm. In small subroutines, as in the example of Figure 5.7, it is often convenient to have more than one RETURN instruction, and there would be no special merit in replacing these by jumps to a common point of return. It is important, however, that a consistent set of conditions should apply at each point of return; for example, in the subroutine of Figure 5.7, the RETURN in each case is made with the value of the result of the subroutine held in the A register.

2. **Avoidance of global references** A subroutine may be said to be **self-contained** if its function can be defined clearly and completely in terms of the parameters it requires and the result it produces. This property is useful for two reasons. Firstly, a self-contained subroutine can be used in more than one context, and, if required, in more than one program; its **requirements** are only those it defines for itself and those implied by its parameters. Secondly, a subroutine that can be defined clearly, completely, and succinctly is more likely to be used correctly within a program.

References to **global** variables within a subroutine weaken this clarity of definition. The requirements of the subroutine must now be defined to include not only its parameters but also the details of the global variables it makes use of. Whenever possible, therefore, it is desirable to write subroutines in ways that avoid global references, and to provide the necessary communication with the program context by means of parameters.

3. Avoidance of side-effects A related point is that a subroutine should have a well-defined *result*, which may be a value it delivers (such as the sum of the elements of an array) or a task it performs (such as exchanging the values of two variable-parameters). If the subroutine, additionally, has some subsidiary **side-effect**, then this is likely to be overlooked in the program design, leading to error. Side-effects can be largely avoided if references to global variables are eliminated, thus reducing the scope for unwanted changes to be made. Side-effects involving changes to values in registers, or values of parameters, can, however, also be significant. It is important that such changes should be recognized as part of the central function of the subroutine or otherwise avoided if possible.

4. Clear and complete specification Underlying everything we have said about the use of **structure** to help us write programs correctly is the idea of a subroutine as a well-defined and clearly understood entity. Assembly language is not the ideal medium to assist understanding, so it is particularly important, in this level of programming, to make liberal use of comments to annotate our programs. When writing a subroutine, in particular, it is useful to preface the instructions with comments which describe succinctly:

1. The function of the subroutine, i.e. the well-defined task which it is to perform.

2. Its entry and exit conditions, i.e. the form of its parameters, and the way in which it returns its result.

3. Any other requirement it has.

4. Any side-effect, including registers whose values may be altered.

Writing these comments is in itself a useful discipline, forcing us to think clearly about the **specification** of a subroutine, and its requirements and side-effects. If carried out properly, the description that results will serve to provide all the information needed to use the subroutine, allowing us to 'forget' the details of its implementation and to concentrate on the wider problems of the overall program structure.

Relocation

We have stressed the value of writing subroutines that are self-contained and independent of the program context in which they appear. A particular aspect of this is the ability to locate the instructions and local variables of a subroutine in any convenient part of the memory. A subroutine that has this property, rather than being tied to a particular set of memory addresses, is said to be **relocatable.**

Relocatability of a subroutine can be achieved in several different ways. If the subroutine makes explicit reference to particular **absolute** addresses, then it cannot be made completely relocatable; the presence of an instruction such as:

$$LOAD \quad A, \ 150 \qquad ; \ A := \ contents \ of \ location \ 150$$

will ensure that the subroutine must make use of this particular memory location. If, conversely, all the absolute memory references made within the subroutine use symbolic identifiers for the locations concerned, then it will be possible for the assembler to allocate different addresses for these each time the subroutine is assembled within a program. In this case **relocation** of the subroutine is achieved by **reassembly** of the source instructions and declarations.

A higher degree of relocatability is achieved if the object code generated by the assembler is itself relocatable. Many assemblers translate the source program, not into **absolute** binary machine code, but into a **relocatable binary** form. In this form, every variable identifier and label in the program is allocated an address which is **relative** to the (undefined) **base address** of the program. Each instruction that refers to an identifier or label defined in this way is translated into a machine-code form which contains a reference to the relative address of the location concerned. These relative references are 'fixed' to absolute memory locations only when the object program is finally **loaded** into the memory. At this stage, the **loader** must add a suitable base address value to each instruction of this form, converting the relocatable binary instructions into their executable absolute machine-code form.

The highest level of relocatability is obtained when the final binary machine-code form of a subroutine is itself location-independent; such a subroutine is said to be **dynamically relocatable.** A subroutine cannot be dynamically relocatable if it makes any reference to absolute addresses, whether as data references or in jump instructions. Thus, for a subroutine to have this property, it must be written to use only **relative** addressing modes for *all* its memory references. The easiest way to achieve this, for data references, is to make use of a stack for all local variables and temporary storage. Stack references are automatically relocated with respect to the stack pointer register. For internal **jumps** within a subroutine to be relocatable, it is necessary that they be translated into some form of relative jump or branch. In many computers, the usual form of a jump instruction uses a destination address that is relative to the current program counter value, and such jumps are inherently relocatable.

5.4   *68000 subroutines

The basic mechanism of subroutines in the 68000 is essentially similar to that described for Papyrus. The 68000 instruction to **call** a subroutine also has the mnemonic JSR, and the 'return' instruction is RTS (return from subroutine). The stack pointer register used by these instructions is one of the **address registers**, A7. In the assembly language, this register may be referred to either as A7 or as SP. The JSR and RTS instructions operate in exactly the same way as their Papyrus equivalents, except that the value stored as the return address is a full 32 bits, the **longword** value of PC, and so the corresponding adjustment to the value of SP increments or decrements it by 4. JSR, like the 68000 JMP instruction, uses a general **effective address** to define the destination for its change of control, which may therefore be defined as a label (translated into an **absolute** address) or, for example, obtained from an address register:

> *JSR   (A1)*   * jump to subroutine whose address is in A1*

There is, however, also a BSR instruction (branch to subroutine), the operand of which must be a simple label, which is translated into a **relative** address.

The 68000 does not use explicit PUSH and POP instructions to manipulate the stack. The reason for this is that the same effects are achieved, in a more general way, by use of the **pre-decrement** and **post-increment** addressing modes with the stack pointer, A7, as address register. The instruction:

> *MOVE   D3,–(A7)*

has exactly the effect of the Papyrus PUSH instruction; the stack pointer register is first decremented (by 2, in this case, to accommodate a word-sized operand), then the value in D3 is stored at the location now pointed to. Similarly:

> *MOVE   (A7)+, D0*

will 'pop' the word at the top of the stack into register D0.

Because these are generally available addressing modes, references to the stack are not restricted to simple pop and push operations using registers. We can, for example, pop a value from the stack directly into memory:

$$MOVE \quad (SP)+, \; SAVETOS$$

and we can also perform other operations involving operands taken from the stack; for example:

$$ADD \quad (SP)+, \; D2 \qquad * \; D2 := D2 + Top \; of \; stack \; value.$$

In these cases, it must always be remembered that the operand referred to will be, effectively, removed from the stack as a result of the operation.

The other advantage of having these general addressing modes available for use with any of the address registers, A0–A7, is that it becomes possible to use them to manipulate more than one stack within the same program. The stack defined by the SP (A7) register must be used for subroutine return addresses, since it is this register that is assumed by the JSR and RTS instructions. We could, however, define a different stack to store subroutine parameters, for example, and this would have the advantage of allowing these to be referenced without the need to first unstack any return address stored.

Suppose, for example, we decide that a stack of size 100 longwords will be sufficient to accommodate all the return addresses we might need to store (allowing subroutine nesting up to a depth of 100), and that 1000 words will suffice for all possible parameter storage requirements. We could set aside space for this by the declarations:

STACKTOP:	*DS.L 100*	* space for return addresses
RASTACKBASE:	*DS.W 1000*	* space for parameter stack
PARAMSTACK:	*DS.W 1*	* base of parameter stack.

Then the instruction:

$$LEA \quad RASTACKBASE, \; A7$$

will load the stack pointer register with the address of the limit of the area set aside for the return address stack, so that the first JSR instruction will store its return address in the last longword of this area. Similarly:

$$LEA \quad PARAMSTACK, \; A6$$

will initialize A6 to the value of the base address for the parameter stack, allowing A6 to be used as the stack pointer for this.

```
* Subroutine to find the larger of two numbers held on a stack
* A6 is the stack pointer used for parameters and result.
* The subroutine also uses the data registers D1 and D2
BIGGER: MOVE    (A6)+, D2       * pop second parameter into D2
        MOVE    (A6)+, D1       * pop first parameter into D1
        CMP     D1, D2          * compare them
        BGT     BIG2            * param2 > param1
        MOVE    D1, -(A6)       * push D1
        RTS                     * and exit

BIG2:   MOVE    D2, -(A6)       * push D2
        RTS                     * and exit
```

Figure 5.19   A simple 68000 subroutine using a stack for parameters

With this organization, the subroutine BIGGER of Figure 5.11, which finds the larger of two numbers held on a stack, could be written in 68000 assembler as shown in Figure 5.19. The calling sequence for this could be:

```
MOVE    FIRST, -(A6)    * Push parameter FIRST
MOVE    SECOND, -(A6)   * Followed by SECOND
JSR     BIGGER          * Find max(FIRST, SECOND)
MOVE    (A6)+, MAX      * Store result
```

Of course, a simple subroutine like this might have more easily been written to accept its parameters in registers; the presence of a number of **data** registers and **address** registers within the 68000 gives us considerable scope to use these for **value** and **reference** parameters. The example of Figure 5.19 does illustrate, however, in a simple way, how a second stack can also be used with convenience for parameters and results. Notice also that this subroutine is **relocatable**; all its memory references are made using the address registers, and the BGT instruction will also be assembled into a relative branch.

Stack manipulation instructions

The 68000 has a number of special instructions that are of use when a stack is used for subroutine parameters.

The PEA (push effective address) instruction is the only explicit 'push' instruction of the 68000, and may be used as a convenient way of placing a **reference** parameter on the main stack, i.e. the stack defined by the A7 register. The instruction is analogous to LEA (load effective address), but in this case the destination of the instruction is not an address register but the stack, and A7 is decremented accordingly. For example:

*PEA   PARAMSPACE   * push address of PARAMSPACE onto stack*

The MOVEM (move multiple registers) instruction is not especially associated with use of a stack, but it is particularly useful if we wish to write subroutines that do not have the side-effect of altering values in registers. The values of any set of data and address registers may be stored in consecutive memory locations by an instruction such as:

MOVEM   D0-D7/A0-A6, REGSTORE

which will save all the data registers, and all the address registers except SP, in an area of memory labelled REGSTORE. We could also be more selective:

*MOVEM   D1/D2/A3, SAVE3   * save 3 register values*

It may often be desirable to save all the register values in this way at the start of a subroutine, and restore them at the end, so that the execution of the subroutine may be said to leave all register values unchanged. In this case, the registers may be saved on a stack by using the instruction in the form:

*MOVEM   D0-D7/A0-A6, -(A7)   * push all registers*

and restored using the post-increment mode.

In Section 5.2, and Figure 5.15, we briefly outlined the use of a stack organization as a way of managing the allocation of memory for local variables within, for example, an implementation of a high-level language. The 68000 has two special instructions to assist in this kind of organization. Recall that each time a procedure is entered, it will be necessary to define a new **local address base** for the local variables declared within the procedure, and on procedure exit, we will want to restore the stack pointer and local address base to their previous values. The LINK and UNLK instructions are designed to achieve these effects. Suppose, for example, a particular procedure uses 72 bytes of memory for its local variable storage. On entry to the procedure, the instruction:

LINK   A0, #-72

will have the following effects:

1. The current contents of A0 are pushed onto the stack, using A7.

2. The new value of SP is placed in A0.

3. SP is further decremented by 72.

The result is to define a region in the stack (a stack **frame**) with a local base address in A0. The previous local frame base address is saved in the stack. If the same procedure were to call itself recursively, repeating the LINK instruction, the stack would appear as in Figure 5.20. Here we see

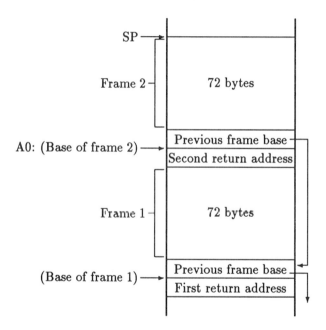

Figure 5.20   State of stack after procedure calls with LINK

that, corresponding to the first call of the procedure, there is a region of the stack, which we have identified as frame 1, within which the local variables of the procedure will be stored. The subsequent recursive call has created a new stack frame, frame 2, on top of this. At any time, the register A0 (assuming it is not otherwise altered) will contain the base address of the *current* frame, and local variables may be referenced using a displacement from this register value. When the procedure terminates, the instruction:

UNLK   A0

will transfer the value in A0 into SP, and then 'pop' the previous frame base address from the stack into A0. This has the effect of restoring both the stack and the frame base pointer, A0, to their previous state, so that, in this example, frame 1 will again become the current frame. Any of the address registers, A0–A6, may be used in this way as a local address base, or frame base pointer.

A 68000 program with subroutines

An example of a program in 68000 assembly language that makes use of subroutines is shown in Figure 5.21. This program calculates the 'scalar product' of two arrays A and B, determined as the sum of $A_i \times B_i$ for all elements of the arrays. The program includes two subroutines. The first, READVEC, is used to read the elements of each array into memory. It is called with the address of an array in A0, and the size of the array in D1. In the main program, space is allocated within the area of memory labelled ARRAYS for storage of the two arrays, and **pointers** to their addresses are stored in longword form in ARRAYA and ARRAYB.

The second subroutine, MULVECS, performs the scalar product calculation. It would again have been possible to pass the parameters in registers, but in this case they have been pushed onto the stack in the calling sequence. The subroutine thus has to 'pop' the return address, storing it in register A0, before it can obtain the other parameters, which are taken off in reverse order: the size of the arrays, followed by their two addresses. After performing the scalar product calculation, the longword result is pushed onto the stack. Finally, exit from the subroutine is made by pushing the return address back onto the stack before performing an RTS instruction. The return *could* have been effected directly using the instruction:

JMP   (A0)

to jump to the return address saved in A0, but there is some virtue in always using RTS to leave a subroutine, as this is always clearly a 'return' instruction. Back in the main program, the result is popped from the stack, and a system function **print_longinteger** used to print it.

```
TTL     SCALPROD
* This program reads in two arrays of n integers, and calculates
* their scalar product, ie sum of A[i]*B[i]

ORG   $1000

                LEA       STACKTOP, A7   * initialize the stack pointer
                read_integer             * read the array size in words
                MOVE      D0, N          * store it in memory
                ASL       #1, D0         * double n to calculate size in by
                LEA       ARRAYS, A0     * A0 := address of arrays
                MOVE.L    A0, ARRAYA     * store pointer to array A
                ADDA      D0, A0         * add size of arrays in bytes
                MOVE.L    A0, ARRAYB     * and store pointer to array B
* now read in the values of the two arrays
                MOVE      N, D1          * size in words in D1
                MOVEA.L ARRAYA, A0       * address in A0
                JSR       READVEC        * read the array A into memory
                MOVE      N, D1
                MOVEA.L ARRAYB, A0
                JSR       READVEC        * read the array B into memory
* calculate their scalar product
                MOVE.L    ARRAYA, -(A7)  * push address of array A
                MOVE.L    ARRAYB, -(A7)  * push address of array B
                MOVE      N, -(A7)       * push size of arrays
                JSR       MULVECS        * form scalar product
                MOVE.L    (A7)+, D0      * pop the result
                print_longinteger        * print it
                TRAP      #0             * and end program


* Subroutine to read the elements of an array into memory
* Array address is passed in A0, size (in words) in D1
* The subroutine also uses D0, and changes A0 and D1
READVEC:  read_integer                   * read an array element into D0
                MOVE      D0, (A0)+      * store in array
                SUBQ      #1, D1         * decrement count of words
                BGT       READVEC        * continue while positive
                RTS                      * then exit
```

```
* Subroutine to calculate the scalar product of two vectors, A and B
* The addresses of A and B, and the size of the vectors, are passed
* on the stack. The result is returned in their place.
* The subroutine also uses D0-D3 and A0-A2
MULVECS:  MOVEA.L  (A7)+, A0      * pop return address
          MOVE     (A7)+, D1      * pop array size
          MOVEA.L  (A7)+, A2      * address of array B
          MOVEA.L  (A7)+, A1      * address of array A
          CLR.L    D2             * use D2 for total
MVLP:     MOVE     (A1)+, D3      * D3 := element from array A
          MULS     (A2)+, D3      * multiply by element from B
          ADD.L    D3, D2         * add into total
          SUBQ     #, D1          * decrement element count
          BGT      MVLP           * and loop
          MOVE.L   D2, -(A7)      * push result onto stack
          MOVE.L   A0, -(A7)      * push return address back
          RTS                     * and use it to return


* Declarations
N:         DS    1
ARRAYA:    DS.L  1                * pointer to array A
ARRAYB:    DS.L  1                * pointer to array B
ARRAYS:    DS.W  1000             * space for arrays
STACK:     DS.L  500              * space for stack
STACKTOP:  DS.L  1                * base of stack

END
```

Figure 5.21   A 68000 program with subroutines

5.5   Exercises

1. In each of the following cases, describe a suitable way to pass parameters to, and return results from, the subroutine:

    (a) a subroutine to test if an unsigned 16-bit value lies within a specified range;

    (b) a subroutine to test if two text strings are identical;

    (c) a subroutine to search a table of (key, value) pairs, where the key is a numeric code of size word, and the value a text string to which the subroutine must return a pointer.

    Write 68000 **calling sequences** for each subroutine.

2. Write a 68000 program that will mimic the behaviour of a lift in a building, starting at the ground floor, ascending to the top floor, and returning to the ground again. As it reaches each floor, the program should display a message of the form

    going up(down): floor 5.

    The program must achieve its effects by the use of a **recursive** subroutine LIFT, which calls itself at every 'floor' until the top of the building is reached.

    Try the program first for a building with a small number of floors; then investigate what happens when the number of floors is so great that the space allocated for your stack is exceeded.

3. Write a subroutine READWORD that will read a single word of text, i.e. a sequence of alphabetic characters. The subroutine should read past any leading 'space' characters, then read the characters of the word, up to and including a non-alphabetic terminating character. Return from the subroutine with a count of the number of letters in the word, and the value of the terminating character. Include this subroutine in a program that reads a piece of text, terminated with some special character, and counts how many words of length 1 letter, 2 letters, ..., up to 12 letters (the maximum) are present in the text.

4. Write a subroutine to test if one integer is a factor of another, i.e. if it divides into it with no remainder.

    Use the subroutine to construct a program that will determine whether some number given as data is a **prime** number.

5. Write a 68000 subroutine to reproduce the effects of the following Pascal procedure:

```
procedure compress(var data: vector; size: integer);
    var i: integer; pos: integer;
    begin
        pos := 0;
        for i := 1 to size do
        begin
            if data[i] <> 0 then
            begin
                pos := pos+1;
                data[pos] := data[i]
            end
        end
    end;
```

where *vector* is of type *array[1..size]* of integer. Include your subroutine in a program to test it.

Chapter 6

Input, output, and interrupts

6.1 Simple input and output operations

Throughout this book, so far, it has been assumed that programs which require to obtain input from (for example) a keyboard, or to print results to a VDU screen, will do so making use of **system functions** provided within the software of the computer. For most programming applications, in most computer systems, this will indeed be so: it is usual for a comprehensive set of **input** and **output routines** to be included as part of the operating system. This is obviously sensible, as these functions will be required by almost all programs, and it would be tedious for us to have to keep rewriting them.

The consequence of this is that in almost all programming, input and output operations are performed using these 'black-box' routines, the details of which are hidden from us. Almost always, this is a good thing; the more that the details of a program can be packaged up and put to one side in this way, the easier it is to concentrate on the problems that only we can solve, of organizing a program to satisfy the needs of the application in hand. In this chapter, however, we will look a little more closely at the form that these input and output subroutines might take. To do so, we must first review our picture of the **hardware** organization of the computer.

Memory-mapped input–output

When the simple von Neumann architectural model was introduced in Chapter 1, we described the processor and memory of the computer as being connected by a **bus**. A bus is simply a set of electrical connections along which binary-coded information can be transmitted from one device to another. When the processor obtains information from the memory, it does so by issuing a **read request** to the bus, along with the address of the memory word required. This information is transmitted along the bus to the memory, which responds by placing the contents of the word addressed on the bus, to be returned to the processor. The transaction is completed when the processor loads this value into an appropriate register which is physically connected to the bus.

A somewhat different sequence is involved when the processor *writes* information into a memory word. In order to distinguish between the steps required for a **write cycle**, as opposed to a **read cycle**, and to deal with other cases and eventualities, the processor and memory communicate using a simple set of rules called a **protocol**. The details of this, however, need not concern us here; the appropriate steps are carried out by the electronic components that comprise the processor and memory in executing, for example, LOAD and STORE instructions. At the primitive programming level, our model of the processor memory relationship is summarized quite adequately by our understanding of the effects of these instructions in program execution.

In the simplest and most commonly used organization, a similar form of communication is used between the processor and the **peripheral devices** of the computer. The actual input and output units—keyboards, VDUs, printers, and so on—are, of course, physically bulky electromechanical devices. They are connected to the bus, however, via electronic **interfaces** in the form of integrated circuit packages, or **chips**, which will probably, like the processor and memory chips, be housed inside the main computer casing. It is these electronic components that, so to speak, 'represent' the peripheral devices in communications with the processor using the defined protocol.

Figure 6.1 illustrates a possible configuration of memory and peripheral devices for a simple computer such as, perhaps, Papyrus. The computer shown has a total of 32K words of memory, which is physically contained in two chips, each of capacity 16K words. Two simple peripheral devices—a keyboard and a VDU monitor—are attached, to enable data in the form of ASCII-coded characters to be transmitted into and out of the system. In this arrangement, each peripheral unit is linked to the bus with a separate interface chip, although in some systems more than one device may be

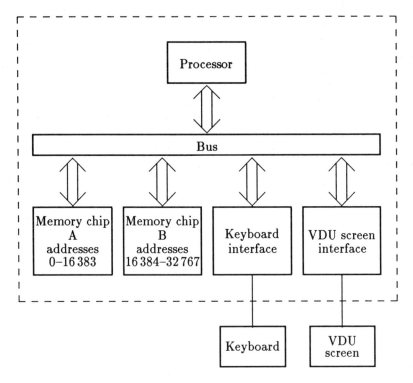

Figure 6.1 Device–bus connections in a simple computer

attached via a single interface. Including the processor, there are in all five chips attached to the bus.

Consider what happens when the processor executes the instruction, for example:

LOAD   A, 850   ; fetch a word from address 850

The address, 850, of the word required will be transmitted via the bus to both the memory chips and to the peripheral device interfaces. However, only the memory chip 'A', which contains the location addressed, will respond to the read request; the other memory chip and the device interfaces will ignore it. They do so because implicit in the way in which they have been connected to the bus is an **encoding** of the addresses for which they are responsible. Memory chip A, in effect, 'knows' that it represents addresses 0–16 383, and chip B that it contains the locations with addresses 16 384–32 767.

It follows that a read request from the processor to, say, address 33 000 will be ignored by both memory devices, and would, ordinarily, lead to an error. There is no reason, however, why one of the peripheral device interfaces should not respond to this request, and this is, in fact, the basis of the way in which the processor communicates with peripheral devices in this form of organization.

In the configuration of Figure 6.1, addresses greater than 32 767 do not correspond to any physical memory locations. It would be possible, therefore, for the keyboard interface chip to be connected to the bus in such a way that it would respond, in some way, to requests from the processor referring to addresses in the range, say, 32 768–33 791. Similarly, the screen interface chip could be configured to respond to the next band of 1024 addresses, starting at address 33 792. The two device interface chips would thus appear to the bus to be each like a 1K memory chip. This way of connecting peripheral devices is called **memory-mapped** input–output, because each device is allocated a set of (otherwise unused) 'addresses' through which communication between the processor and the device takes place.

We put the word 'addresses' in quotes because, in this context, these are not true addresses that correspond to memory locations. As far as the device interface is concerned, each 'address' within its allocated range represents a coded instruction to which it will respond in some defined way. In most cases, only a small number of such codes will be required to enable all the necessary communications with the device to proceed. As far as the processor is concerned, however, its interaction with a peripheral device takes much the same form as with the memory. Input from the keyboard, for example, can be obtained by the processor issuing a read request, via a LOAD instruction, to an appropriate 'address' in the band allocated to the keyboard interface. We will go on to examine this in a little more detail shortly.

One great advantage of memory-mapped input–output is that no special instructions are needed to enable these operations to proceed. This is particularly desirable because peripheral devices are many and varied in nature, and we might need many complex instructions to deal with all cases which might arise. In the memory-mapped arrangement, conversely, we can keep on adding new (and possibly different) devices to the system in the same way as we can add extra memory. Usually, only a few 'addresses' will be required for each device, so the method is very flexible and extensible.

Device polling

The precise details of how input and output operations are performed in any particular computer will depend on the processor instruction set and, more especially, on the characteristics of the device interface chips involved. The simplest kinds of devices are those, like keyboards and character printers, that enable the transmission of a single character at a time. Even for such simple peripherals, there may be differences in the characteristics of the interface chips marketed by different manufacturers. Usually, however, a simple character device interface will appear to the processor to take the form of a set of **registers** which can be referenced via addresses within its allocated band. These registers will include a **status** register which can be inspected to determine the current state of the device, and a **data** register through which information is transmitted.

Let us suppose a Papyrus configuration similar to the machine illustrated in Figure 6.1, with two simple character peripheral devices attached through interfaces of this kind. The keyboard interface has been allocated a 1K band of addresses starting at 32 768, but in fact makes use of only two of these addresses. The interface address 0 (absolute address 32 768) refers to the device status register, and address 1 (absolute 32 769) to its data register. This means, for example, that an instruction:

$$LOAD \quad A, \quad 32768$$

executed by the Papyrus processor, will lead to a read request for this address being placed on the bus. The keyboard interface will respond to this request by placing the contents of its status register on the bus to be loaded into the processor A register. These interactions are illustrated in Figure 6.2, referring to the 'invisible' processor registers IR and MDR which were mentioned in Section 2.2.

From the other side of the interface, the keyboard status and data registers will be affected by operations of the actual keyboard unit. In particular, whenever a key is pressed on the keyboard, the ASCII value of the character thus indicated will be placed in the keyboard data register, and its status register will be set to indicate that this has been done. The keyboard status register, like the processor status register, can represent a number of **conditions** by the setting of individual bits. We will suppose that bit 0 is set to 1 whenever a key is pressed on the keyboard and a character value loaded into the data register, and reset to 0 whenever this character is read from the register via the bus.

In order to 'read' a character that has just been typed on the keyboard, therefore, the processor needs only to LOAD its ASCII value from the address, 32 769, to which the keyboard data register is mapped. In general,

however, it will be necessary first to ensure that a key has been pressed
by examining the status register. Thus, a very simple subroutine to read a
character from the keyboard could take the following form:

```
READCHAR: LOAD A, KBSTATUS ; load from 'address' 32768
     SLR    A, #1          ; shift bit 0 into Carry bit
     JC     CHARIN         ; carry set, shows character waiting
     JMP    READCHAR       ; otherwise loop to try again
CHARIN: LOAD A, KBDATA     ; read the character
     RETURN                ; exit with character in A register
```

Here, we have used the symbolic names KBSTATUS and KBDATA,
which we assume to have been **equivalenced** to the 'addresses' 32 768 and
32 769 respectively, to refer to the keyboard interface registers. The routine
first examines bit 0 of the status register, and if this is found to have the
value 1, goes on to obtain the ASCII value of the character input by loading
this from the data register. If the status register indicates that no key has
been struck, however, the routine must wait for this event to take place.
It does so by repeating the sequence of loading and inspecting the value of
the status register. This apparently endless loop will in fact terminate as
soon as bit 0 of the keyboard status register is altered in response to a key
being pressed.

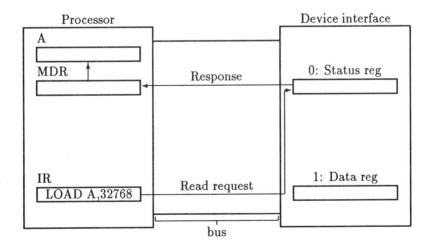

Figure 6.2   Processor–device communication via the bus

This kind of operation is called device **polling**, because the routine repeatedly questions, or 'polls' the device interface to determine its status. Again, we must emphasize that the *details* of this will vary depending on the computer in use and the characteristics of the device interface. In broad outline, however, the routine described exemplifies the simplest kind of character input routine.

The procedure for character output is similar; in this case the device interface must be polled to determine whether it is ready to receive a character to be printed. This is necessary because the actual operation of displaying on the screen a character whose ASCII code is held in the interface data register may take a significant time, during which the data register must not be disturbed. The screen interface will accordingly show in its status register that it is 'busy' until the character printing is complete.

```
PRINTCHAR:PUSH    A              ; save the char. to be printed
PCLP:      LOAD   A, SCSTATUS    ; examine screen status reg.
           SLR    A, #1          ; look at bit 0
           JC     PCLP           ; loop while device busy
           POP    A              ; now ready to print next char.
           STORE  A, SCDATA      ; so put this in screen data reg.
           RETURN
```

Placing a character in the interface data register will initiate the printing of the character, the status register again becoming set to 'busy' while this takes place.

These routines illustrate a possible way of implementing the system functions *read_char* and *print_char* which we have been using in Papyrus program examples. Implementation of *read_integer* and *print_integer* will be more difficult, since the keyboard and screen interfaces only enable transmission of data in **character** form. However, it is not too difficult to see how, for example, an integer can be printed by first decomposing it into an array of digits, and then replacing each of these by their ASCII character equivalents and printing them in sequence. Procedures of this kind will be used within the *read_integer* and *print_integer* system routines to enable all input–output operations to proceed using simple character-based interactions with the device interfaces.

6.2   Interrupts

A potentially serious drawback to the method of performing input and output operations by polling the devices involved is that the speed of operation of these devices is usually very much slower than that of the processor during normal instruction execution. Typically, the execution time for an ordinary instruction may be about 1 microsecond (10^{-6} seconds), whereas transmission of a character to or from a peripheral device may take between 10^{-3} and 10^{-1} seconds, depending on the nature of the device—i.e. between 1000 and 100 000 times as long. This means that our READCHAR routine, for example, may spend what is, in processing time scales, a relatively long time traversing its polling loop waiting for a character to appear in the keyboard data register. The delay may be far longer than this, of course, if no key has been pressed, so that the routine is awaiting a human response!

In many kinds of program, especially in the context of a single user with a personal computer, these delays may not matter. There are cases, however, when such a waste of potentially useful processing time can lead to serious inefficiencies. Worst of all, in the case of a multi-user computer system to which a large number of VDU terminals is attached, it would clearly be quite unacceptable if, each time a program attempted to read in some data from one, all other users were forced to wait for a key to be struck on the appropriate keyboard.

In these cases, repeatedly polling a device to determine its status is not a satisfactory procedure. What is needed, instead, is for a device to take an *active* role in informing the processor that it is ready to proceed. The means by which this is effected is called an **interrupt**.

The interrupt mechanism

An interrupt is a form of automatic subroutine call brought about (usually) by an event occurring *outside* the normal sequence of execution of program instructions—such as, for example, a key being pressed on the keyboard. Because, unlike an ordinary subroutine call, an interrupt is not brought about directly by a specific program action, it can, in general, take place at any point in the execution sequence. The effect is as if a kind of JSR instruction were interposed in the execution sequence at the moment when the interrupt takes place. The destination of this JSR will be the start of an **interrupt service routine** (ISR) whose task is to respond to the event bringing about the interrupt.

Figure 6.3 illustrates this in outline. Here, the main program is executing instructions in a sequence M1, M2, M3, ... We will suppose that, while instruction M3 is being performed, a key is struck on the keyboard, giving rise to an interrupt. The effect will be that as soon as the execution of instruction M3 is complete, a change of control will take place to the instruction I1 which is the start of the ISR. Execution continues through I2, I3, ...until the RETINT instruction (a special form of RETURN) is

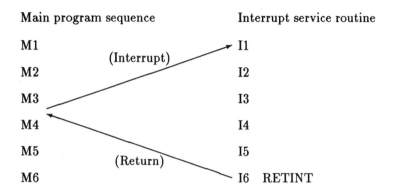

Figure 6.3   Changes of control after an interrupt

obeyed, returning control to the point of interruption.

Just as it is necessary for a JSR instruction to record its return address to allow the subsequent RETURN to take place, so will an interrupt be required to record the program counter value at the point of interruption. In fact, more information than this must be recorded, because it will be necessary for the interrupt (and the ISR) to leave every detail of the program **state** undisturbed. If this were not so, then the occurrence of an interrupt at an arbitrary point in the execution of a program could have undefined consequences. We say that the action of the interrupt must preserve the **context** of the interrupted program. This is done partly as a direct effect of the interrupt mechanism, and partly by the instructions of the interrupt service routine.

In Papyrus, an interrupt brings about the following sequence:

1. The current value of PC is saved, as the return address for the ISR, by 'pushing' it onto the stack.

2. The current value of the status register, SR, is also saved on the stack. This is necessary because an interrupt may occur, for example, in the interval between a condition bit becoming set and the instruction to test that condition. It will be necessary, therefore, for all the status bits to be preserved throughout the ISR.

3. Entry is made to the ISR, at its first instruction. This completes the immediate, 'hardware', effect of the interrupt.

4. Within the ISR, execution of instructions proceeds normally. The purpose of this routine will be to take whatever steps are necessary in

response to the interrupt; for example, to read in a character following the pressing of a key on the keyboard. We will go on to look at this in more detail shortly. It is likely that the ISR will require to make use of A and other registers to carry out its function. In order to do so without affecting the state of the interrupted program, it will be necessary for the ISR to save the values of any registers it requires, in local variables or on the stack, and to restore these before control is returned to the point of interruption.

5. Finally, the RETINT instruction is executed. This reverses the effect of the interrupt itself, i.e. the SR and PC values at the top of the stack are unstacked and restored, returning control to the interrupted sequence. If the ISR has taken care to preserve and restore the interrupted program context, the effect should be that the program can proceed 'unaware' of the interruption.

As with all its characteristics, the way in which Papyrus deals with interrupts is only illustrative of the various forms of this mechanism that may appear on different computers, and is simpler than many. The general principles that apply, however, are constant: in particular, the necessity to preserve the context of the interrupted program in its entirety so that control can be returned following the interrupt to an undisturbed program.

Enabling and disabling interrupts

Interrupts may arise from a number of sources, including, as we have suggested, the pressing of a key on a terminal keyboard. In Section 6.1, however, a method of dealing with keyboard input was outlined that did *not* involve interrupts, and there will be cases when this simple kind of input routine is quite adequate. It will be useful, therefore, to be able to determine within a program whether or not interrupts will arise from events such as keyboard depressions.

In Papyrus, this is controlled using a particular bit, bit 8, within the **status register**. When this bit, the 'interrupts enabled' status, is set to 0, then an event such as a keyboard depression will have no direct effect on the processor, and it will be necessary to poll the device status register to find whether this has taken place. When interrupts are **enabled** by the setting of this status bit to 1, however, then the setting of the keyboard status to 'character waiting' (bit0=1) will invoke an interrupt in the Papyrus processor. In fact, whenever a key is struck and the keyboard status register is set to record this, a signal is sent from the device interface via the bus to Papyrus to report this. When interrupts are **disabled**, Papyrus ignores this signal; when they are **enabled**, it responds by generating an interrupt to suspend the current program sequence, as described above.

The program instruction:

$$LOAD \quad SR, \ \#256 \qquad ;set \ bit \ 8 \ of \ SR$$

will, therefore, be sufficient to enable interrupts, and clearing SR will disable them. When an interrupt takes place, however, further interrupts are automatically disabled: after the current value of SR is pushed onto the stack, bit 8 of SR is cleared prior to entry into the ISR. The reason for this is that, if another interrupt were to take place immediately, the ISR might find it difficult to respond correctly. It is safer, therefore, for interrupts to be disabled, at least temporarily, until the ISR is ready to cope with another. The RETINT instruction will in any case restore the value of SR, automatically restoring the 'interrupts enabled' status at the end of the ISR.

Character input using interrupts

Having described the mechanics of interrupts, let us now see how they can be made use of when performing input of characters from the keyboard. Figure 6.4(a) shows an interrupt service routine, written in PASS, which could be used to respond to a key being struck. We will assume that this routine is entered only as a result of an interrupt arising from this cause. The action taken by the ISR, after saving the context of the interrupted program on the stack, is first to fetch the value of the character input from the keyboard interface data register (using its mapped 'address' KBDATA) into the processor A register. The routine then stores this value in a **buffer**, CHARBUFF. The 'buffer' is simply an array of (in this case) eight memory locations; its purpose is to allow up to eight characters typed in to be saved, or 'buffered' in memory, before any of them are used by the program. The ISR uses the variable CHARPTR1 as an index into the buffer, incrementing it after each character is read until its value would exceed 7, and then resetting it to 0.

The effect of this routine, for a program within which interrupts are enabled, is that each key struck on the keyboard will cause a character to be stored in the buffer, but the main program will otherwise proceed undisturbed as these events take place. If this program now wishes to 'read' a character, it must do so not by interacting directly with the keyboard interface but by examining the buffer, using the routine READCHAR shown in Figure 6.4(b). Provided there is at least one character in the buffer that has not already been 'read' by READCHAR, this routine can simply return with the character in the A register. To ensure that the same character is

---

```
; Interrupt service routine for character input
CHARINISR: PUSH    A
       PUSH  B              ; save context of interrupted program
       LOAD  A, KBDATA      ; fetch char from keyboard data reg.
       LOAD  B, CHARPTR1    ; index to character buffer
       STOREA, CHARBUFF(B)  ; store character in buffer
       SUB   B, #7          ; check for end of buffer
       JZERO ISREXIT        ; if so, CHARPTR1 := 0
       ADD   B, #8          ; otherwise, add 1 to CHARPTR1
ISREXIT: STORE   B, CHARPTR1
       POP   B
       POP   A              ; restore interrupted context
       RETINT               ; and return
```

(a) The interrupt service routine

```
;System routine called from program
READCHAR: LOAD    B, CHARPTR1 ; character input index
       SUB    B, CHARPTR2    ; character fetch index
       JZERO  READCHAR       ; wait if they are equal
       LOAD   B, CHARPTR2    ; 'fetch' index
       LOAD   A, CHARBUFF(B) ; fetch character from buffer
       SUB    B, #7          ; check for end of buffer
       JZERO  RDCHEXIT       ; if so, CHARPTR2 := 0
       ADD    B, #8          ; otherwise, increment CHARPTR2
RDCHEXIT: STORE   B, CHARPTR2
       RETURN                ; A contains character read
```

(b) The read_char routine

Figure 6.4   Routines for character input using interrupts

not read twice, READCHAR uses an index, CHARPTR2, into the buffer, which is advanced each time a character is obtained (and reset to 0 when the end of the buffer is reached, in the same way as CHARPTR1). Figure 6.5 gives an illustration of this buffer, with the two index 'pointers' used by the ISR and the READCHAR routine.

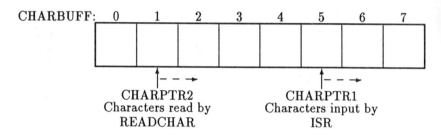

CHARPTR2
Characters read by
READCHAR

CHARPTR1
Characters input by
ISR

Figure 6.5   A character input buffer

If there are no characters waiting to be read in the buffer, then the 'fetch' index CHARPTR2 will 'catch up' with CHARPTR1 so that they both index the same location. In this case, READCHAR must wait for another character to appear in the buffer after a key is struck. It does so by repeating the sequence in which it compares the values of the two pointers until these are different. This apparently endless loop will, in fact, terminate only when an interrupt has intervened. The effect of the interrupt, if and when it occurs, will be to suspend this loop and to enter the ISR of Figure 6.4(a). The result of the ISR will be to change the value of CHARPTR1, so that, when a return into the interrupted routine is made, the next inspection of the two pointers will reveal them to be different.

The routines of Figure 6.4 are not perfect; we have not, for example, taken any steps to deal with the case of the 'input' pointer CHARPTR1 running ahead of the 'fetch' pointer by more than eight characters, so that in this event characters input will be lost. The routines do, however, illustrate some of the advantages of using interrupts for performing input (and, likewise, output). Characters typed in before the program is ready to accept them are not immediately lost; they are, instead, 'buffered' until the program requires them. More importantly, the program will not, in general, have to wait in an unproductive loop while characters are being input; it can be organized to perform useful work until it needs to make use of this data.

Interrupt vectors

When a JSR instruction is performed, the address of the subroutine to which control is transferred is defined by the operand of the instruction. When an interrupt takes place, conversely, no explicit subroutine call instruction is present to direct control into the ISR. How, then, is the address of the ISR determined?

A number of schemes are possible, and used in different computers. In the simplest, all interrupts cause a change of control to a unique address, such as address 0 in memory, which will thus be the first location of the ISR. A slightly more flexible method places the **address** of the ISR in a fixed location, say location 0. This kind of location is sometimes called an interrupt **vector** because the defined location is not itself the ISR address, but *directs* the interrupt to the ISR. The advantage of a **vectored interrupt** mechanism is that it is possible to relocate an ISR anywhere in the memory, and to have different ISRs for use in different circumstances. The program must then ensure that the address of the required ISR is placed in the vector location before any interrupts arises.

The disadvantage of these simple schemes is that interrupts may arise from a number of different sources, including not only peripheral device events such as a key being depressed, but also events within the processor such as errors in the program operation. If all these interrupts are directed to the same ISR, then it will be necessary for the ISR first to determine the reason for the interrupt, by **polling** all the devices in turn, and examining other status indicators as required. In a system with a large number of devices attached, especially, polling each of them whenever an interrupt occurs will be time-consuming.

For this reason, more powerful computers allow interrupts to be vectored through a number of defined locations. For example, the first eight locations in the memory (addresses 0–7) may be used as interrupt vectors, each of which can contain the address of an ISR. When a peripheral device is attached to the system, its interface is configured with the address of the interrupt vector that it must use. Thus, if the keyboard is assigned vector address 3, for example, an interrupt from the keyboard will cause a change of control into the ISR whose address is held in this location. When the device interface sends the interrupt signal on the bus to the processor, it also sends its designated vector address to allow the processor to perform the interrupt operations. Figure 6.6 gives a representation of these transactions. The advantage of this scheme is that different ISRs can now be identified to deal with interrupts from each particular device or group of devices, reducing the amount of polling each must perform.

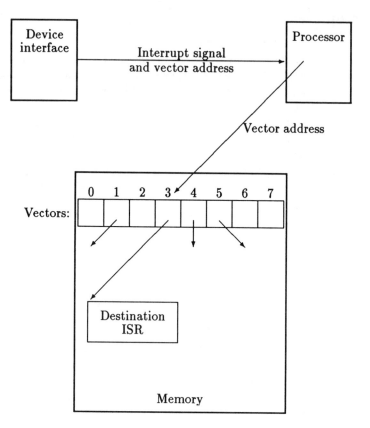

Figure 6.6   Linking to an ISR via an interrupt vector

The significance of interrupts

As we have seen, one advantage of the use of interrupts is that input and output operations can take place without the need for the program to waste time in unproductive loops, waiting for peripheral devices to complete their tasks. An **interrupt-driven** character input routine, for example, can proceed **autonomously**, filling up a buffer with data while the main program execution proceeds undisturbed. This property can be exploited by organizing the program so that, in effect, input operations, output operations, and program execution steps all proceed together, in **parallel**. In programs that involve large amounts of data processing and lengthy computation, this can lead to major reductions in program execution times.

In small-scale programming on personal computers, the gains from this kind of **parallelization** may not justify the effort involved, as programs written in this way are likely to be more complex than would otherwise be the case. In multi-user systems, however, this kind of organization is almost always used by the operating system to manage the overall activity of the system efficiently. When a number of users are interacting with the computer simultaneously, the operating system will try to ensure that each receives a satisfactory **response** from the system, and that their programs are executed as required. This is possible only because the use of interrupts allows one program to proceed while other users are performing input and output operations.

In fact, the role of interrupts in this kind of system is not confined to the management of input and output operations. Interrupts may arise from a variety of sources, including, for example, certain kinds of program errors. In a single-user computer, if a program attempts to overwrite the instructions of some important subroutine, the result will only be harmful to the person using the machine. In a multi-user computer, conversely, it would be quite unacceptable if an error in one user's program were to lead to disaster for some other user. To prevent this, large-scale computers impose controls on, for example, the areas of memory that a program can reference. Any attempt by a program to access any part of the memory outside its allocation will lead to an error, resulting in an interrupt.

To describe in any detail the organization of this kind of operating system, or, indeed, the hardware characteristics required to support it, is outside the scope of this book. It will be sufficient to stress here the central role played by interrupts, as a means by which **control** can be taken from a (user-written) program, which may be malfunctioning or have been taking more than its fair share of time, and passed via an ISR into the operating system which will take appropriate action.

6.3   *68000 device control and interrupts

The 6850 ACIA

The 68000 uses a **memory-mapped** scheme for interacting with peripheral devices, similar in broad outline to that described in Section 6.1. Processor, memory, and device interfaces are attached to a common bus, each device being allocated a set of notional 'addresses' through which communication with the processor takes place. Each kind of device interface that may be used will have its own individual characteristics, so we will here describe only one. This is the MC6850 'Asynchronous Communication Interface Adapter' (ACIA) chip which is, like the MC68000 itself, manufactured by

Motorola. The ACIA interface is very widely used in 68000 computer systems for attaching character peripheral devices such as VDU terminals, and can control both keyboard input and screen output for such a device. In describing its operation, we will assume that it is being used as an interface to a VDU.

The ACIA has four 8-bit registers used in communications with the processor. The **input data** register will contain the ASCII code of the last character entered from the keyboard, and the **output data** register is used to contain a character to be printed on the VDU screen. The **status** register can be examined to determine the current state of the ACIA and its attached devices. Finally, the **control** register, which can be written to by the 68000 processor, is used to contain a code which will determine some aspects of the way in which the interface will behave. Most of the details of these registers, shown in Figure 6.7, need not concern us here; in particular, it will usually only be necessary for the program to initialize the control register with one of a few standard codes.

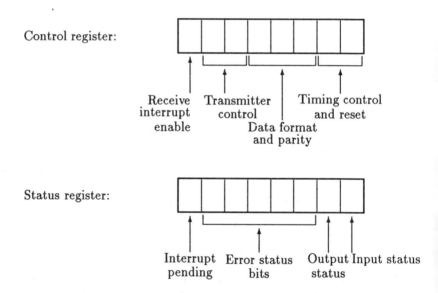

Figure 6.7   The ACIA control and status registers

In the mapping of the ACIA registers onto machine 'addresses', the two data registers are both allocated the same 'address'. This is because the input data register can only be *read* by the processor, and the output data register only *written* to, so a MOVE *from* the common address will always refer to the input register, and a MOVE *to* this address will write into the output register. Similarly, the status register is **read_only** for the processor, and the control register **write_only**, so they too share a common address mapping. The two 'addresses' used refer to the low-order bytes of two adjacent 'words' in the memory map; the actual values of these addresses will be different for different 68000 computer systems (Figure 6.8).

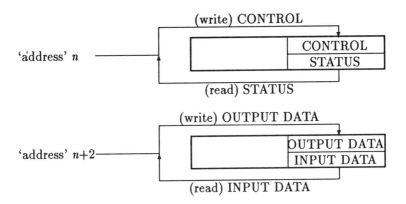

Figure 6.8   Referencing the ACIA interface registers

The status register is used, amongst other things, to record a number of error conditions that may arise in the operation of the device. If we ignore this possibility, then only two bits of the register need be considered. Bit 0 is set to 1 when the **input device** register contains a character, and is cleared when the processor reads this character. Bit 1 is set to 1 when the **output** register is ready to receive a character for display. This bit is cleared when the processor writes to the output data register, and remains clear while the device is 'busy' printing the character.

Simple input and output routines

We can now describe simple subroutines that could be used to perform the **read_char** and **write_char** functions for a simple 'free-standing' 68000 program. We will assume that the 'addresses' of the 6850 registers have been used to define **equivalences** for symbolic names in the program, thus:

```
ACIACONTROL:    EQU $10040    * (or whatever)
ACIASTATUS:     EQU $10040    * same 'address'
ACIAINPUT:      EQU $10042    * adjacent 'word'
ACIAOUTPUT:     EQU $10042
```

Note, again, that these 'addresses' will vary between different 68000-based computer systems.

In a free-standing program (i.e. unless an operating system is present to carry out such administrative tasks) it is necessary to **initialize** the ACIA before any input or output operations are performed. The first stage of this is to **reset** the interface. This is carried out by writing a particular **code**, the number 3, to the **control** register:

> *MOVE.B*   *#3,ACIACONTROL*   * reset the ACIA

It takes a little time for the ACIA to reset itself into a stable state after this instruction is executed, so it may be necessary for the program to wait a little while at this point, perhaps by executing a small 'idle' loop, doing nothing useful for perhaps 1000 cycles.

The next step is to **configure** the ACIA by placing into its control register a code which defines the way in which it will be used. For **polled** input and output, the code hexadecimal 15 is appropriate:

> *MOVE.B*   *#$15,ACIACONTROL*   * configure VDU for polled I/O

These two codes, 3 to reset and $15 to configure, are likely to be all that we need to remember for performing polled input and output on a VDU attached via the ACIA. Once the ACIA has been set up in this way, no further reference to its control register is needed, and the program can continue to perform input and output operations as required.

A character input routine could take the following form:

> *READCHAR:BTST*   *#0, ACIASTATUS* * examine bit 0 of status
>   *BEQ*   *READCHAR*   * loop if zero
>   *MOVE.B* *ACIAINPUT, D0*   * D0 := character input
>   *RTS*

The routine begins by polling the device interface, continually examining bit 0 of its status register until this becomes 1, showing the presence of a character in its data register. This character is then transferred via the bus (using a MOVE.B instruction from the interface address) into register D0. The result is a routine that performs the 'system function' **read_char** which we have used in earlier programs, reading a character from the keyboard into D0.

The **write_char** function could be implemented in a similar way:

```
WRITECHAR:BTST    #1, ACIASTATUS * Examine output status
         BEQ      WRITECHAR      * loop if busy
         MOVE.B   D0, ACIAOUTPUT* put char. in output reg.
         RTS
```

Here it is necessary to test bit 1 of the status register, which will be 0 while the device is busy displaying a previous character. As soon as the interface is ready, this bit becomes 1, and the routine will place the character to be printed in the output register. The ACIA will take over from this point, performing the output of the character to the VDU screen, and recording its output status as 'busy' while this proceeds.

User and supervisor states

Before we can go on to describe the mechanism of interrupts in the 68000, it is necessary to explain a feature of the machine that is not present in simpler computers such as Papyrus. The 68000 has two **modes** of operation, called, respectively, **user state** and **supervisor state**. These two modes are present to help in the implementation of operating systems which are required to **supervise** the overall running of a system within which a number of independent activities may be proceeding.

As we mentioned in our earlier discussion of interrupts and multi-user systems, it is essential that the malfunction of a user-written program should not be allowed to interfere with the activity of other programs or of the operating system itself. For this reason, normal 'user' programs in a 68000 system are executed with the processor in **user state**. In this state, certain kinds of operation are 'illegal', and will lead to an interrupt, suspending the execution of the program. The operating system, conversely, is executed with the processor in **supervisor state**. In this state, the constraints are relaxed, allowing various **privileged** operations to take place, and empowering the operating system to supervise the activity of other programs effectively.

The change from user state to supervisor state is made automatically when an interrupt takes place, so that the ISR begins execution in the more privileged mode of operation. The principal differences between the two states are three: in supervisor state:

1. A number of privileged operations, the use of which is illegal while in user state, become available. These include in particular instructions to modify the **system byte** of the status register, SR.

2. A different stack pointer register is used (and, by implication, a different area of memory is used as a stack). In supervisor state, any reference to register A7 (or SP) is interpreted as a reference to this system stack pointer (SSP) register rather than the user stack pointer (USP) which is used in the user state.

3. **Memory protection** characteristics may be different. It is possible for a 68000-based system to be configured so that certain areas of memory become inaccessible while the processor is in user state, and any attempt to reference these areas will result in an interrupt. This enables, for example, the operating system to be protected from interference by a user program. In supervisor state, conversely, the memory access constraints are relaxed, so that the operating system can not only make use of its own area of memory but also access other areas for the purpose of program loading and system management.

The details of the way in which memory protection is organized will differ between different 68000-based computers and systems, and in simple single-user computers this feature may not be used. Indeed, in this case, there may be relatively little use made of the two modes of operation, and user programs may be written to respond to interrupts directly and, in effect, 'supervise' themselves. In more complex multi-user systems, conversely, it is usual for all **interrupt handling** to be performed by the operating system, and for input and output system functions to be provided for use by user programs.

Interrupt vectors and priorities

The 68000 employs a **vectored** interrupt system, in which the first 1024 bytes of memory are used to contain the interrupt vectors. As each of these is a longword address, this implies that 256 different interrupt vectors can be defined. These vectors, numbered 0–255, are used for various purposes, some of which will be discussed later. Those used to define ISR addresses for peripheral device interrupts are a group of seven vectors, numbered 25–31, occupying the locations with (byte) addresses 100–127.

When a device interrupts the processor it supplies a vector address (or, in fact, in this case, a vector number) which is defined as part of the configuration of the system. The allocation of vector addresses to devices is not entirely arbitrary. The 68000 uses a system of interrupt **priorities** which allows some interrupts to take precedence over others and to be treated more urgently.

The priority of an interrupt is a number in the range 1–7 which is also defined within the device interface. Whereas Papyrus uses a simple 1-bit condition within its status register to determine whether or not interrupts are enabled, the 68000 records within *its* status register a current **processor priority** which determines *which* interrupts will be accepted. The rule is that only those interrupts whose priority is greater than the current processor priority will be accepted (except that priority 7 interrupts, the highest priority, will be accepted in all cases).

Figure 6.9 shows the bit codings for the full status register, including the 'reserved' **system byte** which is inaccessible in user state. The use

System byte	User byte(CCR)

T		S			P_2	P_1	P_0				X	N	Z	V	C

Figure 6.9 The status register, including system byte

made of bit 15 will be mentioned later in this chapter. Bit 13, the **state** bit, is set to 1 to record that the processor is operating in supervisor state, or 0 when in user state. Bits 10–8 record the current processor **priority** as a number in the range 0–7.

When a peripheral device attempts to interrupt the processor, the priority of the interrupt is compared with the processor priority recorded in the status register. If the interrupt priority is less than or equal to the processor priority, the interrupt will not be accepted; in this case, the interrupt will normally remain **pending** until the processor priority is reduced to allow the interrupt to proceed. If, conversely, the interrupt priority is greater than the processor priority, the interrupt takes place, and an entry is made to the ISR whose address is obtained from the designated interrupt vector. In this case, the priority of the interrupt is set into the processor status register, hence becoming the new processor priority.

The effect of this scheme is that if, for example, a device interrupts the processor with priority 4, it will enter an ISR with the processor priority set to this level. Until the processor priority is reset (normally on completion of the ISR), no further interrupts will be accepted if their priority is less than or equal to 4. If, however, an interrupt with a higher priority is invoked, the level 4 ISR will be interrupted so that this more urgent interrupt can be serviced. Execution of the interrupted ISR will, of course, resume when the higher priority ISR has completed.

Vector number 25 (address 100) is normally associated with interrupts of priority 1, and the succeeding six vectors represent priorities 2–7. Use of this system enables some devices (such as, for example, those operating at high speed) to be dealt with more urgently than slower devices.

The operation of exceptions

In the 68000, as in other computers, interrupts can arise both in response to external events communicated via the bus, or as a result of particular actions within the execution of a program, such as an attempt to perform a privileged instruction while in user state. The term **exception** is sometimes used to embrace both kinds of interrupt, and in 68000 terminology, the term 'interrupt' is used only for **external** interrupts (i.e. usually, interrupts from peripheral devices). The system of priorities applies only to these external interrupts, and other exceptions do not, in general, bring about a change in the processor priority.

In other respects, both external interrupts and other exceptions bring about a similar sequence of operations. From the point at which the interrupt is accepted, the sequence, illustrated in Figure 6.10, is as follows:

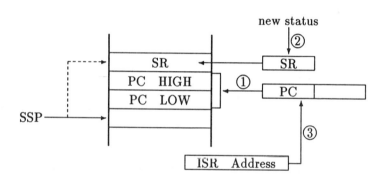

Figure 6.10   The interrupt mechanism

1. The current value of PC (a longword) is pushed onto the **system** stack, followed by the current value of the status register. The stack pointer register used here is the **privileged** register, SSP, which is 'invisible' to programs in user state; the normal 'user' stack and its stack pointer are not affected by the interrupt.

2. Bit 13 of SR is set to 1 to record that the processor is now in **supervisor** state, and (in the case of external interrupts) the priority of the interrupt is set into bits 10–8 of SR, becoming the new processor priority.

3. A change of control is made to the ISR whose address is contained in the vector associated with the exception being processed.

Within the ISR, execution proceeds with the processor in supervisor state, using the system stack for any local stack operations. If, as may be necessary, the ISR requires to inspect the stack of the interrupted program, there are two privileged forms of the MOVE instruction that refer to the user stack pointer register while in supervisor state:

> *MOVE.L   USP, A5   * A5 := value of user SP*
> *MOVE.L   A3, USP   * set USP to address held in A3*

These allow the ISR to transfer the user stack pointer to and from another address register, through which access to the user stack can be made.

The other privileged instructions comprise a number that can change the value of the system byte of SR, and three special instructions: RESET, STOP, and RTE. The instructions that can change SR are MOVE, ANDI, ORI, and EORI, in word-length forms with SR as their destination:

> *MOVE   INITSTATUS, SR   * SR := initial status*
> *ANDI   #$DFFF, SR   * clear bit 13 of SR*

It is necessary for these instructions to be privileged because changing the value of the system byte of SR can change the processor state, and if this were permitted in user state, the protection given by two-state operation would be lost. Note, however, that the condition code register, which is the lower byte of SR, can be changed explicitly by an unprivileged MOVE instruction:

> *MOVE   CONDITIONS, CCR   * CCR := some defined value*

This is defined as a word–length operation, although only the low-order byte of the word is actually used. It is also possible to move *from* the status register, without requiring privilege:

> *MOVE   SR, D0   * D0 := current value of SR*

This allows the status register to be *examined* while in user state, even though its system byte cannot be altered.

The RESET instruction, which has no operands, is used in system initialization to send a special signal on the bus to all external devices, prompting them to set themselves into a defined initial state. The STOP instruction halts the processor, ending the execution of instructions until an interrupt arrives to restart operation. Again, it is essential that this instruction be privileged, as in multi-user operation its effect is to halt the entire system. It is for this reason that we normally use a system call or TRAP instruction to terminate the execution of a *program*, returning control to the operating system rather than halting the processor.

The STOP instruction has an immediate operand, the value of which is moved into SR before the processor is halted. This allows, in particular, the priority level of the processor to be defined, thus determining which interrupt will be able to restart the system:

*STOP   #$0700   * stop until priority 7 interrupt*

68000-based computers have an external 'reset' button which generates a priority 7 interrupt, allowing the system to be restarted in all cases.

The final privileged instruction is RTE, 'return from exception', which is used in most cases at the end of an ISR to return control to the interrupted program. Its effect is to reverse the operation of the interrupt, restoring SR to the value obtained from the system stack, and jumping to the stacked return address. Unless either of these stacked values has been altered within the ISR, execution of the interrupted program will resume from the point of interruption with the processor state and priority level restored to the values pertaining before the interrupt.

Because RTE changes the state of the processor recorded in the system byte of SR, it must be a privileged operation. However, it is sometimes useful in normal user-state programming to save the current value of CCR at the start of a subroutine so that it can be restored when a return to the main program is made. The RTR instruction facilitates this: it loads CCR from a word taken from the top of stack before exiting from a subroutine. Thus, we may organize a subroutine in the following form:

*SOMESUB: MOVE   SR, -(A7)   * push SR onto stack*

   ...
   ...

*RTR   * return, restoring CCR from stack*

Interrupts from the ACIA

In Papyrus, interrupts are enabled or disabled depending on the setting of a single bit in the status register. The 68000, as we have seen, uses a more complex system of priorities to determine which interrupts will be **accepted** at any moment of time. Whether or not a peripheral device *attempts* to interrupt the processor, however, will depend on the state of the device interface. In the case of the ACIA, interrupts are enabled or disabled by the setting of two bits in its **control** register. Bit 7 of this register is set to 1 to enable interrupts on device input, and bit 5 to enable interrupts on device output.

For polled operation of the ACIA, the code $15 was used to configure the control register. This code leaves bits 7 and 5 clear, so that in this state the interface sends no interrupt signals to the processor. If we include in the code the setting of bit 7 to 1, then each time bit 0 of the ACIA status register is set to 1 to indicate a character has been input, an interrupt signal will be sent to the processor. Thus, possible configurations include:

```
MOVE.B    #$95, ACIACONTROL     * enable keyboard interrupts
MOVE.B    #$35, ACIACONTROL     * enable interrupts on output
MOVE.B    #$B5, ACIACONTROL     * enable both interrupts
```

Note that all other bits in the control register are unchanged for all cases of interrupt-driven and polled operation (Figure 6.11).

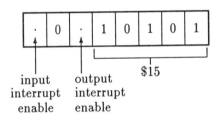

Figure 6.11 Standard setting of the ACIA control register

As a simple example, Figure 6.12 shows routines for printing a string of characters to the ACIA output device (the VDU screen) using interrupts. It is assumed that the ACIA has been initialized (with control register value $15) and that the appropriate interrupt vector location contains the address of the interrupt service routine, OUTPUTISR. The main routine, WRITESTRING, is called in the normal way, using a JSR instruction, with a parameter in A0 showing the address of the string of characters to be printed. It is assumed that this string will be terminated with a byte containing the value 0.

The idea of these routines is that the routine WRITESTRING is called to *set in progress* the output of a string of characters. While output is proceeding, the main program can continue executing, without the need to wait for output to complete. However, if a further attempt to write another string is made, it will be necessary to wait for the first to finish. To deal with such a case, the routines use a 1-byte variable BUSY which is set non-zero to indicate when output of a string is in progress. A special

```
* Routine to output a character string, using interrupts
* Enter with address of string in A0
WRITESTRING:TAS   BUSY              * test and set 'BUSY' marker
       BNE       WRITESTRING        * wait if busy set
       MOVE.L    A0, POINTER        * set up pointer to string
       MOVE.B    #$35, ACIACONTROL  * enable interrupts on output
       RTS                          * exit to continue program


* Interrupt service routine for ACIA output
* Entered whenever the interface is ready to receive a character
OUTPUTISR:MOVEM.L D0/A0, -(SP)      * save regs. for interrupted prog.
       MOVEA.L   POINTER, A0        * pointer to string
       MOVE.B    (A0)+, D0          * get character to print
       BEQ       FINISHED           * end of string
       MOVE.L    A0, POINTER        * save updated pointer
       MOVE.B    D0, ACIAOUTPUT     * put character to device output
       MOVEM.L   (SP)+, D0/A0       * restore interrupted context
       RTE                          * and exit

FINISHED:MOVE.B #$15, ACIACONTROL   * disable interrupts
       CLR.B     BUSY               * record 'no longer busy'
       MOVEM.L   (SP)+, D0/A0       * restore interrupted context
       RTE                          * final exit
```

Figure 6.12   ACIA output routine, with interrupt service routine

instruction, TAS (test and set), is helpful for manipulating this kind of variable. The instruction **tests** a 1-byte operand, setting the condition bits in CCR accordingly, and simultaneously **sets** bit 7 of the byte to 1. The effect of the loop:

$$WRITESTRING: \quad TAS \quad BUSY$$
$$BNE \quad WRITESTRING$$

will, therefore, be to continue cycling endlessly if the BUSY variable was initially set non-zero. If, however, following the intervention of an interrupt, BUSY is cleared, the loop will terminate after again setting BUSY to a non-zero value. The result will be to prevent progress past this point in the routine as long as a previous output is continuing.

Once the BUSY indicator shows the device is ready, WRITESTRING places the string address in the location POINTER, then **enables** output interrupts for the ACIA. There will follow immediately an interrupt from the device interface, showing that it is ready to accept a character. Once this interrupt has been serviced, the main program can continue normal execution, interrupted periodically as each character is output.

Each interrupt brings about an automatic call to the ISR, OUTPUTISR. This first saves the context of the interrupted program; in this case, it is only necessary to save D0 and A0 as no other registers are disturbed. These are placed (like PC and SR) on the system stack (which we assume to have been initialized appropriately). The ISR then takes a character from the string to be printed, places this in the ACIA output register, restores the context of the interrupted program, and exits to allow it to proceed undisturbed by the interrupt. When the device has completed the output of the character, it will signal its readiness to accept another by a further interrupt, leading to a repetition of the ISR. Finally, when the end of the string is reached, the routine disables interrupts for the ACIA and sets BUSY to 0 to allow another string to be printed if required.

These routines provide little more than an outline of the way in which interrupt-driven input and output can be performed on the 68000. In a practical system, it would probably be necessary to provide a range of input and output functions, including both single-character and string operations, and the ISR would need to examine the ACIA status register on every interrupt to determine whether input or output was required. Fortunately, however, we know that most operating systems will take responsibility for interrupt handling, so that only when writing such 'system' software, or in certain specialized applications, is it necessary to program at this level.

Other exceptions

We mentioned earlier that the first 1024 bytes of memory in a 68000 computer are used to contain 256 **exception vectors**, including seven, vectors 25–31, for peripheral device interrupts with priority 1–7. The allocation of these vectors is tabulated in Figure 6.13. Some are unallocated and may

Vector numbers:	
0,1	RESET
2	Bus error
3	Illegal address
4	Illegal instruction
5	Divide by zero
6	CHK
7	TRAPV
8	Privilege violation
9	TRACE
10	Instruction 1010
11	Instruction 1011
12–23	Unallocated
24	Spurious interrupt
25–31	Device interrupts
32–47	TRAP
48–63	Unallocated
64–255	User interrupts

Figure 6.13   Allocation of exception vectors

have different uses in different systems, but a number are reserved for particular exceptions, which will be briefly summarized here.

Error exceptions   A number of error conditions that may arise in the execution of a program will give rise to (different) exceptions in the 68000, i.e. they will bring about interrupt actions via designated vectors. These conditions include execution of an illegal (undefined) instruction, or of a privileged instruction while in user state, attempting to access a word or longword from an odd (byte) address, and division by zero. Errors in the operation of the bus, including attempts to access non-existent memory, will also give rise to interrupts, and a special (priority 7) interrupt is generated when the RESET button on the computer is pressed. All of these exceptions will normally be dealt with by the operating system software, which will include ISR routines to respond to the interrupts and take appropriate remedial action.

Traps In our 68000 program examples, we have used the instruction:

$$TRAP \quad \#0$$

to terminate program execution. This instruction is, in fact, an example of what is sometimes called a **voluntary**, or **software** interrupt. Its effect is to generate an interrupt action, transferring control to an ISR (in supervisor state) via a defined vector. The TRAP instruction has an operand in the range 0–15, and its execution brings about an interrupt via one of the 16 vectors numbered 32–47. We have assumed that the first of these invokes a system routine to terminate the execution of the current program, although this will not be the case in all systems. In general, the TRAP instruction provides a means for calling system routines which may include, for example, input and output routines, and the use to which each TRAP is put will vary between different systems. One difference between TRAP and an ordinary JSR call is that a TRAP routine will execute in supervisor mode and may perform privileged operations.

Tracing In Chapter 3 we introduced the idea of **tracing** a program to obtain a step-by-step execution history. The 68000 processor includes a feature to assist software in performing a program 'trace', by generating an exception (interrupt) after each instruction is executed in a program. This is controlled by bit 15, the **trace bit**, in the system byte of SR. When this bit is set to 1, then at the end of each instruction an interrupt transfers control to an ISR (via vector 9). The interrupt action clears bit 15, so that the ISR itself executes normally, and is thus able, for example, to display the values of registers and memory locations as required. When these actions are complete, return to the interrupted program via RTE will reinstate the TRACE condition, so that a further interrupt will arise after the next instruction.

Special instructions A few special 68000 instructions will generate exception actions in particular cases. The TRAPV instruction will do so if the overflow status, V, is set when it is executed, forcing this to be dealt with by an ISR rather than within the executing program. The CHK instruction is used to check that the value in a data register is less than or equal to some limit, generating an exception if it is not:

$$CHK \quad LIMIT, D3 \qquad * \; check \; 0 \leq D3 \leq LIMIT$$

Finally, there are two unallocated instruction codes (binary 1010 and 1011), the execution of which will give rise to exceptions. The idea behind these is that they may be used in particular systems to provide a **software** implementation of additional instructions, such as, for example, instructions to perform floating-point arithmetic, which are not provided by the 68000 **hardware**. Execution of one of these codes will invoke an ISR that can be written to perform the necessary actions as required.

6.4 Exercises

1. Write a routine READINTEGER for the 68000 that will read a sequence of digits (terminated by a non-numeric character) and construct from them an integer to be returned as the result of the subroutine. Your subroutine should read each character by polling the device interface. You will need to investigate the details of this, including in particular the mapping of the interface registers, on the system you are using.

2. Write an interrupt service routine that will respond to both input and output device interrupts on your computer system. The ISR must:

   (a) poll the device interface to determine which type of interrupt has arisen;

   (b) deal with an input interrupt by reading the character and placing it into an 8-character input buffer;

   (c) deal with an output interrupt by taking a character from an 8-character output buffer and placing it on the device interface;

   (d) when the output buffer becomes empty, disable output interrupts.

   Investigate how to use such a routine within the system you are using.

3. Write a program in 68000 assembly language that will test the reactions of the user. The program should select a printable character by some random procedure, and enter a loop in which this character is printed repeatedly on the screen. To stop the loop, the user must find and strike the key for the same character. His or her 'reaction time' is measured by the number of characters displayed before this has happened. The program should use an interrupt service routine to deal with the key being struck by the user.

Chapter 7

The architectural level in its context

7.1 Physical implementation

We began this book by outlining the so-called 'onion-skin' model of a computer system, expressing the view that the computer can be seen as a series of concentric layers, each of which describes the machine at a different level of understanding. At the **primitive**, or **architectural** level on which we have concentrated, the computer is described as a machine for executing **instructions** in a well-ordered sequence. This is, of course, the level of description most appropriate for understanding how **programs** are performed. To avoid obscuring this picture, we have so far said as little as possible about the layers 'below' the primitive interface, at which the programmer's architectural model is implemented in the physical hardware of the computer. It is appropriate to end our description, however, by placing the primitive level in its context, saying a little more about how it is physically implemented, and also about the layers of software that it supports.

As we have seen, all the types of information that are represented and manipulated within the computer are expressed in the form of **bit-patterns** within bytes and words of memory and in machine registers. It is this binary-coded representation that provides a basis for the physical realization of the machine.

Digital electronics

The *engineering* model of the computer—'inside' the architectural model—represents the machine as a complex electrical circuit. Within this circuit there are a large number of physical connections, along each of which a current may flow during the operation of the machine. For this kind of electrical path, the *presence* of a current is used to represent the transmission of the binary digit 1, while the *absence* of a current represents the value 0. This kind of circuit is called a **digital electronic** circuit, because the relevant characteristic is the presence or absence of current, which can be expressed as a binary digit, rather than the amount of current flowing.

The **state** of the circuit at any time corresponds to the machine state described for the architectural model, and is defined by the presence or absence of current in all of its connections. The state is altered during machine operation by the actions of electronic **components** within the circuit.

Consider the circuit fragment illustrated in Figure 7.1. This shows a

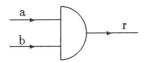

Figure 7.1   An AND gate

single component with three electronic connections. Two of these, labelled a and b, represent electronic *inputs* to the component, along each of which a current may or may not flow. The connection labelled r represents the *output* or result of the operation of the component. In this particular case, the effect of the component is defined to be such that a current will flow in r only if a current flows in the input a *and* in the input b. We can say, therefore, that the component's operation is defined by the expression:

$$r = a \ and \ b$$

and we can describe this component as an AND **gate**.

A very elementary knowledge of physics is sufficient to tell us that Figure 7.1 is incomplete; current flowing into the component from the inputs a or b cannot simply disappear, in any circumstances. In fact, the representation is a conventional one, in which the only electronic connections shown are the **digital logic** connections that carry the binary values which are processed by the operation of the circuit. A fuller picture would show other electrical paths, representing power sources and earth connections. If we take for granted the existence of these, then we can use the representation of Figure 7.1 to express the characteristics of the component that are of interest to us, i.e. its functional properties as a **logic gate**.

A logic gate is so-called because it can be described as performing an elementary logical operation, of the types described in Chapter 4, on binary values represented in the form of electronic **logic levels**, i.e. using the binary interpretation of electrical states outlined above. It is these elementary logic gates that comprise the basic building blocks of an electronic circuit such as a computer processor. Apart from the AND gate of Figure 7.1, it is possible to define, and to construct physically, logic gates to perform other operations such as OR and NOT; the conventional representation of some of these are shown as Figure 7.2. For each of these, the logic level of

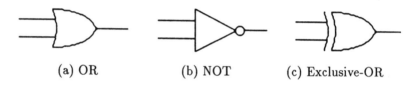

(a) OR   (b) NOT   (c) Exclusive-OR

Figure 7.2   Some elementary logic gates

the output connection is defined by the **truth table** of the component as a function of its input logic levels.

Integrated circuits

Within the computer, the operations performed include not only elementary logic operations on single bits but, for example, operations to perform addition and subtraction on word-length bit-patterns. It is possible, however, to construct these more complex operations using sequences of simple functions of 1-bit values, in much the same way as a high-level language program is decomposed into a sequence of primitive machine instructions.

Suppose, for example, it is required to add two 1-bit values, a and b, to produce a 1-bit *sum*, s, and a *carry*, c. The rule for this would be that a sum 1 is produced if either a or b is 1. If, however, both a and b have the value 1, then $a+b=2$, which must be represented as a sum $s=0$ with a carry of 1.

These rules can be represented in the truth table of Figure 7.3(a), tabulating all possible outcomes of the addition. Another way of describing this

a	b	sum(s)	carry(c)
0	0	0	0
0	1	1	0
1	0	1	0
1	1	0	1

(a)

a	b	p a or b	c a and b	q not(a and b)	s p and q
0	0	0	0	1	0
0	1	1	0	1	1
1	0	1	0	1	1
1	1	1	1	0	0

(b)

Figure 7.3   Truth tables for $a + b$

would be in the form of two **logical expressions**, which could be written:

$$s = a \ or \ b \ and \ not(a \ and \ b)$$
$$c = a \ and \ b$$

The tabulation of Figure 7.3(b) shows these expressions will give the results we require. Now, if we have **elementary logic components** to perform the operations *and, or,* and *not* on electronic logic levels, then we can construct a simple **logic circuit** to produce the outputs s and c required (Figure 7.4).

The circuit of Figure 7.4 is an example of a **half-adder**, so called because it performs only a stage in the processes required to perform a full computational addition. It is clear, however, that continuing the process of construction we have outlined will enable us to design logic circuits to perform complete arithmetic operations on bit-patterns. Within the computer processor, the individual steps involved in the execution of a single instruction will be carried out by logic circuits of this kind.

Physically, a logic circuit is produced in the form of an **integrated circuit** on a single silicon **chip**. The form in which we usually see this is as a 'package' in which the chip itself is enclosed in a plastic protective casing, usually about 2 cm long and 1 cm wide, with a number of metal contacts to enable its connection into a larger circuit. Integrated circuit

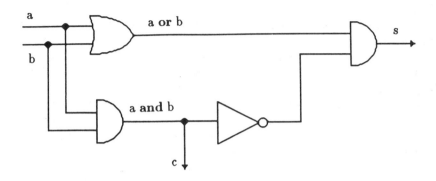

Figure 7.4   A half-adder circuit

(IC) packages of this kind are manufactured to perform elementary logic operations such as AND, and also much more complex functions. Modern technology for **very large scale integration** (VLSI) enables the entire circuit for a computer processor to be manufactured as a single chip, so that most modern computer systems comprise quite a small number of chip packages to carry out the functions of processor, memory, and peripheral device interfacing.

7.2   Software

Our purpose in describing machine-level programming has been primarily to explain the way in which programs are performed by the computer, rather than to impart skills in programming at this level. In fact, most programs are written for use in an environment in which the primitive machine interface is clothed in a layer of software, the purpose of which is to make the computer more attractive and easier to use. The most important components of this **system software** are the **operating system** and the **compilers**.

If the architectural model of the computer defines a machine that executes **instructions** in sequence, the operating system may be said to create an environment for the execution of **programs**. At the simplest level, a single-user operating system will provide facilities for **loading** a program into memory, starting and interrupting its execution, and perhaps for managing a **file store** of programs and other information held on magnetic tapes and disks. In more complex systems, the operating system is required to manage the allocation of memory and other physical resources of the computer, ensuring that each program is able to proceed without interference from others.

In both simple and complex systems, it is likely that the operating system will incorporate routines to perform generally useful system functions such as input and output operations, and will take responsibility for the handling of interrupts. Indeed, as was discussed briefly in Chapter 6, the exploitation of interrupts provides a means by which the operating system can maintain **control** over a machine within which a number of programs may be proceeding concurrently. At this level of use of the system, the computer appears to be performing several tasks simultaneously; however, as we know, within the underlying machine a *single* sequence of instruction execution is proceeding. The operating system reconciles this apparent contradiction by using interrupts to switch control rapidly between the concurrent **processes**.

An operating system carries out its tasks through the execution of program parts or routines which may be invoked in response to interrupts or by calls from user-written programs. Both these system routines and other programs will be *written* in a textual form which may be assembly-language or, more often, a high-level language, and translated into machine-code form by an assembler or **compiler**. We have said, *inter alia*, quite a lot about the relationship between high-level and machine-level program forms in the course of this book. We will only reiterate here the central point: all programs—including as programs both operating systems and compilers—in whatever languages they are written, must ultimately execute as sequences of machine-code instructions.

As even the routines of an operating system may be written in a high-level language, what place is there now for programming in assembly language? The truth is, or should be, very little. Within most systems, there will be small parts, usually involving communication with peripheral devices and other **privileged** operations, for which instructions cannot be generated from ordinary high-level languages. These cases can be dealt with by including within the operating system a small **nucleus** of privileged routines which may have to be written in assembly language.

More rarely, it may be found that the object programs generated by a high-level language compiler are too large in their memory requirements, or execute too slowly, for the application required. Compilers sometimes translate program statements in a relatively simplistic way, and it may be possible to find a shorter and more efficient machine-code equivalent if we write directly in assembly language. The gains from this approach tend to diminish, however, as the programs being written increase in size, because of the difficulty of organizing a large assembly-language program efficiently. We are wise, therefore, to limit the use of assembly language, if at all, to those few routines whose size or speed of execution is particularly critical.

7.3   *Last words on the 68000

Most of the features of the 68000 processor and instruction set have been covered in earlier chapters. There remain, however, a number of instructions and a few incidental details that have not been mentioned, and, for completeness, these will be described briefly here.

Extended arithmetic

We have mentioned in passing the 'X' status bit which is recorded as bit 4 of the status register, but have not described its purpose. This bit is used to assist in arithmetic involving quantities too large to be stored as single words or longwords. In general, the X bit is set or cleared by addition, subtraction, negation, and shift instructions in the same way as the carry bit, C. However, a number of instructions that affect C, including in particular the MOVE instructions which always set C=0, will not change the X status.

The purpose of the X (or **extend**) bit is to allow a *carry* to be propagated in multi-length arithmetic. Suppose, for example, we wish to add two numbers, each of which is stored as a 64-bit quantity in two longwords. We must first add the lower-order longwords, and then add the high-order longwords, including in the latter sum any carry produced from the lower-order addition. The ADDX instruction (add with extend) allows us to do this. If the two quantities are stored in longwords AHIGH, ALOW and BHIGH, BLOW respectively, then the sum could be performed by the following sequence:

```
MOVE.L    ALOW, D0    * D0 := low-order 32 bits of A
ADD.L     BLOW, D0    * D0 := sum of low-order longwords
MOVE.L    AHIGH, D1   * high-order half of A
MOVE.L    BHIGH, D2   * high-order half of B
ADDX.L    D2, D1      * add, including X
```

The first ADD instruction will add the low-order halves of the two quantities, setting the X status to record any carry that results. The two subsequent MOVE instructions will not change X, so that the final ADDX instruction will add the high-order longwords, including in the sum the carry (X) produced by the low-order addition.

The ADDX instruction can only take two forms. It must either, as in the example above, operate on two data registers directly, or on two operands addressed using the address register indirect mode with pre-decrement:

$$ADDX \quad -(A0), \; -(A1)$$

The latter form is intended to facilitate arithmetic on quantities held as sequences of words or longwords in consecutive memory locations.

The SUBX instruction works in a similar way to ADDX, while NEGX (negate with extend) may be used with any of the available forms of effective address. The other special instructions in this group are ROXL and ROXR, to **rotate** with extend, left or right. Unlike the other shift instructions, the ordinary rotate instructions ROL and ROR do not affect the X status. ROXL and ROXR, however, perform a rotate *through* the X bit. A one-place ROXL, for example, will shift the sign bit of the operand into X, and shift the previous value of X into the low-order end of the operand. The effect is to perform a rotate in which X is treated as a 1-bit extension of the operand.

Arithmetic in binary-coded decimal

For certain kinds of application, it is sometimes convenient to represent numbers in memory not in the usual twos complement binary form but in **binary-coded decimal** (BCD) notation. In this form, each decimal digit of a number is represented separately within a 4-bit field of the code. Figure 7.5 gives an example, of the number 39 stored in BCD form in a single byte. The representation is less compact than twos complement binary,

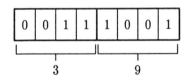

Figure 7.5   The number 39 in binary-coded decimal form

but has the advantage of preserving a very close relationship between the internal storage of numbers and the form in which they are read and printed as sequences of decimal digits.

The instruction ABCD (ADD BCD) will add two numbers expressed in this form, producing a correct decimal sum in BCD notation, and setting C and X if a (decimal) carry results. SBCD performs a BCD subtraction, and NBCD negates a BCD number (by subtracting it from 0, to produce a **tens**

complement result). The instructions operate on values of size byte only, and ABCD and SBCD have the same restrictions on addressing modes as ADDX and SUBX: their operands must be either two data registers, or two memory locations addressed using the pre-decrement address-register indirect mode. Again, the purpose of the latter form is to facilitate arithmetic on strings of BCD bytes stored consecutively in memory.

Because the BCD instructions implicitly assume the use of multi-length arithmetic, they have much in common with the extended arithmetic instructions. The value of the X bit is added or subtracted in every BCD operation, allowing the decimal carry to be propagated through stages of a multi-byte calculation. Both the BCD instructions and the extended-arithmetic instructions also have a special way of setting the Z (zero) status. These instructions will clear Z to indicate a non-zero result for a calculation, but do not set Z to mark a zero result. The effect of this is that, if Z=1 at the start of a multi-length calculation, it will remain set if and only if *each* step in the calculation produces a zero result—which is, of course, what we require if we wish to test for a zero result for the whole sum.

The V and N status bits are not relevant in BCD arithmetic, and the BCD instructions leave them undefined.

Miscellaneous instructions

Finally, there are just a few instructions in the 68000 repertoire that we have not found occasion to describe previously.

The MOVEP (move peripheral data) instruction is designed to facilitate the movement of values to and from device interface registers. Recall from Chapter 6 that the registers of the ACIA occupy the low-order bytes of adjacent 'words' in the address mapping. The MOVEP instruction allows both registers to be accessed simultaneously. Its effect is to move a word or longword from a data register into *alternate* bytes in memory (or, in particular, to the mapped addresses of a device interface), or in the other direction. The only mode available for addressing memory with this instruction is the address-register indirect with displacement (indexed) mode. Thus the instruction:

$$MOVEP \quad 0(A1), \ D2$$

will move the byte whose address is in register A1 into the high-order byte of D2, and the byte whose address is (A1+2) into the low-order half of D2.

The CMPM (compare memory) instruction is just a special form of CMP, setting condition bits to show the result of a comparison. Whereas

CMP compares a memory location with a data register value, CMPM compares the values stored in two memory locations. It is not a completely general store-to-store instruction like MOVE, however, since the only addressing mode that can be used is address register indirect with post-increment:

CMPM (A1)+,(A3)+

Its use is, particularly, to assist comparison of corresponding elements of two arrays.

The TST (test) instruction tests its operand (comparing it with zero), setting the N and Z bits accordingly. The operand may be of size byte, word, or longword, defined using a general effective address form.

SWAP provides a convenient and rapid way of exchanging the low-order and high-order words of a data register, and EXG will exchange the longword values of two registers, which may be either data or address registers:

*SWAP   D5   * interchange halves of longword register*
*EXG   D3, A4 * interchange (longword) D3 and A4*

A group of instructions is provided that will set the value of their operand depending on the result of some condition tested. The operand, which must be of size byte, is set to 0 if the condition is false, or all ones if the condition is true. Thus:

*SEQ   D3   * D3 set true if Z=1*
*SVS   OFLO   * OFLO := true if V status set*

The use of 'all ones' to represent true, and zero for false, is a common convention in high-level language implementations, referred to in Chapter 4. The group of instructions (Scc) comprises tests of all the conditions for which conditional branch (Bcc) instructions are provided (Chapter 3).

Last, and indeed least, is the no operation (NOP) instruction, which has no operand, and no effect other than to occupy a byte of memory and to take a non-zero time in execution. This instruction code will be used by compilers and assemblers to fill bytes in the instruction sequence when, for example, it is necessary to align an instruction to an even address. Otherwise, its only use is likely to be in a loop whose purpose is to idle, i.e. to occupy some time, or perhaps wait for an interrupt.

7.4   Exercises

1. Write a procedure in Pascal (or some other language) that will perform the actions of the half-adder circuit illustrated in Figure 7.5, on variables of type boolean representing individual bits.

   Using this procedure, construct a program that will perform a full addition on two 'words' of 16 bits.

2. Write a high-level language program to **simulate** the behaviour of the 68000 processor. The program should include:

   (a) declarations to represent processor registers and a certain amount of memory;

   (b) a main loop to perform the basic instruction fetch–decode–execute cycle of Chapter 2;

   (c) procedures to simulate the execution of individual instruction types.

   To limit the scale of this problem, you may wish to leave out some details of the 68000; in particular:

   (a) interrupts and peripheral device control;

   (b) some addressing modes;

   (c) some instruction types.

3. Write a 68000 assembly-language program to carry out an opinion poll survey on television viewing habits. The program should ask the following questions and record the responses:

   (a) Do you own a TV?

   (b) How old are you?

   (c) Which of the following programs have you watched in the past week?
   - (i) Dallas.
   - (ii) Dynasty.
   - (iii) etc. ...(up to 10).

   Organize the program to include a subroutine GETRESPONSE which will obtain this information for a single respondent, returning it in the form of a coded bit-pattern. The program should accumulate totals for each category, and calculate the average age of, and number of programs watched by, each respondent. A special response should be provided to display the up-to-date results of the survey.

Appendix

68000 instruction set summary

Key

In the *instruction mnemonics*, the shorthand cc is used to stand for any of the condition code tests possible in conditional branch (Bcc and DBcc) and Set according to condition (Scc) instructions; that is:

cc = EQ | NE | LT | LE | GT | GE | HI | LS | MI | PL | CC | CS | VC | VS | F | T

In the *instruction forms*, various restrictions on the types of **effective address** possible are imposed for different instructions. The following notation is used to describe these:

<ea>	=	any general effective address
<dea>	=	**data effective address**: excludes address register direct (An) mode
<mea>	=	**memory effective address**: excludes register direct modes (Dn and An)
<cea>	=	**control effective address**: excludes register direct, immediate, and pre-decrement and post-increment modes.

The **alterable** address modes <aea>, <adea>, <amea>, and <acea> correspond to <ea>, <dea>, <mea>, and <cea> respectively, with the added exclusion of immediate and program-counter relative modes.

Other notations used:

#< data >	=	immediate operand
#< dn >	=	immediate operand limited to n bits
< lab >	=	address label
An, Am	=	address register
Dn, Dm	=	data register
Rn, Rm	=	address or data register
d(Am)	=	address register indirect with displacement
< reglist >	=	list of registers for MOVEM instruction

Instructions prefixed • are privileged.

In the setting of *status bits*:

-	=	not changed as a result of instruction
*	=	may be changed by instruction
0	=	always cleared by instruction
1	=	always set by instruction
U	=	left undefined after instruction

The reference given in the last column of the table is to the section of the book in which the instruction is described.

Instr.	Form(s)	Size(s)	XNZVC	Ref.
	Data moves			
MOVE	MOVE < ea >, < adea >	L,W,B	- * * 0 0	2.4
	MOVE SR, < adea >	W	- - - - -	6.3
	MOVE < dea >, CCR	W	* * * * *	6.3
•	MOVE < dea >, SR	W	* * * * *	6.3
•	MOVE USP, An	L	- - - - -	6.3
•	MOVE An, USP	L	- - - - -	6.3
MOVEA	MOVEA < ea >, An	L,W	- - - - -	4.3
MOVEQ	MOVEQ #< d8 >, Dn	L	- * * 0 0	3.4
MOVEP	MOVEP Dn, d(Am)	L,W	- - - - -	7.3
	MOVEP d(Am), Dn			
MOVEM	MOVEM < reglist >, acea	L,W	- - - - -	5.4
	MOVEM < reglist >, -(An)			
	MOVEM (An)+, reglist			
	MOVEM < cea >, reglist			
LEA	LEA < cea >, An	L	- - - - -	4.3
	Arithmetic operations			
ADD	ADD < ea >, Dn	L,W,B	* * * * *	2.4
	ADD Dn, < amea >			
ADDA	ADDA < ea >, An	L,W	- - - - -	4.3
ADDI	ADDI #< data >, < adea >	L,W,B	* * * * *	3.4
ADDQ	ADDQ #< d3 >, < aea >	L,W,B	* * * * *	3.4
ADDX	ADDX Dn, Dm	L,W,B	* * * * *	7.3
	ADDX -(An), -(Am)			
SUB	SUB < ea >, Dn	L,W,B	* * * * *	2.4
	SUB Dn, < amea >			
SUBA	SUBA < ea >, An	L,W	- - - - -	4.3
SUBI	SUBI #< data >, < adea >	L,W,B	* * * * *	3.4
SUBQ	SUBQ #< d3 >, < aea >	L,W,B	* * * * *	3.4
SUBX	SUBX Dn, Dm	L,W,B	* * * * *	7.3
	SUBX -(An), -(Am)			
CMP	CMP < ea >, Dn	L,W,B	- * * * *	3.4
CMPA	CMPA < ea >, An	L,W	- * * * *	4.3
CMPI	CMPI #< data >, < adea >	L,W,B	- * * * *	3.4
CMPM	CMPM (An)+, (Am)+	L,W,B	- * * * *	7.3
MULS	MULS < dea >, Dn	W	- * * 0 0	3.4
MULU	MULU < dea >, Dn	W	- * * 0 0	3.4
DIVS	DIVS < dea >, Dn	W	- * * 0 0	3.4
DIVU	DIVU < dea >, Dn	W	- * * 0 0	3.4
CLR	CLR < adea >	L,W,B	- 0 1 0 0	3.4
NEG	NEG < adea >	L,W,B	* * * * *	3.4
NEGX	NEGX < adea >	L,W,B	* * * * *	7.3

Instr.	Form(s)	Size(s)	XNZVC	Ref.
	Logical operations			
AND	AND < dea >, Dn	L,W,B	- * * 0 0	4.4
	AND Dn, < amea >			
ANDI	ANDI #< data >, < adea >	L,W,B	- * * 0 0	4.4
	ANDI #< data >, CCR	B	* * * * *	
•	ANDI #< data >, SR	W	* * * * *	6.3
OR	OR < dea >, Dn	L,W,B	- * * 0 0	4.4
	OR Dn,< amea >			
ORI	ORI #< data >, < adea >	L,W,B	- * * 0 0	4.4
	ORI #< data >, CCR	B	* * * * *	
•	ORI #< data >, SR	W	* * * * *	6.3
EOR	EOR Dn, < adea >	L,W,B	- * * 0 0	4.4
EORI	EORI #< data >, < adea >	L,W,B	- * * 0 0	4.4
	EORI #< data >, CCR	B	* * * * *	
•	EORI #< data >, SR	W	* * * * *	6.3
NOT	NOT < adea >	L,W,B	- * * 0 0	4.4
	Shifts			
ASL/	ASx Dn, Dm	L,W,B	* * * * *	4.4
ASR	ASx #< d3 >, Dm			
	ASx < amea >	W	* * * * *	4.4
LSL/	LSx Dn, Dm	L,W,B	* * * 0 *	4.4
LSR	LSx #< d3 >, Dm			
	LSx < amea >	W	* * * 0 *	4.4
ROL/	ROx Dn, Dm	L,W,B	- * * 0 *	4.4
ROR	ROx #< d3 >, Dm			
	ROx < amea >	W	- * * 0 *	4.4
ROXL/	ROXx Dn, Dm	L,W,B	* * * 0 *	7.3
ROXR	ROXx #< d3 >, Dm			
	ROXx < amea >	W	* * * 0 *	7.3
	Bit inspect and modify			
BTST	BTST Dn, Dm	L	- - * - -	4.4
	BTST #< data >, Dm			
	BTST Dn, < mea >	B	- - * - -	4.4
	BTST #< data >, < mea >			
BSET/	Bxxx Dn, Dm	L	- - * - -	4.4
BCLR/	Bxxx #< data >, Dm			
BCHG	Bxxx Dn, < amea >	B	- - * - -	4.4
	Bxxx #< data >, < amea >			

Instr.	Form(s)	Size(s)	XNZVC	Ref.
	Control changes			
JMP	JMP < cea >	-	- - - - -	3.4
BRA	BRA < lab >	-	- - - - -	3.4
Bcc	Bcc < lab >	-	- - - - -	3.4
DBcc	DBcc Dn, < lab >	-	- - - - -	3.4
JSR	JSR < cea >	-	- - - - -	5.4
BSR	BSR < lab >	-	- - - - -	5.4
RTS	RTS	-	- - - - -	5.4
RTR	RTR	-	* * * * *	6.3
RTE •	RTE	-	* * * * *	6.3
TRAP	TRAP #< d4 >	-	- - - - -	6.3
TRAPV	TRAPV	-	- - - - -	6.3
CHK	CHK < dea >, Dn	W	-*UUU	6.3
STOP •	STOP #< data >	-	- - - - -	6.3
	Test and set operations			
Scc	Scc < adea >	B	- - - - -	7.3
TST	TST < adea >	L,W,B	-**00	7.3
TAS	TAS < adea >	B	-**00	6.3
	Stack operations			
PEA	PEA < cea >	L	- - - - -	5.4
LINK	LINK An, #< data >	-	- - - - -	5.4
UNLK	UNLK An	-	- - - - -	5.4
	Binary-coded decimal operations			
ABCD	ABCD Dn, Dm	B	*U*U*	7.3
	ABCD -(An), -(Am)			
SBCD	SBCD Dn, Dm	B	*U*U*	7.3
	SBCD -(An), -(Am)			
NBCD	NBCD < adea >	B	*U*U*	7.3
	Others			
EXG	EXG Rn, Rm	L	- - - - -	7.3
SWAP	SWAP Dn	W	-**00	7.3
EXT	EXT Dn	L,W	-**00	3.4
RESET •	RESET	-	- - - - -	6.3
NOP	NOP	-	- - - - -	7.3

Index

RE